WILD DEER

Culling, Conservation and Management

by A. J. de NAHLIK

Second extended and revised
edition with new foreword
by Lord Dulverton

Ashford Press Publishing
Southampton
1987

First published by Faber and Faber Ltd 1959
This edition published by Ashford Press Publishing 1987

British Library Cataloguing in Publication Data

de Nahlik, Andrew
    Wild deer: culling, conservation and
    management.—2nd rev. and extended ed.
    1. Deer—Handbooks, manuals, etc.
    I. Title
    636.2'94   SF401.D3
    ISBN 1–85253–002–2

Printed and bound in Great Britain by
Robert Hartnoll(1985) Ltd., Bodmin, Cornwall

To the future generation of 'deer people'

Red deer heads from the collection of Queen Elizabeth I and Queen Elizabeth II, showing the change in antler formation over the last three centuries. (Respective antler length 50 and 32.75 inches.) Allowance should be made, however, for the fact that the latter is a Highland stag, whereas the former is most likely of park origin. *Copyright reserved*

CONTENTS

PART I – WILD DEER

PART II

DEER MANAGEMENT GROUPS

PART III

DEER OF NORTH AMERICA

Tables

Figures

Plates

FOREWORD

by

The Lord Dulverton C.B.E.; T.D; M.A.; D.L.
Past President of the British Deer Society

I am very conscious of it being a great privilege to have been asked to compose this foreword to Andrew de Nahlik's new book on the wild deer. His name is well-known to all of us who are concerned in any way with deer, and I hope that it will become even more widely known when his authoritative book about all aspects of deer reaches the market. He is indeed a devotee to the study of those fascinating creatures of nature, of which he writes, and his knowledge of them is both comprehensive and varied.

He was born the son of a distinguished landowning family in Poland, and was trained by his father to learn about deer from a very early age. He first accompanied his father in pursuit of the Polish roe when he was 4 years old, and shot his first roe-buck and later a red stag a few years after that.

In 1939, eastern Poland was over-run by the Russians, and he himself was apprehended by them. Having somehow escaped from their attentions, he managed to make his way via Hungary and Italy into France, a saga in its own right, where he joined up with the Polish Air Force there. On the fall of France, he was evacuated by the British from St. Jean de Luz, and some little while after that transferred to our own Royal Air Force, with whom he served until 1968, attaining the rank of Wing Commander.

At the ending of the War, his beloved home being in the hands of the Russian Communists, he decided to stay here, and so has remained, having turned his talents to a business career in 1968.

That is something of a background to the man, who for over 40 years has pursued his love of and interest in deer, most of all, but not exclusively, in the country of his adoption. I have no hesitation in commending his new book to all and sundry, not only to deer enthusiasts but to others too, who are attracted to the study of wildlife. As for the select band of deer-stalkers, their blood cannot fail to be stirred by Andrew's exciting if imaginary stalking problems and examples, which are clearly drawn from experience.

Dulverton
Batsford Park
20 March 1987

ABOUT THIS BOOK

A few years ago, my son invited a friend of his to come and shoot pheasant with us; his friend was a young tall Scot, a keen deer stalker. As we were being introduced he said to me: 'I am delighted to meet you, Sir, I weaned on you when I was young'; he was talking about *Wild Deer* (1959), which his mother, also a keen stalker herself, made him read and study before allowing him on the hill with a rifle.

Of course I was flattered, but what he said, meant more to me than being just a compliment for it made me realise that *Wild Deer* managed to make a contribution towards the younger generation's interest in progressive attitude towards deer. It made me feel at the time that maybe, with *Wild Deer* almost unobtainable there was room for something similar, updated, for the benefit of the next and subsequent generations, for my grandchildren and their children. This was the first germ which grew and grew, to culminate in this book and its dedication.

The Deer (Scotland) Act 1959, and *Wild Deer* are 'twins', both appeared in 1959, both were an attempt to bring about a more rational, progressive and constructive attitude towards deer, to help in the realisation that deer had a role to play not only in our environment, but that with a little care and attention, the asset which they represent could be enhanced and realised to the benefit of many individuals and economic benefit of the owners and the country, especially in Scotland.

Since 1959 a number of legislative instruments have come into being to improve and extend the original Act. Their contribution to the well-being of deer has been immeasurable, not only by giving deer a respite from being shot all the year round but also by limiting the weapons which can be used on deer to ensure that the killing is humane.

To realise how the interest in deer has grown and developed in these 20-odd years, all one needs to do is study the current bibliography, articles, research and investigations' reports, concerning deer and compare the volume of these with what existed in 1950 and early 60s. Much scorn has been levelled at *Wild Deer* at the time of its first appearance, because in it, German and other Continental sources had to be used to present the concepts ot the modern ways and means of caring for and understanding deer. By now British material, from simple to very scientific, from practical to theoretical, from children's education to adults' interest, is available, plentiful, and growing, in volume and, in coverage, every year.

But vast as these changes may have been there is room for more. There are still places and people who regard this sort of progress as an infringement of their liberties (by introduction of restrictive legislation) or as an attempt to kill tradition and accepted practices; and I am not talking just of Britain but also other parts of the world where those interested in progressive management of wildlife, including deer, are facing obstacles created by ill practices, lack of understanding, vested interests, impatience and greed, or any other un-endearing characteristics of the human race.

A predominant proportion of deer live in the 'English Speaking World' from Britain, through America, to New Zealand and India. In this World live a vast number of deer of innumerable species. Much of what is written in this book can either be applied directly, or can be adapted with good will and flexibility of mind, to any of the deer species anywhere. It is my ardent hope therefore that there will be readers who, instead of saying 'we have no red, fallow or roe deer here', will say 'what is good enough for the deer in Britain may also apply to our Wapiti, Whitetail, Barasinga, Sambar, Chital, Elk, etc., etc.', study their local deer and selectively and judiciously apply or adjust what is said here to meet their local needs. They may find that as a result not only the quality of deer may improve, but also that deer will make a better contribution to their well-being, and last but not least that their sport will also benefit.

I know that the 'not invented here' is a symdrome that controls many minds and many decisions and not only in relation to deer, but is there really a need to re-invent the wheel over and over again; is it not easier and more effective where practical to just adjust the old invention to the new needs?

A. J. de Nahlik 1986

ACKNOWLEDGEMENTS

This book like the original *Wild Deer* may have been my idea, but without massive outside help and support neither would have had much chance of success. There are many therefore to whom my thanks are due.

In the first place, I have to thank again all those who have made *Wild Deer* (1959) possible, and whose work, contribution and co-operation will live that much longer through this book.

In this book however, in the first place I need to thank all those owners of deer forests and deer holding grounds, the keepers and stalkers whose interest in deer has been and is unflagging, who have been open-minded enough to at least try to follow some of the ideas presented in my works on deer. I know that accepting new and different ideas is never easy especially when these seem strange, challenging traditions, or are for other reasons, difficult to accept. I need to thank those organisations and individuals who in the last 20-odd years investigated and researched deer and published their material and the authors who have written about deer; it is their enthusiasm and perseverance that have improved our knowledge of deer.

I suppose that if it had not been for the foresight, maybe even courage of Faber & Faber, who published *Wild Deer* in the first place, and who have kindly reverted the rights to it to me, this book would have never happened, so amongst the contributors to this book they deserve a special word of thanks. But there are many others: publishers and organisations who have allowed me to use their material — Batsford, The British Deer Society, David & Charles, Deutscher Jagdschutz Verband, Hill Farmers Research Organisation, HMSO, F. C. Meyer Verlag-Munich, Panstwowe Wydawnictwo Rolniczo Lesne-Warsaw, Paul Parey Verlag-Hamburg, Red Deer Commission, Rowett Institute and Tideline Books.

There are also many individuals: my wife and Mrs Piffa Schroder who edited the many additions and changes, Leonard Lee Rue III who provided the photographs of North American deer. Then there is Dr Archie Mac-Diarmid who has generously produced the chapter on the health of red deer and Mr Sandy Mactaggart who provided me with some books on wild-life of North America.

Last, but not least, there are those estate owners who have allowed me to work with them on their deer; hopefully they have benefited from my help; I know that I have learned a great deal from them and their stalkers, as well as their friends and acquaintances with whom I was able to talk deer for many hours, days, months and years.

Ade N
May 1986

DEER STALKING IN BRITAIN

by

G. Kenneth Whitehead

(being the Introduction to "WILD DEER" (1959) and revised for this edition)

Facilities for stalking in Great Btritain equal those of almost any country in Europe even though the size of trophy, particularly in the case of red deer, bears no comparison with some of the immense heads obtainable in parts of Eastern Europe.

However, to the true sportsman trophy-hunting should be of secondary consideration to the pleasures of the hunt and the opportunity of observing wild creatures in their natural haunts. In one respect, therefore, deer stalking on the bare mountainsides of Scotland has one great advantage over its counterpart in the dense forests of Europe, and that the intended victim can generally be seen throughout the whole stalk.

Red deer stalking can be practised in practically every county in Scotland north ot the Glasgow to Edinburgh road, and in particular, in the counties of Caithness, Sutherland, Ross, Inverness, Argyll, Perth and Aberdeen. Red deer are also present in south-west Scotland and on a number of islands off the west coast; these include Arran, Rhum, Jura, Islay, Mull, Skye, Harris and Lewis.

Red deer are well distributed throughout the whole of the northern half of Scotland, and are not just confined to the recognised 'deer forests' — areas which are forests in name only, as for the most part they are entirely devoid of trees. Good stalking can, therefore, be obtained on many of the grouse moors and marginal sheep grounds adjacent to deer country proper. Altogether, Scotland's *recognised* deer forests total about 198 and extend to approximately 3,100,000 acres. Few if any, of the deer forests are entirely fenced today, although fences, many of which are now going into disrepair, separate much of Scotland's deer ground from Forestry Commission ground.

In England, stalking, as practised in Scotland on the open hillside, is only possible in the Lake District and in particular in Martindale Forest — the last remaining true deer forest south of the border. Red deer are present, however, in many Forestry Commission plantations and woodlands — such as Grizdale near Coniston, and Thetford in Norfolk — and in these areas methods of hunting, i.e. high seats and calling, alien to this country but long in use on the continent, are gradually being introduced to replace the hit-and-miss methods of deer drives formerly practised in these districts.

In the south-west of England a large stock of red deer populate the moors and wooded combes around Exmoor. Control here is largely by hunting and the occasional deer drives, so these animals need not be taken into account in this book. Thanks to the superior feeding and shelter it is not unnatural that the West Country stags, on average, produce far stronger heads than anywhere in the British Isles. The record British red deer head — the famous Endsleigh twenty-pointer — came from this district. This stag was found dead in 1950, having apparently met with some accident. The antlers of this wonderful stag measured no less than 114.3 cm (left) and 115.3 cm (right) in length, and *without* frontal bone had an estimated weight of 19 lb (8.5 kg).

Two extremely good heads, however, were shot during the 1956 rut in Thetford forest by two members of the St. Hubert Club, one twenty-one pointer and the other thirteen-pointer. The deer in this heavily wooded district are mostly descended from Warnham Park deer that have escaped capture by the Norwich Staghounds — one of the two packs in England that formerly hunted the 'carted deer', the other being the Mid-Kent, near Maidstone. Hunting of 'carted deer' in England was given up in 1963.

In Scotland the best heads of the past have generally been the result of winter feeding and possibly also of introduction of park blood. Today any head of twelve or fourteen points, combined with a length measurement of 92 cm, is extremely good.

Red deer stalking is also possible in three districts of Ireland — around Kenamare and Muckross in County Kerry, on the Wicklow mountains, and on Glenveagh — an enclosed forest of some 30,000 acres in County Donegal. The only indigenous deer are those in County Kerry.

Roe stalking can be practised in every county in Scotland, but the best areas are undoubtedly to be found in parts of Morayshire, Inverness-shire, Aberdeenshire and Perthshire. The best heads have all come from these counties. Roe also occur on the Islands of Islay, Bute and Seil.

In England roe are plentiful in the eastern and south-eastern parts of the Lake Districts, throughout Northumberland, North Durham and parts of Yorkshire. Elsewhere they occur in the Thetford Forest district, Norfolk and in many woods along the south coast of England between Sussex and Devon. They also occur in Somerset, Wiltshire and Berkshire. It is since the beginning of the last century that roe has reappeared in the southern part of England through introductions at various dates. There are no roe now in Ireland, although a few were introduced at County Sligo during the latter part of the last century.

Although British red deer heads do not compare very favourably with those of the Continent, this cannot be said for roe, and the best heads from Britain are little inferior to the Continental ones, Swedish, perhaps excepted.

In many woods in England and Ireland, as well as in a few places in Scotland, herds of fallow deer roam. These deer are, for the most part, descendants of the stock that escaped from the deer parks during the two world wars and now lead an entirely feral life. They are extremely wary and offer fine stalking at dawn and dusk.

Another deer which has gained a footing in this country is the Japanese sika deer. It first came to this country about the middle of the last century, and animals were liberated in a number of places in England, Scotland and Ireland, descendants of which remain to this day. These districts include the Mull of Kintyre (Argylshire), Lochrosque (Ross-shire), Loch Ness side (Inverness-shire), Langwell (Caithness) and Dawyck (Peebels-shire) in Scotland; Kenmare and Wicklow mountains in Ireland; and in England the New Forest (Hampshire), Purbeck (Dorset), Challock (Kent) and Bolton-by-Bowland (Lancashire). The first stag I ever killed was sika on the Mull of Kintyre over fifty-five years ago, and it can be said that this animal first doctrinated me with 'stag fever' Japs, mainly nocturnal habits, make interesting stalking at dusk or dawn as they emerge from the bracken clumps where they like to lie up during the day time.

The other Asiatic deer — the tiny muntjack or barking deer and the equally small Chinese water deer — have found footing in the wild state in England, whilst distribution of the latter is more or less localised around Northampton, Cambridgeshire and Bedfordshire, the former is rapidly spreading northwards from Woburn in Bedfordshire where it was originally introduced, and has now reached Warwickshire and Staffordshire. The antlers of the muntjack, measuring but a few inches in length, are insignificant, while water-deer bucks have none at all.

In the foregoing I have endeavoured to review briefly the wonderful scope for sport with a rifle which Britain, excluding Wales, offers. There are very few wild deer in Wales. The various methods of going about it have been very aptly dealt with by the author in the following chapters.

Part I

Wild Deer

Chapter I

INTRODUCTION TO DEER

Deer — Their Habits — Habitat and General Information

If anyone were asked to name the most striking feature of deer, surely the antlers ('horns' as some erroneously call them) would be chosen. It is the antlers that are the stalker's most coveted trophy, the breeder–shoot-owner's or tenant's pride and joy, and the naturalist's most useful source of information on vital facts and varied features. Beyond all doubt, then, the antlers are of paramount interest to all who are preoccupied with deer, but are not deer farmers.

Complete chapters are devoted to the antlers later on, so that only general information will be found in these first pages. Antlers are an annual growth. They are shed by deer at certain times of the year and the growth of a new antler occupies a period varying between 120 and 190 days, depending on the species. The new antler will have the same general appearance as its predecessor, though the number of tines may vary from year to year. It used to be the general belief that a tine on each antler was added each year, but the fallacy of the belief has been exposed many times.

When looking at the antlers of a stag it is easy to appreciate what a feat of metabolism such a development represents. No wonder, therefore, that the few male deer which never develop antlers transform the great quantity of food they consume entirely into body-weight. Hummels (for that is what the antlerless stags are called) are therefore greater and heavier than the normal stags — hence in fights of the mating (rutting) season, they are bound to be mighty opponents. Antlers are a product of the hormonal system, hence its imbalance, due to any cause, can result in a malformation of antlers. Similarly, hormonal activities are closely connected with digestive activities, so that permenant, or at best prolonged, upset of the digestive system, caused by illness or wound, can also result in antler deformities.

Deer are basically animals of the forest. They live in the wildest parts where they are least interfered with by man, their main enemy. Since many forests have vanished in Scotland to provide timber for defence, industry, housing, etc. deer have been forced to live in the open; the moors holding deer are still, however, known as deer forests.

1

There are deer of one type or another in most counties of England and Scotland. Basically there are two species indigenous to this country: the red deer and the roe deer. Fallow deer have been imported, and their claim to being native inhabitants is not old; it is, however, older than that of other deer which may be found, such as the Japanese sika, muntjac, etc.

Red Deer

Red deer are the largest wild animals found in the British Isles. The Scottish deer of the Highlands is different from the red deer found elsewhere. It is, above all, smaller. There are three possible reasons for this. Living on the moors, they find feeding of poorer quality than is found in the low-lying and warmer countryside of southern Scotland and England. Also, more of the Scottish deer's efforts must be expended on moving up and down the hillside. The other reason may well be that the English and lowland deer, until comparatively recently the provider of the sport of kings, was better looked after. Indeed, many of the latter have park blood in them of fairly recent origin and have retained in their antlers and body build many characteristics of park deer.

Brian Vesey-Fitzgerald, in his book *British Game*,° says that 'the face of the park deer is long with short and rather narrow forehead and eyes set rather close together, while the Highland deer has a shorter face, blunter muzzle with a wide deep forehead, and eyes wide apart'. Whether these are characteristics which apply particularly to Highland as opposed to park deer it is difficult to say. The same description could apply to European deer, of which there are two 'types', the smaller 'blunt nosed' and the larger 'long nosed'; neither of these is particularly a park deer. In Europe, the smaller type do not appear in the lowlands, but both are quite common in the mountainous areas of Germany, Austria, Hungary and Poland. An even larger type of red deer will be found in New Zealand, living almost entirely in the mountains.

The body build and size are characteristics more informative to the unaccustomed eye. The Highland deer are more muscular in appearance and being smaller appear to be more graceful and agile; other red deer are more heavily built. In keeping with the development of the body the Scottish stag grows a smaller head, thinner and poorer, whereas the English or the southern Scottish stag, even if not a park stag (though possibly with more recent park blood) grows a more massive head. In the following chapters possible reasons for this indubitable fact will be given.

Red deer live in herds. Save during the rutting season, the herds of the mature beasts are segregated, hinds and young ones of both sexes (up to two years old) living separately from stags. The stags join the hind herds just prior to the beginning of the mating season. Here we naturally expect the hummel who, unless he lives alone, can be found in the herds of stags throughout the year.

There is a significant difference between the herds of hill deer and the herds of their woodland brethern. The hill deer herds of 50 or even 100 beasts are not uncommon, whilst the woodland deer are small by com-

° Brian Vesey-Fitzgerald, **British Game** (London, Collins, 1946).

parison, 12 to 24 is about the average. One can assume, that on the open hill there is safety in numbers with a hundred and more eyes scanning the ground for signs of danger. In the woodland on the other hand, small herds find concealment easier.

The herd of stags split up two months before the rutting season opens. The split-up is normally into pairs comprising one old stag and one young one. The old beast spends his time eating and sleeping, building himself up for the strains of the rut; the younger acts as a sentry. When the rut commences, however, the young stag is normally ousted from the herd of hinds his companion has just joined, and the brief alliance is over.

From the deer management point of view, the deer herds on the hill in numbers, give us an opportunity to watch and observe, to note the condition and make an appreciation of the local standard of quality against which the future culling can be exercised. It also gives us an opportunity to count the deer more efficiently. In the woodlands however, where observation, watching and counting is more difficult, there is more of a battle of wits between the men and the beasts, small herds make watching and recording, where frequently no more than a fleeting glimpse is possible, easier.

In their months of segregation by sexes, or together during the rut, stags and hinds move when undisturbed in almost single file, the oldest hind leading. In the rut the stag normally brings up the rear, watching to see that none of his wives strays after a younger stag, or is designedly cut off from the herd by some enterprising youngster.

The rutting date depends on locality, the earliest dates varying between September 15 and October 1; the rut lasts from two to four weeks. The older stags join the hinds earlier, and remain with them for a time, keeping others, weaker or younger stags, at bay. It often happens that when another stag wants to cut off a hind or two from the fringe of the herd of the master stag, the master stag fights the intruder. The victor joins or rejoins the herd; the vanquished has to wait until the master stag (worn out by his love-making and constant vigilance) retires. At that very moment another stag (sometimes more than one) steps in and takes over the herd of hinds; if more than one stag, they either fight for mastery of the herd, or the herd splits into two or three, each stag departing with a small harem.

In spite of the fact that the rut takes place, as already stated, in September or October, it does happen that a single hind will come on heat later in the year, and this might even be as late as January. Stags in the neighbourhood immediately start roaring, and a minor rutting-season-like love match is on. Such happenings not only upset the normal balance of nature, but also cause a considerable strain on stags that happen to be in the vicinity. A stag which has covered a hind in winter often dies of exposure soon afterwards, specially in hard climatic conditions such as may be expected in the Highlands. The calf born as a result of a belated rut will come into the world late in the year, and neither will it be strong enough to survive the following winter nor will the hind have time to recover from the nursing period before the onslaught of winter. Should a hind come on heat therefore after November, it is better on all counts to have it shot, than to expose a number of other animals to considerable hardship.

In the rut the stag develops a voice which he does not possess during the

3

rest of the year. This voice, a lion-like roar, is the stag's challenge and love song. In an area where one stag is a master stag and one or two other stags circle his herd in hopeful anticipation, the roaring duel between the master and the bye-stags is always heard morning and evening and is sometimes carried on throughout the day and night.

In the rut the stag also develops another lion-like characteristic, namely a mane on his neck. The mane is retained throughout the winter and shed when the winter coat is changed to the summer one. After the rut the stags retire and are normally not seen for three to four weeks. During that time they rest and feed, preparing themselves for the rigours of winter.

Calves are dropped by the hinds after a period of about eight month's gestation, in late May or early June, usually near the mother-hind's own birth place. Newly born calves are spotted; in the first day or two they are able to stagger about on widely splayed legs, and need mother's help; after a few days they become quite mobile however, and follow the mother normally. The spots disappear when the young animal starts changing its first coat to a winter coat. Until it can move the calf is odourless: this and its spots, which serve as camouflage, are nature's defence against enemies; the fox, wild-cat, dog, eagle, etc. Calves remain with their mothers for as long as two years, but always for at least two winters.

A two-year old stag joins the herd of stags after its second winter.

The red deer's natural habitat is the thick of the forest; there they live, moving to the feeding places outside the forest in the early morning and the late evening specially when the food in the woodland is scarce. For these reasons they remain often unseen and this fact may, in some districts, lead people to an underestimation of their numbers. Their diet is such that, under normal circumstances, they do not need to leave their normal habitat of forest or moor, for feeding.

The Scottish hill deer move about more than the woodland deer; sometimes they move quite considerable distances to better food, better shelter, trying to escape from human intrusion or getting away from fly and midge infested lower ground. But there is also a large scale migration, of a more permanent nature especially when deer find themselves cut off from their normal wintering ground or rutting stands, by tracts of land being fenced for afforestation or other purposes. Provision of artificial feeding may be essential to prevent this, and on this subject we shall enlarge in Chapters IV and XXVI.

Red deer, in spite of their size, are most agile and graceful animals. When forced they will clear a six-foot obstacle with ease and grace of movement. At the least disturbance, whatever its nature, deer will move up wind, their sense of smell and hearing being their main defence against both agression and lurking danger. Red deer's eyesight is much poorer than that of roe and fallow deer, and is rarely relied upon solely for warning of approaching peril.

Once the spots disappear from the calf, the colour will alternate between the greyish-brown of its winter coat and the rich red-brown of the summer one. The summer coat is short and often shiny; the winter coat is long and dull and it becomes greyer as the coat-changing time approaches.

Fallow Deer

Generally speaking, fallow deer are smaller than red deer, but fallow, specially park-bred, have been known to weigh as much as fifteen stone. In striking contrast Highland red deer have been known to weigh less than ten and a half.

There are three, if not more, types of fallow, the difference between them being mainly in the colouring of their coats; dark grey sometimes appears to be true black (and is often called black fallow); then there are mottled fallow, with white spots, and plain white. As each of these three basic colours admits of variations, each type has its subdivisions based on colour.

Of these three basic types, the white fallow are all of park blood, the dark grey are the generically wild variety, and the spotted represent the south European imported blood. The spotted fallow has the white spots ranged along its flank in lines; these markings are far more pronounced in the summer coat and all but disappear in the winter.

Fallow have a black or dark grey-brown line of long hair along the centre of their back; in white fallow, this line is less marked and is white or yellow-white. Fallow are gregarious and gather in much smaller herds than red deer; does and bucks run together from October till spring; from March to April they often segregate by sexes.

The rut takes place in the latter part of October and is of short duration, but if a doe comes on heat later, she will be covered by a buck. The recommendation already made, that a doe likely to occasion a late rut should be shot, is here equally applicable (see pages 3, 83 for reference to same state of affairs with a red hind).

Unlike the red deer, fallow do not develop a special voice of challenge nor do they fight as red deer, but they have been known to kill one another. In the rutting season the buck develop a rolling grunt, a voice similar to that used solely as a warning when they are frightened at other times of the year. In the rutting time however, the barking can be heard quite often without any such apparent reason. Does cough as a warning signal, and call the young by giving a bleating sound rather like the short bleat of a goat or sheep.

Plate IA   Fallow fawn

5

Fawns (for illustration, see Plate IA) are dropped in May to June after a gestation period of eight months.They are capable of following their mother within a few hours of being born. Fallow's food consists of grass, young shoots, forest fruit, chestnuts, acorns, etc. all found within their natural surroundings; and unless forced into the open by lack of natural food, fallow prefer to remain under cover. In the hours of daylight fallow remain in the thickest of the thick wood, but being by nature restless and shy, can be seen moving from one thicket to another during the day, in search of new cover. Their powers of hearing, smell and eyesight are excellent, better than those of red deer, and they are extremely cautious.

Fallow's gait is characteristic, quite unlike that of the red and roe deer; they run by jumping on all four legs, and appear therefore, jumping as they do in little leaps, to be slow. In fact, they are extremely fast. Fallow running between thickets, even undisturbed, will clear a six-foot obstacle with ease. When chased, they have been known to jump easily a seven-foot fence.

Roe Deer

As red deer is the largest deer native to the British Isles, so the roe is the smallest; not only the smallest, but the most attractive of the three. It is interesting to learn that roe have not changed the form of their antlers since prehistoric days (Plate II), whereas both red deer and fallow deer have, so far as antlers are concerned, deteriorated considerably. The buck sheds his antlers in about October and by May his antlers are regrown and cleaned of velvet.

Plate IB   2 year old roe doe

Like the other deer, roe are gregarious, but live in the smallest groups of all, six beasts being probably the most that are likely to be seen together. On their feeding grounds, more than one group of roe can be seen, but they arrive and leave separately as different 'families'. Twos and threes are the most common grouping, with the fawns in addition.

The rut takes place basically between July 20 and August 10, but the date may vary, as it is influenced by weather conditions and the geographical latitude. The farther north, the later the rut will begin. The roe's mating is a remarkable thing to watch. First of all there is movement of the beasts hither and thither all day long; the does, pursued by the bucks, are always darting into view in some fresh spot. In their chase does run in circles, the buck following, and these circles do not vary much; so that in the forests where roe are numerous, roe 'rings', as they are known, can actually be found worn into the earth and grass, and remain well marked throughout the year. The centres of the rings, which are normally in the meadow, are single bushes or small trees.

Buck do not move far; throughout the year, when a buck has his antlers fully grown, he wanders along the perimeter of his 'domain' marking it by his antlers on the bushes and fraying the bark. That area, during the rut, is the one where he will court his doe. Should the doe, however, decide to wander, the buck is quite likely to follow, returning when the rut is over. Normally a buck will defend his area, rather than fight for the favours of a particular doe.

Fawns are dropped in early June, after a gestation period of ten months, and follow their mothers after two to four weeks, remaining with her for a year. Like the red and fallow deer the fawns are spotted and odourless until they can run and thus avoid the predators, the spots vanish at the time of their changing from summer to first winter coat.

The normal colour of roe is red in summer, bright on the back, paler on the underbelly, sometimes becoming greyish-white or orange-grey. The winter coat is dirty grey. There are variations in the summer colour from reddish-chestnut, with a white patch on the underthroat, and muzzle, which are peculiar in the British Isles to the Scottish roe, to very dark grey, almost black which can be found in some roe of the Eastern Counties, and which come originally from the Schaumburger Wald in Lower Saxony or Würthemberg. The influence of this dark grey or black German roe on the roe of the Eastern Counties, means that here, darker coloured beasts than elsewhere can be found; their coat is shorter and shinier in summer than that of other roe. The winter coat of all roe is rather long, dark grey and dull.

Roe are generically deer of the forest and woods. Being night feeders they move principally between dusk and dawn, and by virtue of their size as well as their nocturnal habits they are not often seen, hence the common belief that they are rare. In fact there are more roe than any other deer. They can be found in most counties of Britain. The time when roe can be found comparatively easily is after a cold night's rain or heavy dew, sunning themselves in the afternoon in the wind-sheltered and sunny wood clearings. This is more common among roe than among the other deer.

Like red and fallow deer, the roe normally finds all his food within his habitat, but if forced by hunger he will leave the forest and feed in the agricultural neighbourhood, creating some damage. His favourite food outside the forest is clover and unripe corn, which, being by nature greedy, he cannot normally resist.

It has been underlined when describing each species of the deer that they should find their food within their normal habitat of woods, or the

7

moors of the Highlands. Under normal conditions the basic feeding for deer is provided by the growth of the woodland meadow, by the green annual undergrowth, the bi-annual growth, young self-seeded bushes and trees, tree and other plantations. Among trees and bushes, the deciduous ones are of better food value than most of the coniferous, and it is to them that the deer will normally gravitate. Variety of food is, however, very important and monotypic food is never very satisfying to them. It is for this reason that coniferous woods (having little undergrowth) when they carry deer, do not often provide sufficient natural feeding for deer. Food must come therefore from elsewhere, and it can be found in the fields. Can one thus wonder that deer raid the fields to amplify their diet?

Generally speaking, these are the factors which decide habitat: sufficiency of cover, and protection against the intrusion of man; suffiency of natural food in the vicinity (ideally, the immediate vicinity) ; and lesser factors such as availability of water, suitability of climate, presence of animals with which they can live in harmony, and absence of hostile animals.

Plate IC
Pricket stag
(staggie)

Plate II   Similarity of roe antlers over ages

Roebuck(pleistocene) from excava-
vations at Charing Cross. London.

a) Roe of Pleistocene
(c. 50000 B.C.), 7¾in
long

b) Roe's present-day antler,
8¾in long

c) Antler of a doe

Chapter II

DEER DAMAGE —
DAMAGE CONTROL

The evaluation of damage done by deer to useful plants of field and forest has undergone considerable changes throughout the ages, the variable factor being the value of venison — staple diet in many parts at many times and valuable also as industrial material — and of considerable potential food value at all times, compared with the value of damaged field crops or trees. The main re-evaluation of damage came, generally speaking, in two separate stages: the first at a time when, due to overpopulation of deer, considerable damage to crops was suffered by farmers, the value of these crops being out of all proportion to the value which would be obtained for venison: the second when afforestation was developed on a scientific basis with the aim of providing badly needed timber for the internal use of the country.

With the development of modern countries in the last few decades the importance of deer from most aspects diminished, whereas the value of the deer-damaged crops to the economy of the countries concerned soared — hence the problem.

This problem had often been tackled in the press without a conclusion being reached or a suggestion as to counter-measures being made, short of a wild recommendation that deer should be decimated if not exterminated. This attitude was basically due to the fact that only a few people understood the problem completely.

Complete understanding of it must, of course, be based on cause and effect. Therefore the reasons for the damage will occupy the first part of this chapter; then the prevention of damage will be easier to understand and follow.

Damage by game is inevitable. The damage done by 'small game', fur and feather, is comparatively small; deer can create greater damage. Damage is done in the search for food. The larger the animal searching for food, the greater the damage; the greater the damage, the greater the cost of upkeep of deer. It is necessary therefore to strike a balance between the value of game, be it big or small, and the value of the damage. If we can balance the account, or at the worst show an acceptable loss, we are on the way to solving the problem; otherwise the problem is how to combat

9

the damage or decrease it to an acceptable level. As far as small game is concerned we are prepared to accept some damage and with the other overheads offset it against our income from renting the shooting, selling the game and having a certain amount of sport ourselves.

With deer we are not generally quite so indulgent, possibly owing to lack of interest, possibly to lack of understanding of an industrial and sporting ready market.

The problem facing us is best represented graphically by a 'family tree' of deer damage problems embracing a variety of questions. Subsequently we shall look at each part of this 'family tree' and consider each question individually with a view to reaching a solution, however tentative (Table I).

TABLE 1   Systems of preventing deer damage[*]

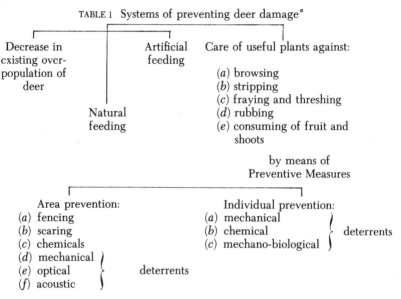

These, then, are the problems and the possible counteractions and remedies, which, as will be seen, may be broadly grouped under two headings, therapy (i.e. action *post factum* to repair damage done) and prevention (i.e. preventives and precautions against damage being done or which may be done in the future). Therapy is a problem for the botanist, forester or farmer; we therefore propose to deal principally with prevention, dividing it into headings to correspond with the 'family tree'. The question of therapy will remain untouched, for the specialists just mentioned are well aware of the damage done and well prepared to play their part in checking it.

Overpopulation

Recommendations regarding the proper density of deer population are contained in a separate chapter; the influence of overpopulation on deer

[*] Based on Dr F.Türcke, *Mittel gegen Wildschäden und ihre Anwendung* (Munich, Hamburg, F. C. Meyer, 1953).

damage is obvious, and the advantages of maintaining the right density need no explanation.

Feeding

Natural and artificial

We must not lose sight of the fact that the male of the species during a period varying from 120 to 190 days each year, must devote an enormous proportion of the vitality acquired from food to the rebuilding of antlers. To no less an extent the female of the species, during the period of gestation and lactation, require considerable quantities of food, admittedly of different chemical constituents, for their own, and the born and unborn young ones' sustenance. In a word they all must feed and feed well.

A stag, to produce a head of antlers weighing 12–20 lb, must derive from his food some 3½ lb of calcium, as well as 3–5 lb of phosphorus during the period of the antler build-up.

Hinds, during gestation and lactation, require ¼ lb albumen $\frac{1}{30}$ lb calcium, and $\frac{1}{30}$ lb phosphorus each day.

Table 2 represents the daily feeding requirements of red deer. The requirements are for stags weighing approximately 350 lb live weight, and hinds approximately 240 lb. In areas where the weights are higher or lower, the total consumption should be reduced or increased in direct proportion.

The amount of food required by hinds is as follows; the lower figure shown in the table for uncovered hinds; the higher figure in the period of lactation. Hinds in gestation require a quantity approximately between the figures stated.

TABLE 2 Deer food°

	Dry substance (lb)	Nitro-free substances (lb)	Digestive albumen (lb)	Total fresh food (approx.) (lb)	Dry food content (lb)
Stags	6–8	3–4	0.3–0.5	22	14
Hinds	4–7	1.5–3	0.1–0.8	13	7

By its digestive and hormonal reproduction, the stag or buck builds up its antlers. The chemical consistency of these is as follows (Table 3).

TABLE 3 Deer food — chemical contents°

	%		%		%
H_2O . . .	9.7	K_2O . . .	0.1	SiO_2 . . .	0.03
CaO . . .	28.37	P_2O_5 . . .	22.4	N	5.8
MgO . . .	0.6	CO_2 . . .	3.0	N-free substance	29.0
Na_2O . . .	0.7	SO_3	0.3		

° Tables 2, 3 and 4 are based on Dr Oloff's *Rotwild — Jagd und Hege in aller Welt* (Heinzwolf Kölzig Verlag, Dusseldorf, 1955)

TABLE 4 Levels of damage*

Wild forest, without artificial feeding:	Conifers	Mixed	Deciduous
Browsing	5–7	1–3	0.1
Stripping	5	2	0.2
Wild forest, with artificially provided balanced diet:			
Browsing	1–3	damage is negligible –	
Stripping	1–2	below 0.1%	

The multitude of chemical components shows that the bulk comes from food which a stag must find in order to allow for nature's normal evolution.

It will be seen that unless the feeding conditions in the deer forest where we wish, or are by force of nature compelled, to maintain deer, are such that the chemical components can readily be found and in sufficient quantities to meet nature's requirements, the deer will be forced to find them somewhere somehow. This they will do by raiding the agricultural areas in the neighbourhood, where most of their needs can be satisfied, and it goes without saying that they will inevitably damage the useful plants of the forest, in many of which certain of the chemical components required by deer are to be found. By now, we should be able to see that some of the damage, a considerable percentage of it, is the result of the animals' search for what nutritionists call 'a balanced diet'. In order to prevent that damage, therefore, we must attempt to balance deers' diet artificially — to make available the elements they naturally crave, in a readily accessible spot.

The damage one can expect from deer is represented in Table 4. The table shows damage by percentage of the total crop of the forest, where two red deer live in an area of approximately 250 acres.

These artificial additions to the diet can be in the form of small fields of ¼–½ acre in size, arranged in suitable locations and sown with suitably selected crops which will attract deer, giving them their dietetic requirements, and will divert them from the tree plantations and fields where they would otherwise look for the balancing factor in their diet. The alternative is to provide fodder, fresh and dry, at times of necessity. The recommended crops and types of fodder will be found in the chapter on feeding deer. Furthermore, it is possible to move deer from one area to another by gradually rearranging the locations of artificial feedings towards the area where we wish to concentrate our deer. This process may be slow, but is normally a workable proposition.

It is difficult to produce an abstract diet, and it is advisable to consult local farmers as to the feeding matter deer are seeking, and to adjust the feeding matter provided accordingly. On the whole, however, such crops such as grass, clover, oats, wild rye, buckwheat, potato, turnips, beet, lupin, lucerne, sweet-corn, cabbage, and fruit-bearing bushes and trees will normally produce the required results.

In addition to 'green' and manufactured food sown, planted or laid out, in certain areas where minerals are scarce in their natural form, minerals should be provided in the form of licks. Of these, cattle salt licks mixed with powdered clay are the cheapest and easiest to procure and arrange. Where deer food includes a large proportion of cellular substances (such as heather), rumen ammonia salts will help better digestion; where phosphorous is in short natural supply, traces of it should be added to licks or other food.

Winter is the lean period for all game, and just as small game are normally fed by the owners and shooting tenants, so deer, specially in areas where snowfalls are heavy, should be fed. To this end a mixture of hay and clover, possibly oats if these can be spared, serves a good purpose. From the point of view of damage, artificial feeding will prevent stripping and browsing, the two actions which, particularly during a frosty winter, can cause considerable damage.

Hay and clover thus laid out should be fresh, not musty. Musty hay can play havoc with deer's digestion. Normally deer will not touch musty food, but if forced by hunger will eat anything, with disastrous results.

Physiological Needs

Damage by fraying, rubbing, breaking, threshing

A large proportion of damage is created not by the physical needs but by the physiological ones. This damage consists of fraying, rubbing, breaking and threshing. The main damage in this group is that done by the males of all species during the period of cleaning the velvet off the antler, and marking the area of an individual's domain. The growth of antlers is described elsewhere, but it should be said here that during a formative period of 120 to 190 days each year the antlers undergo their development. Until the final phase is reached antlers are a living tissue with blood vessels running through them. At the final stages of development the blood vessels are sealed off and the antler becomes hard and physically dead. During the formative stage it is covered by a protective coat known as velvet. It is conceivable, but not as yet proved, that the drying blood and hardening of the antler cause a feeling of irritation in the upper parts of the head and along the antlers, not unlike that which accompanies the drying of blood and healing of a wound. Consequently the deer rub the head and the antlers against solid or semi-solid obstacles such as branches of trees, bushes, etc. While the antler is still in velvet, the damage, if any, is negligible and in fact the deer normally avoid afforested areas for fear of damaging their antlers, until the final stage, when the velvet is being rubbed off to expose the bare rough and hard surface of the antler. The rubbing of antlers results in the bark of the young trees and bushes being stripped off, hence its name of fraying. Later in the year, trees and bushes are again exposed to attack by deer antlers, just before and during the mating. This time the fraying often gives place to downright threshing, and even breaking of young trees. This action can be attributed to two causes: one is the marking of the area of activity of a particular beast, the marking of its march; the other is the using up of the extra vitality accumulated prior to the rutting season and to furnish a show of strength; it is the last, in particular, that can result in breaking of young trees, especially where red deer are concerned.

Threshing by red deer rarely concentrates on very young plants, for they have smoother bark, thus not abrasive enough to help rub off the drying velvet and too supple to offer much resistance. Threshing tends to be concentrated therefore on young trees with rough bark which are sturdy, therefore in softwood areas probably 5 to 10 years old. The time of the year when threshing is evident, in antler cleaning, is July to September and rutting time, September and October. But is happens outside these times when deer become frustrated for whatever reason, more frequent reasons being, finding themselves fenced in and unable to get out, high level of competition for food with other animals, disturbance in feeding areas (such as hikers) and high ratio of stags to hinds (in excess of 1 stag to 2 or 3 hinds). Needless to say there is a very close correlation between the density of deer and the extent and ferocity of damage.

It may have been noted by some, that this type of damage is normally confined to the outskirts of the thickets and coverts. In this fact lies the answer to the problem in preventive action to be taken. In those areas where deer are known to reside, when the time comes for weeding, cleaning and thinning of the plantation of trees, a belt of 2 to 10 yards wide (5-yard belt for plantation larger than 10 acres) of complete wilderness should be left surrounding the plantation. It will be to this belt that the damaging activities of deer will in the main be confined, and only negligible, if any, damage will be found in the plantation proper. The belts can be cleaned up at the time when the young trees in the plantation have passed the dangerous age. It will often be found that within the belt a number of trees have survived and new trees can be planted in the place of the damaged ones. In the case of coniferous plantations, it is advisable also to sow a belt of deciduous trees or bushes, which deer prefer, and will concentrate their damaging activities on them. The remains of these trees and bushes can again be cleared away as soon as the conifers have passed the dangerous age, or can be left as fire-breaks.

Bark stripping is an activity almost completely confined to, and always started by, the female of the species. This again is a result of food shortage and can be counteracted by artificial feeding. It is doubtful whether the hinds and does find in the bark any particular substance they are short of other than the minerals and the 'bulk'; if it is so, then hay and salt will give them sufficient sustenance to stop or decrease the stripping. The stripping is done with the front teeth of the lower jaw in an upward, striking movement, and the bark looks as if it has been taken off with a blunt pen-knife. It has been suggested that this type of damage is connected with the development of the teeth. In fairness to deer, it must be stated here that this type of damage can be attributed to sheep also, which in many parts can be found grazing in deer-inhabited areas.

Stripping is normally prevalent from late autumn to spring, especially in hard weather — hence the suggestion that it is 'bulk' that deer obtain from it in place of dead leaves and dried substances.

Against the group of damaging activities described as physiological there are not many preventive measures which can be taken. The one described above, the wild belts, is the only one by means of which the habits of deer can be confined to a space provided for them. It is impossible, of course,

14

to ensure that by the adoption of this system damage will be completely confined and none will be done outside the belts, but in general the bulk of the damage will be restricted to that area. It is for this reason that artificial means of damage prevention have been developed and are being employed, abroad.

Prevention of Deer Damage — Mechanical Measures

If, or when one sees the extent of damage sometimes done by deer and evaluates it, it is not surprising that deer are not popular and that in some radical circles people talk of total extermination where the only good deer is a dead deer. In some respects however we, the humans, may be only some humans, are as culpable for deer damage as deer are themselves. It is we who have allowed the environment to develop in a manner where deer damage is not only inevitable but is likely to increase to our cost and often to the cost to deer themselves. In our (the humans) race for survival in increasing numbers, in the race for resources and for income, we have wiped out from our mind any consideration that deer also have to live. We have given deer some land to live on, without bothering to control their numbers in taking away land from them by fencing, we have not considered their need to move, for whatever reason, and even to this day when the deer have gained themselves some recognition because they are also a resource that we can utilise, we have not done much to evaluate the capacity potential of the land we have generously allowed them to live in.

Having said all this, one has to recognise that we need to protect our investment and our needs and therefore have to protect against deer damage.

Fencing

Fencing is a useful and proper protection against deer. To be useful and proper however it should be planned so that it does not completely disrupt the life of deer on the adjoining land. Where large tracts of land are fenced in for planting or for agriculture rarely is a study of deer movements undertaken as a part of the planning process; where some recognition is given to deer herds need to move, the 'right of way' given to them is often in the places which are not suitable, forcing the deer to move along the routes which are not habitual to them and often are quite unacceptable to their instincts. Deer will not move any distance in a deep gully where they are unable to watch out for danger, along the boggy bottom of a valley or a glen where they are appreciably slowed down or along a ridge where they can be observed and where they are exposed to weather. We also tend to enclose large tracts of land and force deer to 'trespass' onto other landowners' property resulting in an unexpected influx of deer on one area and complete emigration from another. But badly planned fence has also an impact on the fencer. Deer cut off the hill, have been known to break even a very sturdy fence, jump even a high fence or, under different

15

circumstances they gather up against the fence in large numbers and even perish there; this last eventuality is not unlikely if the weather suddenly turns cold and snowy and deer try to escape to warmer lower ground.

It is also often not recognised or remembered that deer may get into the fenced-in area sooner or later; whether they force their way through the fence, jump it or take an opportunity to get in while the fence is damaged, or in the last resort have been caught up while the ground was being fenced, is of no consequence. What is of consequence is, that, once in, they will probably wish to get out be it for food, escape from flies or midges, to join in the rut, or whatever other reason.Once fenced and unable to get out they will become frustrated and will start doing damage; the damage will take the shape of tree threshing and fraying by the males and bark stripping by both sexes.Of course they will try to break out and may be successful in so doing, damaging the fence and allowing themselves and others access.To ensure against this deer leaps should be provided allowing deer to escape out, but not allowing them to return. Provision of deer leaps had been widely practised in deer parks with a high degree of success but has eluded the deer fence planners of today. Ideally deer leaps should be provided in the location of deer paths at the fence and in the corners facing the natural deer ground.They should slope gently up, be covered with moss or grass and have a sheer drop of 4½ to 5 feet on the 'away' side, ideally over a down slope and never against an up slope providing a take off for a jump in.

It goes without saying that a fence which is too weak, too low or if comprising just wires with gaps too wide, will not be deer proof for long and is a waste of money.The Red Deer Commission (*Red Deer Management*, HMSO) gives specifications for satisfactory fencing as follows:

Line wire fencing. In a low ground situation where the fence can be inspected regularily — eleven wire fence of spring steel wire. At metre intervals wire droppers which lock onto the wires and have ends twisted round the wire; staples or wooden droppers are not recommended. Posts should be not further apart than 10 metres (30 feet) with strainers at 350 metre intervals.

Two piece netting. Rylock type hinged joint or welded mesh to a minimum height of 6 ft (1.83 m) strung on three wires of spring steel and attached to it wire lashing rods. Posts in hill country should not be more than 16 ft (5 m) apart with strainers not more than 656 ft (200 m) apart — this interval can be exceeded over level ground which is not subject to snow drifting.

One-piece netting. The continental type strung on 3 spring steel line wires and attached by lashing rods. The spacing of posts and strainers should be as for the two piece netting fence.

Sheep netting. An alternative to welded mesh or rylock type, but at the 14 gauge which is needed tends to be expensive.

Combined fencing. 18 gauge rabbit netting backed by not less than 4 line wire with C6/90/30 rylock type on the bottom and hinged joint or welded mesh on the top.

Electric Fencing

In the recent years electric fencing has started being used as protection against deer. There are certain requirements which have to be met to make the fence effective. 1. Current should be 5000 volts pulsing from the mains or a heavy duty battery of 12 volts (one battery will energise up to 6 km (3·6 miles) . 2. The earthing must take into account the type of undersoil. 3. The ground immediately under the fence should be cleaned and periodically sprayed with herbicide to avoid small shorts from wet grasses and rougher vegetation. 4. Ideally there should be either a light reflecting wire or light reflecting tape in the fence to make it visible from a distance (but never electrified sheep netting).

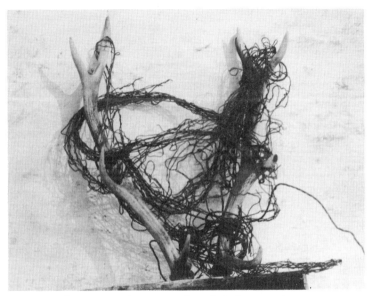

Plate III   . . . but never electrified sheep netting . . .

The effectiveness of electric fence may disappear during winter in snow.

The advantage of electric fence is that it can be moved easily and therefore can be used as a short term protection (say for 5— 6 years) while a plantation is vulnerable, or as a block for a damaged fence.

Note: It has been found useful, in all types of fencing to install a strand of wire 3 feet off the ground and 3 feet off the fence as a stand off fence on the deer side. Even when not electrified such a wire increases the effectiveness of the fence.

(Manufacturers/ importers° Wolseley Webb Ltd. Whitton, Birmingham or Ridley & Son, Stockbridge, Hampshire).

Prevention of Damage — Feeding

A large proportion of damage done by deer is in their quest for food and therein lies at least the partial answer to damage protection.

Not only additional food at the time of need, food shortage and rapid development, but also food additives will not only help in reducing the search for forbidden food but will often be instrumental in improving the quality of body and antler. Whichever form the help takes, the important thing to bear in mind is that to be effective it must be provided in the time of greatest need and it must be lasting and not sporadic.

Whatever shape the supplementary food takes, be it in the form of additional fodder, planted food or media which improves the digestion ability of the animals (such as rumen ammonia) must continue during the lean period when the hinds carry their young and stags grow their antlers, and while natural food is in short supply. Interruption for any length of time will cause a rapid increase of hunger and once this happens the animals will tend to move to better feeding, more food in the fields, etc. Feeding only when snow is on the ground for a fews days in January is not adequate; if nothing else deer unaccustomed to perhaps strange food will not take it in adequate quantities initially. Ideally one should start when the natural food starts becoming scarce, say November, and carry on until adequate quantity of natural food is available to sustain the pregnant or lactating females and antler growing males.

The practical difficulty of feeding deer on the hill is well appreciated, but one can use ponies or vehicles which are sent up to collect the culled hinds for the purpose of delivering fodder. Feeding on the verges of low land bordering on agriculture or forestry is putting temptation in the deers' way and misses many animals living in more remote areas.

It will often be found that hinds especially take slowly to strange forms of food and if this happens, an admixture of food familar to them like corn cobs, beet, or potatoes can be added.

Among the additives to food, in such areas where deer consume quantities of woody material — twigs or heather, rumen ammonia should be provided to help in breaking up cellulose substances.

Where deer resort to stripping bark which may threaten the life of parts of the forest supplementary feeds can be provided; researched in Poland and reported in 1981[*] are the following:

1. *Silage* made of bark strips and twigs mixed with growths attractive to deer (cabbage leaves or beet leaves) in proportion 1 : 1 : 1. Pine bark with cabbage leaves in proportion 3 : 7 (The latter is slower in being accepted because the bark needs more chewing, but at the same time they are better digested and a better measure against bark stripping.) Silage is taken by deer more eagerly in frosty weather than in mild weather.

2. *Bark.* A simple exercise indicated the quantities of bark stripped by deer from standing pines. As an alternative felled tree logs can be provided using trees 8 to 12 years to 60 years old. These logs are placed on supports 30 to 50 cm above the ground. Deer manage to strip 80% of the bark so provided (100% if the logs were occasionally rolled).

[*] E. Szukiel, *Acta Theriologica*, vol. 26, 19 (Warsaw, I.B.L., 1981) 319–30.

Note: Deer stripping a pine 7 to 8 years old can obtain between 5 and 20 grams of bark depending on the variety of pine, whereas a felled tree of 30 cm diameter at the base and 20 metres long provides between 5 and 13 kg of bark. Such quantity of bark is equivalent to some 650 to 1300 trees attacked on one side only, where trees of 8 to 18 years are being stripped.

See also Appendix 1/II 'Identification of damage'.

Protection by 'acoustic means'

The acoustic preventives are normally classified as area preventives. These consist of anything which makes a noise, hung along the edge of the plantation, suspended semi-freely to encourage noise to be made at the slightest breeze. Tin cans with a weight inside are popular and effective, as far as this system can ever be effective. Before deciding to use such a system we must consider its drawbacks. At a period of complete calm the deer may get into the area thus safeguarded, and should the breeze spring up when deer are inside they may be kept there for some time; for this reason, the method requires periodical inspections with a view of taking the 'acoustic fence' down and letting out any deer which may have got inside. In addition should the deer be trapped inside during a gale they are quite likely to panic as a result of the noise made all around them and to stampede, creating greater damage than they would have done in the normal course of events in the unprotected area.

In the recent years, electric/electronic acoustic deterrents have been developed. They sound a deer-scaring signal either at random intervals, for use in protection of areas, or, are activated by car headlights, for use along the roads, to protect both the deer and the road-users from accidents.

Protection by optical preventives

The optical preventives are similar in basic conception to the acoustic ones, the difference being that instead of noise-making implements we hang up strips of coloured rags, or tin foil, and place scarecrows here and there. This method is efficient for a short time only, unless the lines of optical scares are moved from time to time. Reflectors placed on stakes along the roads and reflecting traffic headlights into the deer territory have also been proved as being very effective.

Chemical Deterrents

Chemical deterrents, marketed or home-made are being used but their popularity seems to go through a number of recurring peaks and troughs. Some require hand painting or dubbing and are therefore labour intensive and for this reason not always suited to large-scale application; several can be sprayed by the agricultural, ground or air, spraying. The durability of most leaves something to be desired; in wet weather they get washed off and their smell deteriorates. Surprisingly, some of the home-made ones, which are based on manure, specially with creosote admixture seem to leave a deterring quality through taste buds, for even after the smell had disappeared, deer do not come back to browse on the sprayed areas for some time.

In the same way various industrial chemicals may be applied to this end. Here, however, care must be taken as some of the very efficient chemical deterrents will kill plants or at least damage them; others will keep not only deer away but also small game. A series of experiments has therefore been undertaken on the Continent to establish the degree to which chemicals can be used without deleterious effects on other forms of life and numerous firms have produced their own results in the form of manufactured deer deterring mixtures.

In general, the basic chemicals acting as deterrents are as follows: coal tar, wood tar, secondary oil-refining produce, sulphites, resins, minerals and organic products.

From that multiplicity of chemical groups, Meyer, in 1939, selected the following:[*]

(a) Carbolic; heavy lubricating oil; solution of copper sulphate.

(b) Tar emulsion; emulsion of animal oil.

(c) Non-soluble high molecular and thick hydrocarbons, ramified or neutralised through C, Br, CN, O, CO, SH, NO_2, or COOH

(d) Lower grades of petroleum products.

(e) Fatty acids which have retained their aldehydes.

(f) Cattle fats; cattle blood; Vaseline; acid-free oils.

(g) Technical benzol, chlorinated and mixed with water or whitewash.

(h) Anthropin.

In practically all cases these chemicals cannot be used pure and require additions in order to neutralise their harmful effects on various forms of growth and few only can be used in their basic form. The bulk of them are applied by spraying or brushing on, or dripping from containers, thus forming an odour barrier.

Individual Protection of Trees

In many instances, when young plants require protection and where fencing is not appropriate, individual tree protectors can be used (Fig. 1).

Individual tree protectors can be home-made but these days, when labour and material costs are high, they seem more appropriate for use in garden than woodland plantings.

Two types of manufactured protectors are on the market however, both made of polythene. One a spiral strip which winds around the plant; this remains effective only if it is checked, and rewound should the young branches protrude between the spiral twists. The other, usually made of translucent polythene, is in a form of a square sleeve which is slipped over

[*]Dr F.Türcke, *Mittel gegen Wildschäden und ihre Anwendung*, (Munich, Hamburg, F.C. Meyer, 1953).

the plant at the time of planting. This protector requires no further attention and furthermore encourages the upward growth of the young plant. In areas exposed to wind, it is safer to stake the protectors, otherwise they tend to fall down and bend or even break the plants. In hot sunny weather, the sleeve tends to cook the plant unless it is placed with an adequate gap from the ground to allow air circulation.

Fig.1   Individual protection of young trees

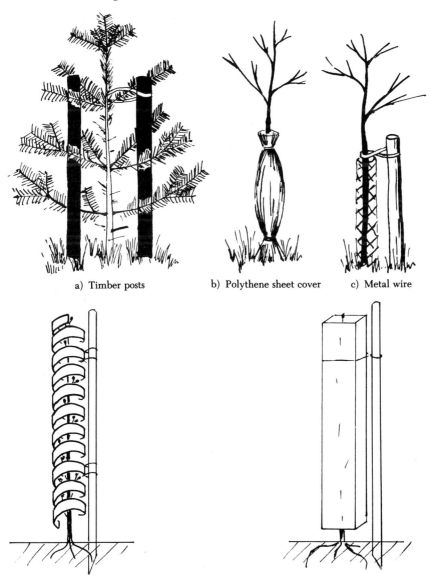

a) Timber posts   b) Polythene sheet cover   c) Metal wire

d) Manufactured polythene protectors
L. Spiral   R. Sleeve

21

Part damaged	Appearance of damage	Season	Type of damage	Evidence		Species responsible
Stem or trunk	Bark stripped in well-defined pieces. Toothmarks parallel and more or less vertical	Dormant	Winter bark stripping	Width of toothmark	Height above ground	
				8–9 mm	0.3–1.7 m	Red
				4–5 mm	0.5–0.6 m	Roe
					<1 m	Fallow/Sika
	Bark stripped in small pieces. Toothmarks parallel and oblique. Often on lower branches and stem	Dormant	Bark nibbling	2.5 mm	<0.5 m	Rabbit
				3 mm	<0.6 m	Hare
				<1.3 mm	<0.15 m	Voles
		Mostly Mar.–Jun.	Bark nibbling		any	Squirrel
	Bark stripped in vertical bands	Active	Summer stripping	Evidence of species present – slots, droppings		Deer
	Bark torn off in strips often on one side. Few or no broken side branches. Wood underneath scored	1 Feb.–20 May	Fraying (velvet)	Height		
					<0.80 m	Roe
		15 July–15 Sept.			<1.80 m	Red
		1 July–31 Aug.			<1.60 m	Fallow/Sika
	Bark torn off in strips, often all round stem, side branches twisted and broken	1 Apr.–15 Aug.	Fraying (territory)		<0.80 m	Roe
		15 Sep.–31 Oct.	Fraying (velvet and rut)		<1.80 m	Red
		15 Sep.–31 Oct.			<1.60 m	Fallow
					0.17–0.5 m	Muntjac
		Mar.–Apr.	Spring fraying		<1.80 m <1.60 m	Red Fallow
		Nov.–Dec.	Fraying (Rut)	Stems <12 mm	15–38 mm	Chinese Water deer
	Stems prodded into holes (mostly conifers)	Sept.–Nov.	Fraying (Rut)	Stems <10 cm		Sika
Buds or twigs	Buds and twigs eaten – cut ends rough with chewed appearance	Dormant	Winter browsing	Maximum height of damage		
				1.50 m		Red
				1.40 m		Fallow
				1.15 m		Roe
				56–86 cm		**Muntjac
		Active	Summer browsing (mostly hardwoods)	Height-species as winter + indication of species, i.e. tracks, droppings, hair		Deer
	Buds and twigs eaten. Cut ends a clean oblique sheared appearance	Dormant	Winter browsing	Width of incisor	Height of damage	
				2.5 mm	<0.50 m	Rabbit
				3 mm	<0.70 m	***Hare
				+ indications of species, i.e. tracks, droppings, holes		
	Buds or ends of shoots picked off	Early spring	Leaf flush	On young plants <.60 m + indication of species, i.e. tracks, droppings, feathers		Capercaillie or Blackcock

Note:
°R. Prior *Trees and Deer*, Batsford 1983.
**Muntjac frequently browse to the second height by standing on their hind legs.
***Bitten twig often lying on the ground below.

Chapter III

DEER DENSITY — STOCK CONTROL — PLANNED SHOOTING — STOCK ADJUSTMENT — CULL SELECTION PRINCIPLES

Density

No matter what damage protection methods are used, or planned for the future, they are doomed to failure if the numbers of deer are not controlled, and maintained at a density level which the ground can carry. That density level depends on the feeding potential of the locality not in absolute terms but related to the acceptable level of damage, to the level of damage which can be economically (or emotionally) sustained.

Deer density however, has the influence not only on the level of damage but also on the condition of the deer. In areas where conditions are poor but damage potential is high the numbers need to be low, whereas where conditions are good and damage risk is low, they can be higher. The Scottish deer living on the hill without competition with other (domestic) animals, and with the damage on the hill being of comparatively low importance, can live at fairly high density; here the dangers of overpopulation are that too high a density will cause deterioration in the quality of deer and may be the reason for marauding on agricultural or forestry land. On the whole, a density on the hill accepted in Scotland as reasonable is that of some 20 to 25 acres per head of deer. At this level deer seem to maintain their condition, but if an improvement in the condition of deer is required, the density may have to be reduced by as much as 20%. Experience from a fairly good hill with fair conditions, but limited cover from weather, shows that reduction in population by 17% resulted in improvements of carcass weight by 5% in three years. At the same time the antler quality improved appreciably but abreast of careful and intensive selective culling.

The density figure cannot be used in absolute terms and generally applied as the feeding potential of the hill varies from place to place and the danger of marauding also varies, to a degree depending on fencing, proximity of arable land or forestry, natural barriers between the hill and arable land, etc.

There are methods of assessing the capacity of deer on a given ground; some of these are simple others complex and they give a mix of results which do not necessarily agree with each other. The complex ones previously published° are repeated in Appendix 1 to this chapter.

A frequently used and simple yardstick of density applied on the Continent in an open and mature forest gives a density of 1 red deer to 150 acres. This is applied in forests of mixed conifer and broadleaf variety and could not be used in the typical current forest in Britain which is coniferous and close-planted where feeding potential is appreciably lower, unless a very progressive planting regime is adopted on the lines suggested in Chapter X.

It stands to reason that deer density is not a static figure but has to be changed in relation to the vulnerability of the environment: for instance at the planting stage, the density needs to be low, it can be allowed to rise as the trees mature, because by the time most conifers are at the age of say 8 to 15 years the danger of damage is of a lower order; once the canopy has closed and consequently the ground growth dies, the density needs to be reduced to prevent stripping within the forest and wandering to other areas. Of course the relationship between the tree age to damage vulnerability is different in a broadleaf forest where trees grow more slowly. Here the trees become less vulnerable to damage probably at the age of 12 years, but the forest does not close its canopy as effectively as the coniferous one, and there is usually more ground growth to sustain deer.

One hears of mixed woodland where 100 deer inhabit 3,000 acres: density of 1 : 30 acres; another coniferous forest of 30,000 acres inhabited by 200 deer: density of 1 : 150 acres.

In the 3,000 acre forest, having reduced the density to 1 : 100 acres a dramatic reduction in the level of damage had been achieved.

In yet another forest of 10,000 acres of conifers, a cull of 900 deer was executed in two years (say 450 deer per year), as a measure to reduce damage level. Such cull alone represents a culling rate of 1 deer to 22 acres, hence the density must have been much higher for there were numerous deer left in the forest after the cull.

No wonder the forest owners were concerned about deer damage!

Unfortunately little conclusive and acceptable research had been published so far in Britain. Various organisations are conducting research and when published there may be further useful guidance. The research is a complex and time consuming one, for not only does it need to consider the nutritional value of thousands of plants but also establish the levels of acceptable damage and economic density of different areas where geophysical conditions specially soils and weather factors differ, and it is not only red deer but also others that need to be included.

° A.J. de Nahlik, *Wild Deer* (London, Faber & Faber, 1959) and *Deer Management* (Newton Abbot, David & Charles, 1974).

Sex Ratio

Next consideration must be given to the proportion between the sexes.

There are nearly as many schools of thought on this subject as there are countries where deer are managed and recognised as game. The generally accepted ideal, common to all schools is that 1 : 1 male to female. The figure which has the greatest support and which causes comparatively least worry with good results is that quoted below, but it is difficult to attain. The practical application of the adjustment of sex proportion shows, that, without deterring results about which we shall talk later, the following can be accepted: Red deer, 1 stag to 1.5 hinds (excluding young of less than eighteen months — this proportion can be applied to the areas considered as good or poor and can be exceeded to 1 : 2 in the very good areas, however, 1 : 1.5 should not be otherwise exceeded. Fallow deer, 1 buck to 2 does, and roe 1 : 3, are acceptable for good and very good areas, and in poor areas does should be decreased by one-half.

There are several reasons why the proportions indicated above should be adhered to. The reasons are perhaps best represented by Dr H.B. Oloff.°

In order to achieve an improvement in the quality of antlers of deer, the relative unbalance between the sexes by overweight in the number of either stags or hinds must be avoided. Such unbalance will in the first place result in the loss, by wandering away, of the best, heaviest and strongest stags, and cause deterioration and consequent disturbance of our aim of planned breeding and shooting.

The results are even worse in their aftermath. The proportionate percentage figure of the female of the species increases. The shortage of stags results in weak and poor beasts amassing their herds of hinds and by covering them during during the rutting season, propagating poor blood; while the good, strong stags stray away.

Dr Oloff adds further

It is therefore necessary firmly to regulate the relative numbers of the sexes at the earliest moment, in particular by the shooting of surplus hinds or does, and by selecting the ages of the beasts to be left behind.

The graphs and the tables which follow represent the gradual adjustments which are required to be made, in abstract examples.

One may well wonder why the best stags should stray away when there is too much competition by other stags, or even if too many hinds are in evidence. This is difficult to explain, and a sight which may be seen in Scotland, of a stag leading a herd of some dozens of hinds, may seem to cast doubt on that statement. The case is difficult to base on facts which disprove it. The suggestion put forward is, *inter alia*, that a good stag, knowing his value, cannot stand the everlasting company of bye stags, and being forced to fight on one side of the herd for the integrity of his harem, while other stags round up a part of the herd on the other side.

Red deer are animals with some notion of fair play. Cases have been known of two stags selecting the fighting ground so as to allow both animals

° *Jagd und Hege in Aller Welt*, chapter 'Rotwild'.

to find foothold on equally firm terrain, neither starting the fight with his back down the slope, allowing the other to charge down-hill. Stags are, however, unscrupulous where'stealing the other one's wives' is concerned, specially when an old wily master stag defends the herd; the younger ones or the weaker will play all manner of tricks, fair or unfair, but avoiding straight fight. These tricks are not popular with the master stag; here is one possible explanation of the strange-seeming situation.

Imagination can bring many solutions to that question and it will be difficult to disprove any. One explanation of this problem of the Scottish herds may be that the beasts are forced to live in certain areas where they are least interfered with by human intrusion, where food is available and space provided. Going up-hill may well mean, specially in the latter part of the rutting season, entering the snow area; going down invading the human-inhabited area before the time when for the purpose of survival it is absolutely necessary. Remaining with the herd even at the cost of enduring against the competition from other stags may be thus the best solution if not the only one.

Shooting Plan

Table 5 shows planned shooting of red deer on an area approximately 20,000 acres (capacity assessed on the Tables in Appendix 1 to this chapter) where the existing stock of deer stands at 80, and the sex proportion is 1 : 3. In this example, the task is to adjust the proportion of sexes without changing the overall number of heads (see also Fig. 2) .

TABLE 5 Stock adjustment — red deer

Age:	1	2	3	4	5	6	7	8	9	10	11	12	Total	Remarks
1st year														Note the number
Stags	6	5	4	1	1	1	1	1	-	-	-	-	20	of young stags and
shot				— none —									nil	predominance of
Hinds	6	4	16	— total 34 —									60	hinds – no stags are
shot	3	1	4	— total 12 mainly barren —									20	shot first year, and
2nd year														only the bare mini-
Stags	11	6	5	4	1	1	1	1	1	-	-	-	31	mum in subsequent
shot	3	2	1	-	-	-	-	-	-	-	-	-	6	years.
Hinds	11	3	3	12	— total 22 —								51	
shot	5	-	-	-	— total 6 —								11	
3rd year														
Stags	10	8	4	4	4	1	1	1	1	1	-	-	35	
shot	4	1	-	-	-	-	-	-	-	1	-	-	6	
Hinds	12	6	3	3	12	— total 16 —							52	
shot	6	1	-	-	2	— total 3 oldest —							12	
4th year														
Stags	11	6	7	4	4	4	1	1	1	1	-	-	40	
shot	3	-	-	-	-	1	-	-	1	-	-	-	5	
Hinds	12	6	5	3	3	10	— total 13 —						52	
shot	6	1	-	-	-	2	— total 3 —						12	
5th year														
Stags	11	8	6	7	4	4	3	1	1	-	1	-	46	
shot	4	2	-	1	-	-	-	-	-	-	1	-	8	
Hinds	12	6	5	5	3	3	8	— total 10 —					52	
shot	6	1	-	-	-	-	1	— total 4 —					12	
Stags	7	6	6	6	4	4	3	1	1	-	-	-	38	State after five-years' planned shooting has been in operation.
Hinds	6	5	5	5	3	3	7	— total 6 —					40	

Note: The examples in this section are based on H. Dziegielewski, *Przewodnik Informator Lowiecki* (P.W.R-L., Warsaw, 1955) and refer to the areas of deer habitat in Poland, where great efforts to improve deer stock are being made. The density of deer population is therefore on our, or even on many Continental standards, very low. In some parts an arbitrary density is advocated, as follows: Red deer : 1 : 250/280 acres; Fallow : 1 : 60/80 acres; Roe : 1 : 25/50 acres.

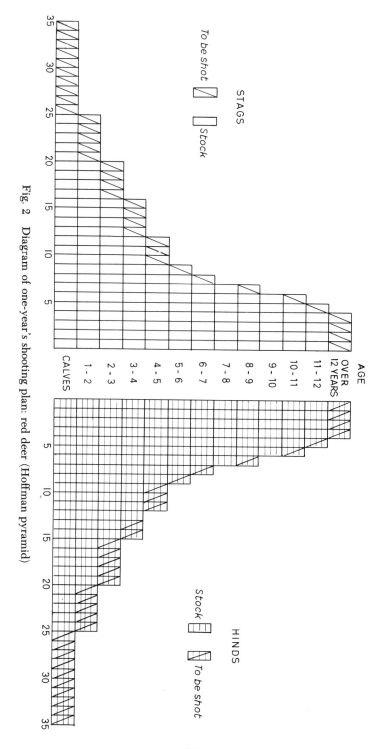

Fig. 2   Diagram of one-year's shooting plan: red deer (Hoffman pyramid)

The consequent adjustment which still remains is to distribute the ages more evenly on the basis of the following table of percentages:

TABLE 6 Percentages shot — red deer

	% of the total number	Shoot in the year
Prickets and calves . .	20	20% birth rate
2nd year		
3rd year	37	44% age group
4th year		
5th year		
6th year	28	12% age group
7th year		
8th year		
9th year and older . .	15	24% age group
	100	100

TABLE 7 Stock adjustment – fallow deer

Age:	1	2	3	4	5	6	7	8	9	Total	Remarks
1st year											As a result of a very
Buck	13	12	7	3	2	–	1	–	–	38	high birth rate of
shot	3	1	1	2	–	–	–	–	–	7	fallow deer very high
Does	18	20	13	10	14	total 17				92	proportion of birth rate
shot	5	7	–	–	3	total 4				19	must be shot as long as
2nd year											there is an overweight
Buck	27	10	11	6	1	2	–	1	–	58	of does.
shot	17	3	2	1	–	–	–	–	–	23	The prickets and young
Does	27	13	13	13	10	11	total 13			100	does of weak mothers
shot	17	5	5	5	3	2	total 8			45	must be shot first.
3rd year											In the shooting of
Buck	20	10	7	9	5	1	2	–	1	54	mature does, the
shot	12	4	2	2	1	–	1	–	–	22	barren ones should
Does	20	10	8	8	8	7	9	total 5		75	be shot first.
shot	10	3	2	1	1	1	4	total 3		25	
4th year											
Buck	18	8	6	5	7	4	1	1	1	51	
shot	10	2	1	1	2	1	–	–	1	18	
Does	18	10	7	6	7	7	6	5	2	68	
shot	6	4	2	2	3	3	2	5	2	29	
5th year											
Buck	12	8	6	5	4	5	3	1	1	45	
shot	6	2	2	1	–	1	–	–	–	12	
Does	12	12	6	5	4	4	4	4	–	51	
shot	6	6	2	2	–	–	–	2	–	18	
Buck	6	6	4	4	4	4	3	1	1	33	State after five-years'
Does	6	6	4	3	4	4	4	2	–	33	planned shooting has been in operation

A similar table for the planned shooting of fallow deer will be presented on the assumption that in an area of 18,000 acres the capacity is 66. The initial stock which is the starting point of the plan is 38 buck and 92 does (total of 130); our aim is to adjust to a proportion of 1 : 1. The five-year shooting plan will be thus (see also Fig. 3A):

A. FALLOW DEER

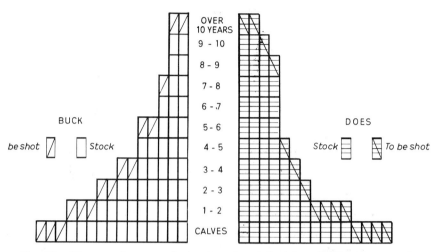

Fig. 3A Diagram of one-year's shooting plan: fallow deer (Hoffman pyramid)

The proportionate build-up by ages should be continued to the following percentage formula:

TABLE 8 Percentages shot – fallow deer

	% of the total number	Shoot in the year
Prickets and calves . .	22	20% birth rate
2nd year . . . . . ⎫		
3rd year . . . . . ⎬	38	25% age group
4th year . . . . . ⎭		
5th year to 8th year . .	22	22% age group
9th year and older . .	18	33% age group
	100	100

Lastly we come to the problem of the planned shooting of roe deer. Assuming that the area with which we are dealing is of 17,000 acres and that the initial count reveals that some 232 roe deer are present on the area, of which 51 are buck and 181 does, giving the approximate proportion of sexes 1 : 3.5. Our aim is to establish the sexes in the proportion of 1 : 1. From the tables quoted before we know that this, being forest of very good quality, can carry 144 head of roe. The shooting plan will be thus (see also Fig. 3B):

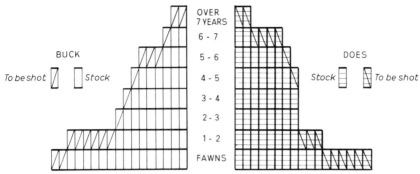

B. ROE DEER

Fig. 3B Diagram of one-year's shooting plan: roe deer (Hoffman pyramid)

TABLE 9 Stock adjustment – roe deer

Age:	1	2	3	4	5	6	7	8	Total	Remarks
1st year										On the initial takeover
Buck	30	15	3	3	–	–	–	–	51	of the forest, by the
shot	–	–	–	–	–	–	–	–	–	time the count was
Does	50	19	20	26	32	34	–	–	181	completed it was too
shot	–	–	–	–	–	–	–	–	–	late to carry out any
2nd year										shooting in the first
Buck	50	30	15	3	3	–	–	–	101	year. The number of
shot	21	8	–	–	–	–	–	–	29	does allotted to ages is
Does	52	50	19	20	26	32	34	–	233	largely hypothetical as
shot	27	20	–	–	–	8	25	–	80	it would be impossible
3rd year										to assess their ages quite
Buck	51	29	22	15	3	3	–	–	123	so accurately.
shot	34	9	2	3	1	2	–	–	51	
Does	51	25	30	19	20	26	24	9	204	The correct number of
shot	34	7	10	–	–	6	4	9	70	buck reached in the
4th year										third year.
Buck	47	17	20	20	12	2	1	–	119	
shot	27	4	4	6	4	1	1	–	47	
Does	47	17	18	20	19	20	20	20	181	
shot	27	3	2	4	3	4	10	20	73	
5th year										
Buck	35	20	13	16	14	8	1	–	107	
shot	20	3	2	4	2	4	–	–	35	
Does	35	20	14	16	16	16	16	10	143	
shot	20	6	1	2	2	8	8	10	57	
6th year	(5th year of planned shooting)									
Buck	23	15	17	11	12	12	4	1	100	
shot	16	4	2	–	2	3	1	–	28	
Does	28	15	14	13	14	14	8	8	114	
shot	15	5	2	1	3	5	3	8	42	
Buck	12	11	15	11	10	9	3	1	72	State after six years'
Does	13	10	12	12	11	9	5	–	72	planned shooting has been in operation.

We have achieved the required overall number and the right proportion of sexes 1 : 1, but the age proportion is still slightly wrong. For roe the percentage apportioning of ages should be approximately as Table 10.

TABLE 10 Percentages culled – roe deer

	% of the total number	Shoot in the year
Fawns	30	30% birth rate
1–3 year old	24	27% age group
4–5 year old	26	20% age group
6 and older	20	23% age group
	100	100

The tables as represented do look somewhat frightening, To adjust the age proportion exactly is a task on which a number of very experienced stalkers would have to be employed, a task which, for the purposes of scientific experiment might be feasible but to a private tenant neither practible nor possible unless he had unlimited financial and manpower resources.

These tables are therefore to serve as a guide based on theory. The practical application of the theory will be elaborated upon below, when the practical application of the planned shootings is discussed.

If one were to generalise about planned shooting it would be fair to say that the beasts which should be left for breeding are the medium-aged and those which are to form our breeding stock in the future; the older male animals are generally kept as potential trophies and not as part of the breeding stock. It is important that among the young animals which are shot, all the weak and late-born should be taken first of all, followed by those which are malformed or come from malformed stock.

Shooting of malformed stock should be given high priority. Badly formed stags or bucks, barren hinds and does, and sick or badly wounded deer which have little chance of surviving without the wounds being reflected in future antler formations should be shot, preferably before the rutting season.

Here, of course, 'deer recognition' is of the greatest importance. In order to facilitate this part of planned shooting, two chapters are later devoted to deer recognition.

The above shooting planning relates to deer management for sport and trophies. A different approach is needed if deer are managed for venison production (not deer farming), the approach is described in Chapter XXIV 'Business Objectives'.

The Preparation of the Shooting Plan.

It will be seen by now that the basis of our plan is the area under control and the number of deer therein.

The number of deer is a difficult figure to arrive at. First of all it must be considered within the complex of a forest or a forest block holding deer, and not necessarily within the tenancy or estate. This is especially important where the deer population is of a shifting nature, for part of the year residing in one area and then wandering to another. It will be seen therefore that the count must be done on the whole of the deer holding area, but its implications applied to the tenancy or estate only.

It has been said before that a certain density of deer population can be acceptable with a minimum tolerable damage being done by deer. This density will apply to a specific area which may have to exclude the acreages under human habitation and cultivation (farm or forestry) and even cattle grazing, unless deer are to be tolerated in fields and grassland grazing.

These considerations may be vital, because control of deer needs to be viewed in two different ways which may, but need not be complementary.

In the context and tenor of this book we are basically looking at the control and adjustment of deer numbers as measures which are needed in managing deer, to optimise the condition and therefore quality of deer. We are therefore concentrating on taking out the surpluses which are unwanted, in a sequence of priority: poor quality animals, calves and yearlings which cannot be sustained, old animals past the optimum development and females, the surplus of which may lead to excessive recruitment. The accent is on numbers in relation to the condition and quality of deer and the environment, within the acceptable limits of damage.

There is however, another approach where the accent is on managing the environment, within which deer need to be controlled for the benefit of the environment and therefore probably with a less tolerant approach to damage, but with an acceptance of continued existence of deer. The accent is therefore on optimising the quality of the environment (therefore including field and silvicultural crops), where the deer, whilst accepted have to take the second place and therefore number control is more important than quality.

It is easier to find a compromise between the two approaches in open hill deer management than in woodland, if for no other reason than it is easier to count, to ascertain and establish quality criteria, and in a manner of speech execute the cull, on open hill. But this does not mean that under woodland conditions such a compromise is impossible even if one accepts that it is difficult. It is sometimes better however, to forgo the demands of deer quality and concentrate on numbers, than forgo deer altogether under the pressure from human interests.

Having determined the acreage of the deer holding we must apply the density figure to the overall number of deer which we can economically hold. From this overall figure the number of stags/bucks, and hinds/does can be easily arrived at, it being remembered that although generally speaking a sex proportion of 1 : 1 is advocated, more hinds/does than stags/bucks can be accepted; but when the adjustment is completed this proportion should be maintained. Increases in the numbers of hind/does are acceptable as long as they do not result in the straying of the old stags/bucks, or deterioration of the antlers. Should either of these events take place, a return must be made to the recommended proportion with the minimum of delay.

The most difficult part of the preparation of the shooting plan (specially on the first occasion) which recurs each year, is the counting.

Counting of deer should take place during the latter part of winter, preferably at the end of February and early in March. Where deer-keepers and stalkers are employed the counting can be done by keen observation of the deer, and by noting their movements, thus establishing an approximate total. An experienced keeper or stalker should be able after a month's observation, to arrive at a figure with an acceptable margin of error. This method is not advocated when a first count is being carried out, specially in the forest, but is a very safe way of determining the ages of the beasts.

A useful method of counting deer, if dry fodder of a type attractive to deer, or salt licks, are provided and in regular use in winter, is to count deer coming to use these during mornings and evenings (in hard winter even during the day).

A similar method, widely used, is to count deer coming out to feed in the fields and glades early mornings and late evenings; this method is especially successful where parcels of woodland are broken by cultivated fields and woodland glades.

In both, a number of people are needed to allow for simultaneous observation in a number of selected locations in fair proximity of each other, and on a consecutive number of mornings and evenings, preferably in sunny weather (never in rain).

A method of deer counting increasingly used is that of moving deer through a line of observers cum counters. Deer are moved very gently, with the 'beaters' and 'counters' recording the sightings.

Not all deer will be counted in the woodlands whichever method is used; some will slip through unseen, others will just not move and a correction factor needs to be applied normally to the results. Suggested correction factors, depending on type of deer counted (the smaller they are the more likely it is they will escape recording) are as follows: 1.4 to 1.7 in individual observations over a number of outings, 1.3 to 1.6 in simultaneous observation by observers over a number of consecutive outings, 1.2 to 1.3 in moving deer through observers. Of course, the experiecne of observers is also a factor in accuracy of observations.

In individual observations and simultaneous observations the following formula is applied:

$$\frac{\text{Total number of deer observed}}{\text{number of mornings and evenings}} \times \text{correction factor.}$$

Both the individual observation and simultaneous observation can be used as a sample. Here a record from a representative sample of observation locations is created and applied to a larger area using a simple sampling technique. In very simple terms: Observations from sample areas covering

20 acres show 5 deer, therefore the total area of 100 acres equals 25 deer. In this approach it is imperative that the 'sample locations' are not selected because one knows that deer are there, or because they offer easy observation but that they are a truly representative sample of the environment in which the deer live. In young plantations high seats, suitably located, can be used for this purpose, in older woodlands observation may have to be done from ground level, but rides with high seats can be used if the area is well provided with rides, thus allowing a number of observation points.

During the observation by individuals a record should be kept starting with precise identification of the observation point, or observers route, on the map, and complemented and supported by notes which are best made on a standard format such as suggested in Figs 4, 5 and 6. Such notes can then be plotted on the map and analysed, using the indicated direction of animals' movements as a means helping to protect against double counting.

Ultimately, the maps will show the preferred location of deer, and can be used as means of introducing stalkers or guests to the area.

Fig. 4   Individual observation record

Location..Date ....

Weather..Wind Direction..

Sighting/Tracking		Sighted, number	Tracked, number	Direction of move
Stags	Old			
	Medium			
	Young			
	Pricketts			
Hinds	Old			
	Medium			
	Young			
	Calves			

Other comments ....

....

Recorded by ....

Fig 5 Roe deer census

Date ....

Estate .... Position/Beat ....

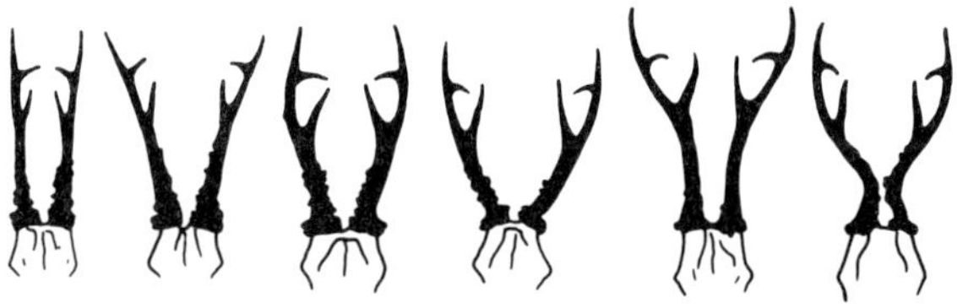

1 2 3 4 5 6

7

8

Direction clock

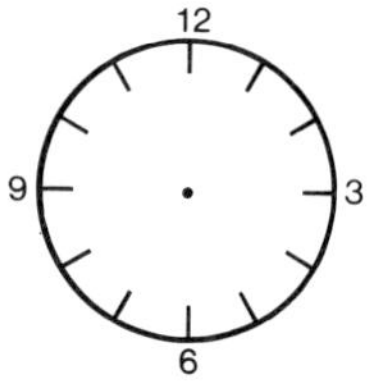

Buck									
M	Shape								
	Dir'n								
Y	Shape								
	Dir'n								
Doe									
M	No								
	Dir'n								
Y	No								
	Dir'n								
Kid/Fawn									
	No								
	Dir'n								

Recorded by ....

The other system of counting deer, by driving the beasts with a number of beaters through the line of 'observers', can be used where the areas in question are sufficiently small to make a proposition of this sort a practicable one. By this method neighbouring blocks of forest can be driven with not less than two days between drives to allow the deer to return to their normal habitation in between. The driving must be done slowly during the hours of mid-day when the deer are not on their way to or from the feeding grounds.

In Chapter XX, 'The Count', a description of the method advocated by the Red Deer Commission and widely used in Scotland, is also given.

If a count has been carried out and either an age assessment has not been made, or we have doubts as to its accuracy, the following expedient can be adopted at any time before the opening of the season: during reconnaissance in the forest a note is made of the numbers of deer of each sex observed over a period of not less than seven consecutive days in a given area (the area must be the same each time). On the observations made and assessment of ages produced, a percentage figure of each can be found, and this percentage figure applied to the overall number of deer should represent a reasonably accurate picture of the numbers in each age group — accurate for planning the shooting in the following season.

By now we have covered the theory of planned shooting, and the practice of deer counting. Next we must cover the practical aspects of planned deer shooting.

We have admitted that planned shooting as accurate as has been represented earlier in this chapter, is not a practical proposition under normal conditions, if for no other reason, because the differences in ages of some beasts are too small for us to assess, specially when two neighbouring age groups are concerned. Furthermore, no allowance has as yet been made for the shooting of poor beasts, definitely not wanted in our forest, such as old or barren hinds and does, malformed and old stags and bucks, weak and late-born calves and fawns.

In the practical working out of the shooting plan, the males are normally divided into two groups, Old (Group I) and Young (Group II) ; and by perfection of antlers into two sub-groups, Good (Section A) and Bad (Section B). From these divisions a diagrammatic cross can be produced (Table 11). (But see also — Cull — selection principles, page 32).

TABLE 11 Division into groups

	Old (I)	Young (II)
Good 'A'	IA	IIA
Bad 'B'	IB	IIB

Having thus subdivided our deer into four broad categories, we must consider how to allot the various species to groups as far as age is concerned.

Age classification, very much simpler than that represented in the preceding pages, depends on the advance in antler and body development. Once we have settled the dividing line between young and old our schematic tabular representation can be completed but for the assessment of 'good' and 'bad' antlers, a subject which will be covered in a separate chapter.

The age classification is basically as follows (Table 12):

TABLE 12 Age classification

	Young	*Old*
Red deer	1–7	8 upwards
Fallow deer	1–6	7 upwards
Roe deer	1–4	5 upwards

The dividing line, however, fluctuates with the area, Red deer are generally considered to reach maturity at the age of seven, but in many areas maturity is reached later (Northern Scotland), or earlier (park deer). Fallow deer up to the age of five continue to develop the palmation of their antlers and therefore one does not consider the fallow mature until he has reached the age of six. With roe one can take the age of four as being the prime of their development almost everywhere, possibly because there is almost no influence from park breeding. The fact that a beast has reached maturity does not necessarily qualify it for classification as 'old'. This classification is normally confined to beasts which have started to show signs of being 'past their prime'. The first sign of this is the 'going back' (also referred to as setting back or deterioration) of their antlers. There is sufficient information in the chapter dealing with antlers to allow only a cursory glance being given to this problem here. In the widest and broadest possible sense we shall assume that a year after any male deer has reached maturity he will start 'going back' and can therefore be considered old. If in addition from local knowledge we make allowance for local conditions, we can fill the vertical columns of our chart of the division of deer, having age as a guide and the actual condition of the animal as the deciding factor in it.

It is for this reason that in deer recognition upon which decisions as to the design of the shooting plan are based, a knowledge of the location is so important a factor. Deer react to variations in feeding, changes of atmospheric conditions, blood-stock, etc and these must remain in the foreground when consideration is being given to the shooting plan.

A formula which may be of assistance in the preparation of the shooting plan is shown in Fig. 6.

In the woodland, having worked out a shooting plan for the entire deer forest area, it is now necessary to prepare one for each block of 300–500 acres or any other greater area which may be well defined. The best scheme is to divide the plan proportionately between the blocks and arrange a shooting plan for each, working out a formula for the entire forest and one

FOREST: _____ BLOCK _____

RED DEER

	STAGS OLD Good	STAGS OLD Poor	STAGS YOUNG Good	STAGS YOUNG Poor	STAGS TOTAL	HINDS Mature	HINDS Barren & Weak	CALVES less than 2 years Male	CALVES less than 2 years Female	GRAND TOTAL
Total count March 198–										
Proposed plan for 198– season										
Estimated recruitment* 198– season										
Estimated loss to other causes in 198–										
TOTAL LEFT IN AREA										

FALLOW DEER

	BUCK OLD Good	BUCK OLD Poor	BUCK YOUNG Good	BUCK YOUNG Poor	BUCK TOTAL	DOES Mature	DOES Barren & Weak	CALVES less than 2 years Male	CALVES less than 2 years Female	GRAND TOTAL
Total count March 198–										
Proposed plan for 198– season										
Estimated recruitment* 198– season										
Estimated loss to other causes in 198–										
TOTAL LEFT IN AREA										

ROE DEER

	BUCK OLD Good	BUCK OLD Poor	BUCK YOUNG Good	BUCK YOUNG Poor	BUCK TOTAL	DOES Mature	DOES Barren & Weak	FAWNS less than 2 years Male	FAWNS less than 2 years Female	GRAND TOTAL
Total count March 198–										
Proposed plan for 198– season										
Estimated recruitment* 198– season										
Estimated loss to other causes in 198–										
TOTAL LEFT IN AREA										

* Recruitment = calf or fawn survivors after their first winter.

Fig. 6   Page from Shooting Plan

for each block. It is wrong to fulfil the plan for the whole complex of forest by shooting more beasts in one area than in another unless the count reveals an excessive number of deer there and a shortage in the neighbouring area.

The same principle applies on the Scottish hill, except that the 'blocks' may run into thousands of acres representing the natural deer holding areas like glens or groups of glens or even complete deer forest or deer estate.

It is, however, quite acceptable to shoot an extra beast in one block if a neighbouring block is to be undershot in the season by one animal, provided that the animals are from the same group.

Cull — Selection Principles

One hears or reads occasionally, down and out arguments on how best to establish the deer's age, at the same time it is rare that one hears of the reasons why and when an accurate estimation or definition of age is important. It may be useful therefore to put the age estimation into its proper perspective specially in relation to wild deer and their stalking.

No doubt, that for some scientific purposes accurate definition of age would be important; for instance in an investigation of susceptibility of deer to some viruses, sex maturity and many others. In deer farming, the age at which the deer should be killed or sold on hoof would have its impact. Deer farming is easily disposed of for deer can be easily tagged on the farm (as indeed they could be tagged in parks).

In managing wild deer, the consideration is usually what deer to cull and what to leave. To this end those who make such decision need to be able to distinguish a shootable (cull) beast from the non-shootable one. That person has to age the animal on the hoof at distance using the body and antler recognition for guidance; it is only on rare occasions that tagging, and therefore easier means of recognition are available. It is after the beast had been culled that there is a need to confirm the visual estimation of age and this way confirm the correctness of the decision to cull. In this exercise, absolute accuracy is not needed.

To arrive at his decision the stalker (professional or sporting) needs to establish the age group of the animal in question: Young; Mature, Old, and quality grouping, shootable or non-shootable.

Selection — Stags and Bucks

Culling is an activity primarily aimed at the control of numbers of deer in total, and by sexes, so that a suitable number of stags, hinds and calves is retained on the ground.

It is not unlike a similar activity in farming — cattle or pig or other livestock. The capacity of the farm is limited and if the farmer has a breeding stock, there comes a time when he has to dispose of his surplus. The stock he does not need for breeding may be sold for meat, some beasts may be sold to other farmers on the hoof but a good cross section of quality beasts is retained. A good farmer follows established principles of age and quality of stock retained, breaking it down to breeding bulls, cows and heifers, or, boars and sows, all distributed within a span of ages, and when even his highly valued beast reaches a certain age it is disposed of like the other surplus stock.

Culling deer has exactly the same underlying principles.

A deer manager knows his objectives; his deer number is controlled by the capacity of his land; the stag to hind ratio is controlled by his business objectives (see Chapter XXIV), if he runs his forest for stalking and venison he will aim at a ratio of about 1 : 1 and not in excess of 1 : 2 stags to hinds. If the forest is managed for venison production the ratio will be about 1 : 3.

In contrast with a farmer, a deer manager has no precise knowledge of the age of each of his animals, their exact condition, parentage, calving record, etc. He has to rely on his experience, and decides on the quality and value of each animal by his ability to visually evaluate. The more information he can gather from observation and ideally from the knowledge of each beast (and he ought to know and recognise most of his beasts from year to year) the better will be his decision with regard to culling.

In his evaluation by observation, he needs to approximate the age of the beasts and in relation to the age, evaluate the quality both being related to the business objectives.

When deer are managed for stalking and venison, he will want to have deer, specially stags, of good age and high quality of antler and weight and to this end he will watch his stags until he spots irrefutable indication of going back. Once this point is reached, even the best animal must be considered to be shootable. Obviously the animals of poor quality are shootable as soon as their quality inadequancies are spotted.

To ensure however that there is a constant supply of good old beasts, he will also ensure that the culling retains a proportion of animals across the ages.

On the other hand, where deer are managed for venison the culling differs widely. Once the beast has fully developed in body (at the age of 5 to 7 years) it can be culled, for its increase in weight after that age is only marginal and food consumption for each pound weight added high, and therefore uneconomical. Here the quality of antler is of less interest, the stags are no more and no less than the means by which calves are produced, and the hinds' value lies in their reproductive capacity. High number of hinds is retained because a high recruitment rate is needed for good quality and quantity of venison. All this having been said however, the overall number of animals on the land has to be controlled in relation to the feeding potential.

Whichever is the business objective, deer for stalking or deer for venison the ability to age the beasts on the hoof is an important one to the stalker. One has to accept however that the ageing accuracy need not be very precise; if evaluation of age ± 1 year by tooth formation is adequate, it stands to reason that the evaluation of age by visual observation must be less accurate and for all practical purposes the need is limited to being able to group the beasts into groups of Young (0–3 years) , Mature (4–8 years) and Old (8 or 9 years and older) with a classification of shootable or non-shootable alongside the age.

If this classification is accepted, the only refinement to it, specially where the management is for stalking, is in distinction between the shootable and non-shootable young stags from the first to third head, where errors are easy to make.

Here however, it is necessary to be critical of the selection of deer in the cull by the stalking community, be they professional or sportsmen. Far too many deer, young and for their age well developed are not recognised for what they are, but are shot as rubbish. This is a sad indictment on those who do the culling who, as a result do both the deer and the deer owners a disservice. Deer need improving through careful culling, not only because through improvement the owners income will increase (as a result of increased quantity of venison and higher possible fees for trophies, but also through improvement, the well-being of animals is better assured).

A deeper, more self-critical study of deer shot is needed and lessons learned from such analyses be used in the future.

Fig. 7   Cull Guide Summary Red Deer

	Non-shootable	Shootable
	a Calves of 4–7 months are culled as a part of the hind cull, the deciding factor being age & condition of the hind or condition of the calf	
YOUNG 0–3 years	b Yearlings–those with antler longer than the ears c 2-year-old–long antler and antlers with tines (brows and/or top fork) and d Exceptionally long or thick antler tine-less but with bulges & kinks.	b Yearlings with short antlers c 2-year-old, spikers, unless exceptionally long, thick and with bulges or kinks.
MATURE 4–7 years (hill) 4–8 years (wood)	a 6-pointers and better with fair length and weight up the antler b 'Normal' and better heads with signs of future development	a Short or spiker heads b Antlers with fewer than 4 points at the bottom of the age group and fewer than 8 points at the top of the group c Heads from third head on triangular in profile d Heads below the 'norm' for the locality with no signs of development
OLD beyond 8 years (hill) or 9 years (wood)	Well developed antlers at least 8 points with good weight	a Poorly developed antlers irregular, ugly in appearance b Good quality heads showing signs of going back for 2 consecutive years c All stags of a known age of 14 years and more (better cull than die)

Notes: 1 The statements above are for guidance; a hill which is cold, exposed with poor quality feeding will call for a set of lower criteria than one with good shelter and certainly woodland.

2 Woodland red deer develop more quickly and grow stronger heads, live longer and therefore age bracketing may need adjusting

3 Where captive deer have access to plenty of food the above criteria can not be applied.

Appendix 1/III Deer Density

It was the Red Deer Commission that sounded a warning about the overpopulation of deer and high density level. In 1959, a figure of 180,000 deer with a density of 17–39 acres per head of deer population was quoted; in 1977 a new figure of 270,000 deer was quoted. This figure does not necessarily represent an increase in deer population by 90,000 but could represent a better technique in counting and specially greater area coverage. Whichever figure is accurate, it represents an undoubted overpopulation and attempts have been made to counter it. Two fronts of attack are needed — heavier culling to reduce the overall numbers and searching for a density figure which is acceptable in relation to damage (forestry and agriculture); overgrazing the hill and well-being of deer do not equate.

Some research on deer density and related damage levels had been done and more is in progress.

D. Welch[°] relates damage by browsing to red deer density; in a study, density is established by dung deposits — the density of dung pellet groups over a given area. The formula or relationship is as follows:

Rate of browsing damage on birch saplings = 2.97
Rate of dung pellet groups per 100 m² per week = 1.09

The study suggests that at a level of 0.5 dung pellet groups per 100 m² per week, damage is negligible and that such density represents a deer density in the area between 65.6 and 131 acres per head of deer. This is very valuable information, for two reasons; firstly it appears to be the first study of this sort in Britain carried out scientifically and with the sole purpose of serving the 'deer cause'; secondly, it supports some of the continental findings upon relationship between damage by deer and deer density. It is also worthy of note that as deer are fond of birch, one could expect the damage to brich saplings to be high.

In spite of the fact that much research on deer density has been carried out in various continental countries, there are still vast differences of opinion as to the densities recommended. These differences can be accounted for by the variety of approaches and attitudes to deer problems, the variety of geophysical conditions and, above all, the different aims and methods. Nevertheless, whichever method or approach is adopted, none would support the density of deer as high as that in Scotland.

There are other factors which have to come into consideration and have an important bearing upon the approach to deer density calculation and studies, among these is the important question of which interest is to benefit: forestry and/or agriculture or deer, or is there a suitable and economic compromise:

1. *The origin of the forest.* A naturally regenerated forest is by its character richer in undergrowth and stronger in tree growth and development, and in consequence has greater resistance to deer damage with a better recovery capability than an artificially planted forest.

° Nature Conservancy, Range Ecology Research, 1st Report, 1970.

2. *Location.* A forest bordering on pasture-land, to which deer have free access, allows for a greater density of deer within it than one which is fenced.
3. *Geophysical conditions.* Rain, and particularly snowfall level, is a very important factor because snow cover forces deer to browse on tree and other growth; thus in a high snowfall area deer density may have to be kept at a lower level than in a similar low snowfall area.
4. *Feeding.* A forest in which deer have and are being fed as a matter of course, thus countering damage, can sustain a higher deer density than another where no feeding is done or where feeding is only sporadic.
5. *Condition of deer.* The aim is to maintain high quality deer or low level of overgrazing or damage.

Professor Müller° bases his theory of deer density to incidence of damage ratio on the level of damage acceptable to forestry interests; he finds that incidences of damage over an area, through browsing of 10–15 per cent, through fraying of 5 per cent, are acceptable. He bases this assertion upon the approach to tree survival where a pine or similar tree should survive 50 per cent damage because this species has a high recovery potential.

In his detailed working of density he examines the food potential of various species of trees and also differentiates between young and old trees, in that he classifies them by species and age and allots feeding coefficients to each age group.

TABLE A   Müller's feeding coefficient

	Forest age						
	1–5	6–10	11–20	21–40	41–60	61–80	81–100
Pine Larch }	50–70	5–25	0	10–26	30–50	45–65	45–65
Fir Red fir }	40–60	40–60	0	0	0	25–45	45–65
Oak Birch }	60–80	60–80	35–55	50–70	55–75	55–75	60–80
Alder	50–70	15–25	15–25	20–40	20–40	45–65	55–75
Beech	40–60	0	0	0	0	10–20	20–40

Müller then relates the coefficients of species and age of trees by percentages to the overall area of deer-inhabited range. The outcome of his calculation is not vastly different from Ueckerman's.°° Table A is of particular interest, however, because it suggests firmly that in some types of woodland the value of natural food provided by the woodland's ground growth is very small. Müller then applies the Mottl formula:

° Unpublished lectures; Dept of Forestry and Game, University of Eberswalde, 1967.
°° E. Ueckerman. *Wildstandbewirtschaftung und Wildschadenhuttung beim Rehwild* (Neuwid, 1957).

$$D = \frac{A \times C}{R} \quad \text{Where:}$$

D is the density value
A is the area covered by each type of growth
C is the coefficient for each type
R is the total area inhabited by deer

and subsequently applies the density points in Mottl's Density Points Table (Table B).

TABLE B   Mottl's density points

Density points	Acres per head of red deer
above 100	100
92–100	122–100
85–90	176–122
41–84	273–176
31–40	500–273
21–30	600–500

In connection with this table a further stipulation must be made; that is, if other deer are present on the range with red deer, a conversion can be applied of two fallow deer to one red deer and four or five roe deer to one red deer.

Mottl ° himself worked out a different method of estimation of density, relating the deer-inhabited area to the type of growth which provides the feeding base. He also provides coefficients which he then applies to his formula mentioned above, as indicated in the Table C.

Ueckerman°° provides some very useful guides on the subject of density which he established after prolonged research, but I have seen a very much simplified method attributed to him which simply allows 100 to 164 acres per head of red deer, 25 to 123 acres to fallow deer and 22 to 82 to roe deer, moving within these brackets according to the value of naturally found feeding matter.

TABLE C   Mottl's coefficient of feeding values

1	Area of bush	179
2	Grass meadows in old deciduous woodlands	78
3	Grass meadows in old conifer woodlands	65
4	Grass meadows in old mixed wood	66
5	Grass, wood clearings, heath	48
6	Meadows, cultivation and other feeding areas within the range	56

° S. Mottl, *A Caseagainst Damage by Deer* (Czechoslovak Government Publication, 1954) and *Feeding of Deer* (Prague, Biologia, 1957).
°° E. Ueckerman. *Das Damwild* (Hamburg, P.Parey, 1956).

The Hungarian Government, which controls the forestry interests in that country, has officially established the following densities throughout Hungary:

190 acres per head of red deer
120 acres per head of fallow deer
50 acres per head of roe deer

A much more demanding method, one obviously established for 'playing safe', has been suggested by the author. It is based on a number of works from the Continent.°

This method relies on grading deer habitat quality of feeding potential, as follows:

Forest
Very good area. An area of forest so graded is considered to be one which, as a complex, is not smaller than 15,000 acres, with small fields and meadows within it. The ground is fertile, allowing for luscious growth of deciduous and coniferous trees (or deciduous only); grass in the undergrowth is of the sweet variety; a good proportion of wild undergrowth is available. Fresh flowing water is available within the area and is easily accessible to the deer.

Good area. A rather cut-up area of forest with a preponderance of conifers; a comparatively small quantity of flowing water; folding or mountainous land, few meadows and feeding areas; limited dense undergrowth.

Poor area. Sandy soil; very dry or marshy land; heather and grass of the sour kind; little sweet grass (but heather and sweet grass form an area which may be considered *good* if the two are mixed and the grass of the sour variety is in a minority); peat, conifers with soft mossy undergrowth.

Field and Moorland
Very good area. Fertile, well cultivated and drained, with wide variety of crops; forest areas in blocks of 60–100 acres within easy reach.

Good area. Mixed land, well watered, in parts covered with scrub or smaller than 60-acre copses; total area of the block less than 7,500 acres (scrub included).

Poor area. Sandy soil, moorland, heather and dry grass in preponderance.

Having categorised the land, the densities which can be applied are as shown in Table D. In the 'playing safe' policy negligible damage by resident

° S. Dziegielwski, *Jeleń* (Warsaw, 1970); Z. Pielowski, *Sarna* (Warsaw, 1970); H. Miszewski (ed), *Przewodnik Informator Lowieck* (Warsaw, 1955); T. Paslowski, *Lowiectwo* (Warsaw, 1971).

TABLE D   'Playing safe'

Density Table			
	Acres per head of deer		
	Forest	*Field*	*Moor*
Very good area			
Red deer	250	°	300
Fallow deer	125	300	°
Roe deer	50	150	100
Good area			
Red deer	500	°	400
Fallow deer	175	400	°
Roe deer	80	200	200
Poor area			
Red deer	750	°	500
Fallow deer	250	600	°
Roe deer	150	300	300

° Unsuitable for this deer

TABLE E   Ueckerman–cultivation points

1 *Percentage of forest within the area*		*Percentage of meadows within the area*	
%0	pts 7	%0	pts 9
1–20	8	1–4	10
21–40	11	5–10	13
41–60	13	11–20	17
61–80	16	21 and over	22
81 and over	18		

2 *Geology*			
Sand downs		Shell lime	35
(diluvium, alluvium)	14	Glacial deposits	18
Red sandstone	20	Granite	20
Basalt, quartz	23	Oolitic limestone	30

3 *Afforestation*			
Spruce, over 50%	pts 10	Pine, over 50%	pts 13
Mixed forest at least three types			
of tree at 10–50% of area, each	15		
oak up to 309	15	oak up to 50%	21
oak up to 40%	18	oak 60% and over	25

deer has been the prime consideration, and no other preventative methods have been contemplated.

Ueckerman has been mentioned before. His method of establishing deer density is too important not to be described in some detail.

His calculation of the optimum figure for the deer density is based on allotting a figure value to such items as the type of afforestation and its surface area, its bordering with other types of land, and the geology of the terrain. Score points are then applied which are translated into recommended density figures (Table E) for the area of 1,000 acres.

Points appropriate to the area by its characteristics are totalled and land grading is arrived at as in Table F.

TABLE F   Land grading

Very good areas	71 pts total
Good areas	61–70 pts
Medium areas	51–60 pts
Poor areas	41–50 pts

According to the 'goodness' of the area, the deer density is read off from Table G.

TABLE G   Deer density per 1000 acres

Points Score	Roe deer	Fallow deer ·	Fallow deer †	Red deer
40–45	6	4	8	3
46–50	8			
51–55	10	10	14	4
56–60	12			
61–65	14	14	20	
66–70	16			
71–75	18			6
76–80	20	20	28	
81–85	22			

None of the figures quoted can be considered as absolute; they can vary by as much as 30 per cent.

Appendix 2/III. Minimising Damage

There are some trees which are particularly attractive, even among the species which are grown extensively: red oak (*Quercus rubra*), for example, among the hardwoods; all the willows, and many poplars. Lodgepole pine (*P. contorta*) stands out as a particularly succulent conifer; Lawson's cypress is also high on the list; larches, although less palatable, are very vulnerable to fraying by roe, even several years after planting.

R. Prior, *Trees and Deer* (London, Batsford, 1983).

A few species are recognised as low on the list of preferences: Corsican pine (*P. nigra*) is often left alone. Szukiel states that in Poland the grey alder (*A. incana*) is also resistant to deer browsing. For those who attempt to establish a ground layer of cover for the benefit of game, two low-growing shrubs may be grown without protection. Snowberry (*Symphoricarpos rivularis*) flourishes on alkaline soil, to the extent that it can get out of control. Shallon (*Gaultheria shallon*) produces low cover in acid conditions. Deer hardly ever touch either species. In *The Ecology of Red Deer* by Mitchell, Staines and Welch, the following table of research findings is given.

Author	Area	Highly preferred	Preferred	Seldom or never browsed
Sablina (1959)	White Russia	*Salix* *Populus tremula* *Fraxinus* *Quercus*	*Sorbus aucuparia* *Betula*	*Tilia* *Carpinus*
Dzięciotowski (1970c)	Poland	*Quercus petraea* *Salix caprea* *Sorbus aucuparia* *Corylus*	*Acer platanoides* *Carpinus* *Prunus serotina* *Frangula alnus*	*Pinus sylvestris* *Funiperus*
Bobek, Weiner & Zieliński (1972)*	Poland	*Populus tremula* *Salix caprea* *Frangula alnus*	*Quercus robur*	*Tilia cordata* *Carpinus* *Betula*
Ueckermann (1960)	West Germany	*Populus tremula* *Quercus borealis* *Abies* *Acer platanoides* *Fraxinus* *Quercus*	*Pinus sylvestris* *Picea abies* *Fagus* *Pseudotsuga* *Larix*	*Picea sitchensis* *Alnus* *Betula*
Ahlén (1956a)	S. Sweden	*Fraxinus* *Salix* *Frangula Alnus*	*Betula*	*Alnus*
Chard (1966)	NW. England	*Juniperus* *Quercus borealis* *Pinus contorta* *Picea abies*	*Larix* *Acer pseudo-platanus* *Pinus sylvestris* *Quercus* *Betula*	*Picea sitchensis* *Fagus sylvatica* *Alnus glutinosa*

*Includes roe deer browsing

See also Table 4

Chapter IV

FEEDING OF DEER

F eeding deer does not necessarily imply providing extra food to supplement what they usually find in their environment, but providing a feeding platform in the environment on which deer can sustain themselves adequately to meet the objectives of deer management.

The spectrum which these objectives may represent stretches from retaining the status quo — we are satisfied with things as they are to the extreme of seeking and achieving the maximum development potential of deer. Between these two there will be a multitude of degrees of adjusting the feeding platform to obtain stages of marginal improvement of quality, create conditions under which numbers can be increased, decrease numbers in order to allow for quality improvement (with or without artificial assistance) and many others as far as the imagination can stretch.

Having said this much — the upper extreme of seeking maximum development potential is obviously outside the purpose and scope of this book for it has to look at an experimental investigation often under clinical conditions far outside the means of an average landowner. When such investigations are conducted however, much is revealed which is of direct interest to the deer forest owner. One such experiment had been conducted by the Rowett Institute of Aberdeen in conjunction with the Hill Farming Research Organisation. Not only is that experiment of interest because it blazes the trail in Britain but also because in it calves of red deer caught randomly on a number of estates were used and therefore the experiments do not apply to a specific strain of deer. What the experiment has illustrated is, that hill calves respond to a suitable and balanced diet, by body and antler development which hitherto would have been thought impossible. Fuller information is in Appendix 1 to this Chapter.

In *Wild Deer* account had been given of the Schneeberg experiment which, under wild park conditions produced quite dramatic improvements in the quality of deer. The objective of that experiment, conducted with commitment of large resources was to seek establishment of harmony between the interests of forest and agriculture with the interests of deer. At Schneeberg however, large scale additional feeding and introduction of high quality deer had been resorted to. Importantly however the experiment also proved that with suitable feeding, very considerable improvements of

50

quality of antler (and body weight) can be achieved. Some of the achievements are shown in Tables 13 and 14.

One can gain much encouragement, specially from the Scottish exper-

TABLE 13 Schneeberg Table I

	Number of tines	
	Poor heads	Best heads
FIRST GENERATION		
3-year-old	10	14
4 ,, ,, ...	9	17
5 ,, ,, ...	14	18
6 ,, ,, ...	14	20
7 ,, ,, ...	15	20
8 ,, ,, ...	15	26
9 ,, ,, ...	15	22
10 ,, ,, ...	14	23
SECOND GENERATION		
3-year-old	12	19
4 ,, ,, ...	14	24
5 ,, ,, ...	15	24
6 ,, ,, ...	17	27
7 ,, ,, ...	17	29
8 ,, ,, ...	17	26
9 ,, ,, ...	17	28
10 ,, ,, ...	16	33

TABLE 14 Schneeberg Table II

Age	Year	Weight of antler (kg)	Mean length of beams (cm)	Mean length of brow (cm)	Mean circumf. of burrs (cm)	Mean circumf. of beams		Tines	International points score
						lower	upper		
2	1933	3.35	88.5	28.9	12.4	14.1	12.3	11	155.6°
3	1934	5.07	95.3	31.6	23.9	16.7	14.4	13	176.8°
4	1935	7.64	116.4	37.5	25.6	17.7	15.1	14	201.0°
5	1936	9.55	113.4	37.5	28.5	19.7	16.0	17	216.3°
6	1937	10.18	121.0	42.5	27.7	19.8	16.2	17	222.1°
7	1938	11.00	127.7	42.2	29.4	21.5	17.2	17	240.5°
8	1939	11.00	130.5	40.5	30.3	22.0	18.0	19	247.0°
9	1940	10.5	126.5	22.7	30.6	22.2	19.0	20	234.0°°
10	1941	12.0	117.0	24.0	31.8	22.0	18.0	16	225.2°°

Notes
° Conditions: Ideal Feeding.
°° Deterioration sets in due to lack of the balanced diet required to maintain further progress.

iment, if one is aiming at improvements of the Scottish hill deer, for the Rowett/Hill Farming Research Organisation results prove that there is a quality potential in hill deer which is dormant only because of the adverse living conditions which exist in Scotland, and that feeding improvement could achieve fairly quick results. (See Plate IV)

The spectrum of such improvements is wide:

(a) Decrease of the number of deer on the given area of land to increase the quality of food available per head;

(b) Improvement of the quality of food by simple soil dressing which encourages the growth of sweet grasses, widely known and practised by farmers for the benefit of hill sheep and cattle;

(c) Draining;

(d) Sowing of grass and other fodder seeds to provide a better value fodder; and

(e) Provision of salt licks and rumen ammonia licks, to help digestion of cellular substances; to mention just a few simple and comparatively inexpensive ones.

Of course one could go very much further and grow small fields of crops attractive to deer, plant trees and shrubs attractive to deer (Appendix 2 to this Chapter), providing additional food and feeding compounds specially at the time of need, etc. The pressing question that will play a role is the economics and the return one expect from such investment.

Appendix 2 to this chapter gives an analysis of the food value of those plants which deer find in their natural surroundings under normal circumstances, and the nutritional values of the additional food which may be made available to deer during the winter months. These requirements must not be looked upon in too detailed a fashion, nor must one assume that all the plants mentioned should be provided. Deer, like humans, seek variety in their food and avoid monotonous feeding. Consideration should be given therefore to the overall balance of chemical, calorific and vitamin values, by provision of a variety of suitable feeding-matter containing the required components. Items such as calcium and phosphorous salts, however, need to be provided in such forms as will allow easy and complete assimilation. This can be done by experimenting. Generally speaking, the mineral salts are introduced into the digestive system through the consumption of green fermented feeding-stuff; the assimilation of mineral components in these is almost complete. Hay and other dehydrated fodder allows a normal absorption of only 50–60 per cent of the mineral contents. One can therefore accept that from mixed fodder provided for deer something in the region of 70–80 per cent of their mineral contents is assimilated.

It has been said already that the deer's greatest need for food is during the antler-forming period, when a good food-supply and provision of minerals is of prime importance if good stock is to be maintained, and during gestation and lactation. The provision of these for stags and hinds should be as follows: Calcium (CaO) 2 oz (54 g); Phosphoric salts (P_2O_5) 1.5 oz (46 g); albumen 1.3 lb; nitrogen-free substance 4 lb; overall 8–11 lb per head per day, including the dry food-stuffs serving as 'bulk'.

Vitamins play an important role in the general development of deer and

Plate IV Development of hill deer under experimental conditions

a) 2 years old. Born 1 June 1972; weight   b) 2 years old. Born 29 May 1972; weight
5kg. Photograph March 1974; 113kg   7kg. Photograph March 1974; 135kg

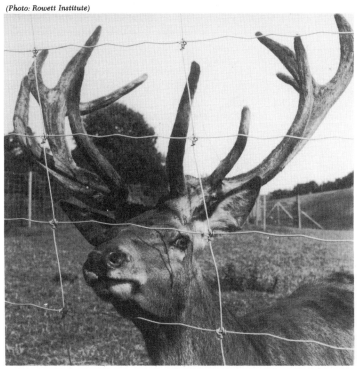

c) Fully mature. Born on the hill 1971. Caught the same year and reared on Glensaugh Deer Farm

so Vitamin D 4,000–6,000 units, Vitamin C 3 grains, Vitamin A 0.01–0.02 grains per head per day is recommended. These quantities are of course, what may be called a forced diet for rapid and vast improvement of stock by provision of ideal feeding conditions regardless of cost, but it shows how much needs to be done to achieve optimum results, and on how little deer in many parts have to live, still being expected to produce good trophies and to supply high-grade venison!

When the feeding requirements of deer under the headings 'damage prevention' and 'stock breeding' are compared it will be noted that only a quarter of the latter is needed to satisfy the needs of the former.

There are circumstances where no amount of feeding will bring about the desired improvement of antler quality; there are forests where the inherent antler characteristics are very deeply inbred. In such circumstances one may have to turn to restocking.

In restocking, antler and body formation must be our guide. If the antler-spread of the local beasts is narrow, new blood must provide extra spread. If the antlers locally are short and thin but of good spread, the new stock must be long and thick; if the beasts are small the new stock must be larger. In introducing new deer (specially red deer) to an area, care must be taken as the newcomers may be ousted by the local stags during the rutting season. It is advisable therefore, to introduce new deer to an area soon after the rut has ended or at the very end of the winter. During both these periods deer appear to be calmer, specially after the mating season has just ended.

Not only the characteristics of antlers but also their quality will vary with area, age, health, etc. Heredity plays a strong role. An illustration of inheritance of faults and similarity of form in the antlers of roe, will be found in Plate V. The following description will elaborate the point.

A stag, a well developed eighteen-pointer, had a badly formed and short trey and a slight deformity of the curve of the antler in the shape of a kink. Apart from that he was an exceptional animal with uncommonly long antlers. He was a master stag in his area for two years and in the rutting season always had a few hinds with him. As soon as his offspring started growing up, however, it was found that his deformity was passed to them, in some being only slightly marked, in others, however, quite as strong as in their ancestors. In order to stop the deformity spreading he and his sons had to be shot. In spite of the fact that all his male descendants were shot, the deformity was passed through the female line.

Plate V   Examples of antler similarity in buck of the same area

 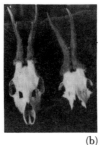

(a)   (b)

b) Inheritance of antler characteristic is shown here in the relation between the 'grandfather' and the 'grandson'. Note the kink in the right antler. The head on the left, shot in 1939 as a 4 year old buck, the one on the right (his grandson), shot in 1948 aged 10-11 years. The apparent increase in the kink of the head on the right can be ascribed to its extreme age, because many buck of the forest where these were shot start going back from the fifth year.

Appendix 1/IV: Deer Development — Experimental Conditions (Rowett Institute Experiment°)

The investigations were conducted in the 1970s by the Rowett Research Institute and Hill Farming Research Organisation, at the Institute itself at Aberdeen and at Glensaugh Experimental Farm.

The experiments were, admittedly, conducted under clinical conditions which cannot be repeated on the hill or in the forest, but they provided some fascinating information about the development potential of the Scottish hill deer.

In the early 1970s some 44 stags and 94 hind calves were taken off the hill from a variety of estates in all parts of Scotland. The selection was therefore a completely random one. Additionally in 1972 and 1973 25 stag and 27 hind calves were born from the previously captured ones.

The calves were fed on cow's milk substitute made up as for bovine calves and weaned to dried grass with home-made concentrates and proprietary lamb fattening pellets, with variations for experimental purposes.

From the records kept the conversion efficiency of the calves had been ascertained. In the first 8 weeks in captivity the calves consumed 1.24 kg of milk substitute, 1.01 kg of lamb pellets and 0.11 kg of hay for every 1 kg weight they gained. A group kept on dry feed consumed 5.1 kg dry feed for 1 kg body weight gained. The calves were weaned to artificially dried grass and lamb pellets. The overall results were as below:

Stag calves: at birth average weight 8.1 kg; by December 47 kg
Hind calves: at birth average weight 7.0 kg; by December 42 kg

By March (therefore at age of some 9–10 months) the weights were 55 kg and 45 kg respectively showing a deceleration in body build-up during the first winter, but at the age of 14 months the weights moved to 70–90 kg for hinds and 80–100 kg for stags. After that age/body weight increases were only marginal.

These results suggest that given suitable feeding conditions, many Scottish deer could develop both an antler and the body to a size far in excess of those seen on the hill (See Plates IVA and IVB).

The analysis of antler development shows some quite staggering results:

	Age of 14m			Age of 26m			Age of 39m		
	Length (cm)	Weight (grm)	No. of tines	Length	Weight	No. of tines	Length	Weight	No. of tines
On the "Farm"	17–42	20–250	2–3	42–52	380–580	4–8	no stags at that age kept on the farm		
At the Institute	14–32	140–510	2–5	30–50°°	860–4100	6–12°°	72°°°	1800°°°	10°°°

Notes: Most antlers have been sawn off when dry for reasons of safety.

° *Farming the Red Deer*, Department of Agriculture and Fisheries for Scotland (London, HMSO, 1974).

°° Some malformations of antler through contact with the pens, gates, etc.

°°° One stag only.

Appendix 2/IV: Crops, Shrubs and Trees for Deer°

A. Food plants for deer

1. Harvested, stored and hand-fed (either main crop or rejects).

(a) concentrate food (autumn)

		Red°	Roe°
Apples	*Malus sylvestris*	+ +	+ +
Barley	*Hordeum vulgare* (grain)	+ +	+ +
Beet, sugar	*Beta rapa*	+ +	+
Carrots	*Daucus carota*	+ +	+ +
Maize	*Zea mays* (grain)	+ +	+ +
	corn-cob silage	+ +	+
	whole plant silage	+ +	
Mangolds	*Beta vulgaris*	+ +	+
Oats	*Avena sativa* (grain)	+ +	+ +
Potatoes	*Solanum tuberosum*	+ +	+
Rye	*Secale cereale* (grain)	+ +	+ +
Swedes	*Brassica napus*	+ +	+
Wheat	*Triticum aestivum* (grain)	+ +	+ +

(b) maintenance food (winter)
Silage made from whole plants and fruit-husks

		Red	Roe
Apples	*Malus sylvestris*	+ +	+ +
Artichokes, Jerusalem	*Helianthus tuberosus* (herb silage)	+ +	
Beet, fodder	*Beta vulgaris*	+ +	+ +
Beet, sugar	*Beta rapa*	+ +	+ +
Grass-silage		+ +	
Hay		+ +	
Mangolds	*Beta vulgaris*	+ +	+ +

2. Crops for summer/autumn feed
(the species in bold type also for winter feed)

		Red	Roe
Artichokes, Jerusalem	*Helianthus tuberosus*	+ +	+ +
Beet, fodder	*Beta vulgaris*	+ +	+ +
Beet, sugar	*Beta rapa*	+ +	+ +
Buckwheat	*Fagopyrum esculentum*	+ +	+ +
Kale	*Brassica oleracea*	+ +	+ +
Linseed	*Linum usitatissimum*	+	+
Lupin, annual sweet	*Lupinus* spp.	+ +	+ +
Maize	*Zea mays*	+ +	+
Mustard	*Sinapis alba*	+ +	
Oats	*Avena sativa*	+ +	+ +
Peas	*Pisum arvense*	+ +	+ +
Radish, fodder	*Raphanus sativus campestris*	+ +	
Rape	*Brassica napus*	+ +	+
Rye	*Secale cereale*	+ +	+ +
Seradella	*Ornithopus sativus*	+ +	
Spurry	*Spergula arvensis*	+ +	
Sunflower	*Helianthus anuus*	+ +	
Swedes	*Brassica napus*	+ +	+
Turnips, stubble (Tyfon)	*Brassica rapa*	+	
Vetches	*Vicia sativa*	+ +	+
Wheat	*Triticum aestivum*	+ +	+ +

°R. Prior, *Trees and Deer*, Batsford, London, 1983

3. *Grasses and clovers*

		Red	Roe
Bent grass	*Agrostis* spp.	+	+
Clover alsike	*Trifolium hybridum*	+ +	+
Clover red	*Trifolium pretense*	+ +	+ +
Fescue	*Festuca* spp.	+	+
Foxtail	*Alopecusus* spp.	+	+
Lucerne	*Medicago sativa*	+ +	+ +
Meadow grass – smooth	*Poa pratensis*	+ +	+
Medick black	*Medicago lupulina*	+ +	+
Ryegrass, perennial	*Lolium perenne*	+	
Sainfoin	*Onobrychis sativa*	+ +	+ +
Timothy	*Phleum pratense*	+ +	
Trefoil	*Trifolium resupinatum*	+ +	+
White melilot	*Melitotus albus*	+ +	
Yorkshire fog	*Holcus lanatus*	+	

Note
°Relative benefit to red deer and roe indicated by number of crosses. Fallow and sika have similar tastes to red deer, depending on the location.

Feed plots
1 Mixtures must be chosen according to the soil and climate, and they must receive suitable fertiliser if they are to flourish and prove attractive to the deer. The following suggestions have been evolved in consultation with Farmacre Seeds Ltd, Tilston, Malpas, Cheshire, from whom seed may be obtained.

Mixture A: fodder root mixture for use on medium to good agricultural land and with reasonable applications of compound fertiliser. The constituents are reasonably winter-hardy and can be expected to last into January.
  Sow May to July.

1.00 kg Thousand Headed Kale
1.00 kg Maris Kestrel Kale
0.50 kg Purple Top Swede
0.50 kg Giant Rape
0.50 kg Tyfon Stubble Turnip
0.25 kg Green Globe Turnip

———

3.7 kg per acre (9.25 kg per hectare)

Mixture B: fodder root mixture for upland areas and less fertile conditions. This mixture does however require reasonable soil and will not thrive in very acid conditions.
  Sow July.

3.50 kg Giant Rape
0.50 kg Green Globe Turnip
6.00 kg Danish Italian Ryegrass

———

9.50 kg per acre (23.5 kg per hectare)

Chapter V

DEER RECOGNITION AND AGE DISTINCTION

In the preceding chapter we have seen that in preparing a shooting plan age and perfection of antler-form play an important role. Even more, we have seen that on these two factors we shall base the decision as to which beasts are to be shot first, which may be allowed to see the rut through before being shot, and which must not be shot in any circumstances.

What we have not yet seen is how to recognise these beasts when they are on foot.

The estimation of age by the body of a beast is a matter of practice, coupled with a knowledge of the locality. We have shown already what a great role is played in the development of deer by feeding conditions and the value of blood-stock as well as by climatic conditions, and it is quite possible that because of these influences no comparison can be struck between the deer of one area and those of another. What better example than the difference between Scottish red deer and say, deer of northern or western England? Otherwise than in very general outline these two are unlike — they differ in body size, antlers, many of their habits. Purely by virtue of the fact that they live in different environments their past is different and so is their *modus vivendi*.

Serious thought must therefore be given to the particular locality under observation: only then can we approach the question of judging ages and the animals' value to our stock.

Antler Development Cycle

The red deer antler development cycle is represented in this chapter in diagrammatic form and illustrated with photographs (see Fig. 8). These show the relationship between age and the phases of antler development. The illustrations will present a much clearer picture than a lengthy description.

A calf dropped in May/June does not develop an antler in the first year of life. Only the pedicles grow, forming by the end of the calendar year two bulging knobs which sometimes remain covered with skin and sometimes perforate it and cover themselves with a horn-like substance.

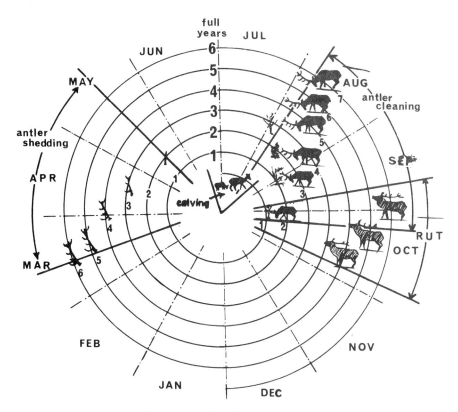

Fig. 8   Red deer development cycle

From the first winter of its life, however, the calf starts developing small antlers. These, compared with those of fully grown males, are late in their development and are not cleared of velvet sometimes until September in red deer, and June in roe. By the time the antlers are cleaned they should be at least the length of the ears, regardless of the species of deer, and preferably longer. The well-developed young stag (staggie) of one and a half years should have developed such antlers (single point or forked, blunt at the tine points). Short but heavily built antlers are also acceptable, specially if the weight of the antler is in its upper part. Those which are likely to form a crown at an early age may well have the top of the beam not only blunt but flattened, and sometimes a small fork or a minute crown may be marked. In areas where stags are generally well developed, it is safe to assume that prickets (staggies) with very short beams at that age can be shot during autumn or even earlier, as soon as the poor quality of their antlers can be safely decided upon; in areas where the average head is poor and royals are few and far between, only very weak prickets and those with knobs should be shot, unless, of course, the yield of that year is heavy and there are too many beasts on the terrain.

Having finished developing his first head late, the pricket will shed his antlers late. It is not uncommon to see them carrying their antlers as late as May of the following year, when nearly two years old. New antlers start forming immediately the first head is shed and by the end of August, sometimes by mid-September, the antlers (second head — third year of life) are cleaned of velvet.

This is the stage when the battle for good blood must start, if it has not started earlier. Under very good conditions the second head should be at least an eight-pointer, in medium and poor conditions a well marked six-pointer or very well marked four-pointer, in which the weight is well up and the tine ends are blunt, showing signs of further development.

There is no doubt at all that a switch in his second head (third year), with no tines but just a single-pronged beam regardless of length must be shot. A poorly marked four- or six-pointer must be judged subject to local conditions but if we are striving for blood improvement and purification, should be shot. It is no exaggeration to say that under optimum conditions a second head can be royal with three on top each side.

To lay down hard-and-fast rules, however, is impossible. An indication of a poor head in a young stag is often a brow tine which is very long, where the trey (if any) is short. A well-developed stag should have a brow shorter than the trey and other tine ends, all tines being blunt and indicating further development. The beam of a stag with a good future should be thinner low down, becoming thicker in the upper parts. The tine ends should be blunt and dark. If the second head has developed a brow and bey, regardless of the length of the brow and beam, the stag should be preserved and watched in the future (See Plate VI).

The second head is shed in April and the third head starts growing by the end of that month or the beginning of May, and should be cleaned of velvet by August or even as late as early September.

Plate VI Good and poor red deer antler development

a) A development over a period of 2 years showing retained characteristics.

b) Quick distinction between poor and good heads: (left) head inscribable into a rectangle in a head with a future (right) head inscribable into a triangle will never be a first class trophy

a)   b)

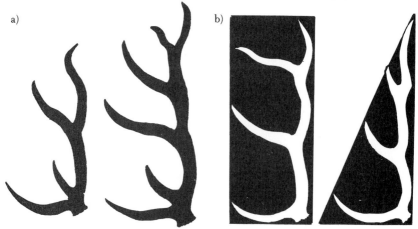

based on 'Das Ansprechen des Hirsches' - Karl Lotze (Shaper - Hanover)

c) Antler development in first four heads

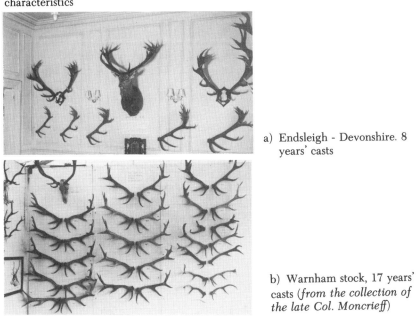

Good
development

Medium
development

Poor
development

Plate VII Development of good red deer heads retaining the main shape
characteristics

a) Endsleigh - Devonshire. 8
years' casts

b) Warnham stock, 17 years'
casts (*from the collection of
the late Col. Moncrieff*)

The antlers of a stag with a good future should have the following characteristics: brows should be longer than beys and equal to the treys; the beam should have its centre of gravity high (comparatively thin low down and thicker high up), the tine ends of the brow should be blunt and so should the top of the beam where the crown should be well marked (if the crown in that area develop at all).

A head without a future is one which has a thick beam low down, narrowing towards the top, no crowns or signs of them developing, long brows, and short treys (shorter than half the length of the beam between the brow and trey).

The formation of the crown, even if it is ugly in appearance, plays no role at this age — if the crown is there, the stag has a good future.

It should be appreciated by now that a stag carrying his third head (in the fourth year of life) must be shot if he is a tineless switch, a forked head (four pointer), or a weak six-pointer with long brows and short tops, all sharp pointed.

Beys, low-set treys, blunt treys and top tines, earn good marks.

The third head is shed at the end of March, and the fourth head cleaned by the end of July or during August, very much depending on the weather and the climatic conditions.

There is little difference between the characteristics of the third and fourth heads (fourth and fifth year of life). One thing, however, is certain by this time, if the stag is going to have a crown it should be formed in his fourth head, unless the absence of it is due to grave undernourishment.

From now on the beams will thicken and the thickness of the upper beam, which was a good characteristic at the younger age, will start spreading downwards. The tines will elongate and by the time the sixth head is reached they will start getting white ends. The beys should be showing signs of developing if they are going to appear at all. The beyless antler is not necessarily a poor antler, but an antler with beys is a better one. Now the appearance of the antler is important. A stag who has reached the medium-age group should have a good spread, long tines, thick beam, tines slightly curved upwards. The tines may be pointed by now but should not be too thin. A very thin elongated tine means that the animal is reaching the end of its development. This condition is difficult to describe accurately; the tine-ends definitely do appear too thin and slender compared with the thickness of the beam. The stag without crowns at this age, as has already been said is unlikely to develop them, and providing that royal and better stags are about in some numbers, can be shot; where royals are few, a well-proportioned ten-pointer with heavy antlers can well be kept. The narrow and misshaped stags which are not royals should be shot as unwanted stock.

We should be able by now to form some idea of good and bad stags in the young and medium age groups.

The older the stag grows the thicker, longer and heavier his head should become, provided that feeding conditions remain constant. It is possible that the number of tines will vary from year to year, both up and downwards, specially with heads considerably better than royal. The variation should not normally exceed two points from year to year, and where a temporary decrease takes place, a marked increase in weight or

Plate VIII   Examples of good heads

a) England (Norfolk)

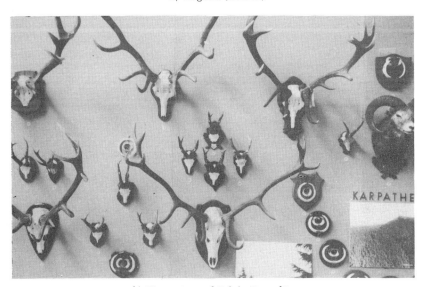

b) Hungarian and Polish Carpathians

c) Carpathians

length should normally accompany it. The main characteristics of the antler will, of course, remain throughout (Plate VII) provided that no mechanical damage deformity of antler by illness, wounds or frost takes place. The results of these are described in the chapter dealing with the malformations of antlers.

A fully mature stag will deteriorate sooner or later, depending very much on the conditions under which he has been living. This setting back will normally take place sometime after the seventh head has been shed but may happen as late as the fifteenth or later year of life. The setting back (deterioration or going back as it is called) must be carefully watched and allowed to carry on for a year or two in order to ensure that it is not temporary, and only after then can the stag be shot as being past his prime. (For illustrations of good heads see Plate VIII.)

This is the extent to which antlers can be our guide. Antlers are, however, not sufficient as a sole guide to age, as they change their form, shape and degree of perfection from one place to another. For that reason another guide must be used.

Red Deer

Body Development as Guide to Age Estimation

There are not many of us do not know Disney's proverbial Bambi. For those who do not, he has long ears on a small head with two big black eyes, a long neck and an ever-inquisitive look. Thus a deer below the age of one year.

As the head-bones develop and the head enlarges towards its normal size, so the ears lose their appearance of vastness and the eyes do not strike us as being so large. The neck starts filling in and losing the almost ridiculous disproportion of length to thickness, and appears somehow shorter than in the first year.

A three-year-old male beast is not quite full size, but its appearance is not yet mature. Until the age of three or four the face is long; the nose seems to protrude in an odd way; the neck, compared with the now full-sized body, is still thin, but towards the end of this period appears to be slightly pouchy in the underside. Longish hair appears on the underneck of a stag, the rest of the neck being still covered with hair of the same length as elsewhere. The back above the shoulders is straight. The head is kept high.

With advancing age the face loses the appearance of protruding as it fills in, the hitherto pointed muzzle becomes blunter and the depth of the face increases. The neck as it fills in looks shorter and this effect is even more marked as the pouch of the underneck increases, and the mane grows round the stag's neck. An old stag looks thick set in the neck.

The shoulders, which until the age of four or thereabouts formed a straight line from the rump to the base of the neck, start protruding upwards in about the fifth or sixth year, and by the time the beast reaches the eighth or ninth year the line of the neck breaks above the shoulder, falling down from there both forwards towards the base of the neck and back towards the rump. This characteristic is more marked in stags than hinds, in whom the back does not change its outline to an extent where it can greatly assist in age estimation.

We have said that the head of the young stag is held high. This impression is exaggerated by the fact that the neck is curved in the shape of a sickle, at the top of which is the head, at the bottom the base of the neck. The lower curve of the neck has the appearance of a pouch. With increasing age the upper curve straightens out and fills in, and by the time the beast has reached the eighth year it is almost straight, though the curve of the underneck remains. A really old beast's neck runs in a straight line from behind the ears to a point a few inches forward of the shoulder. Furthermore, the mane which stags develop gives an impression of the neck being curved outwards, thus increasing the impression of thickness.

These factors affect the appearance of the carrying position of the head and form a picture of an animal thickset round the neck and shoulders. In addition however, the head position changes. The young stag, whether walking, running or standing still, carries the head high, the angle of the upper nose bone to the horizontal being somewhere about 30°. As the beast ages, so the head is lowered. The lowering is gradual: to start with the differences each year are almost too small to notice, but at the age of eleven to twelve years in red, and six in roe deer, the drop becomes quicker so that by the age of fourteen to sixteen years and nine, respectively, the neck and line of the back adopt in relation to one another the form of a very shallow inverted letter V, in which the high point is the shoulder, sloping downwards from there to the rump and head. The silhouette of a stag walking undisturbed, standing or even trotting slowly, is a tell-tale feature of age. When startled, an old stag will lift his head up to look round and listen or sniff the air, but as soon as he is satisfied that there is no danger the head will drop very soon to its previous position where the nose bones form almost a right-angle with the horizontal (see Fig. 9 and Plate IX A, B).

It is common, in many countries on the Continent, when talking about a very old stag, seen from the rear or the front more or less as a silhouette, to say that, 'He looked as if his antlers were growing from his stomach'. The illustrations in this chapter will provide an adequate idea of the appearance thus described.

The hope that on having read these descriptions, one will be able to look at any stag and assess its age at a glance, is wishful thinking. As with everything else in 'deer matters' local knowledge is quite indispensable; without it, and without experience gained by bitter disappointments and mistakes, an accurate age assessment on sight, of a stag's age cannot be made. Even the most experienced stalkers come across cases by which, for all their knowledge of the ground and local experience, they are baffled. There is only one way of judging the age with any accuracy, and that is by the teeth of the beast. To this topic a separate chapter is devoted. This may be an opportune moment however, now that we are dealing with 'recognition', to give an outline of the characteristics of the deer heads.

Fig. 9   Red deer body recognition

3 years   Yearling   4-6 years

7-8 years

Very old   Old

Old hind   Calf   Weak hind

Plate IX A) Red deer recognition by body build (park)

2-3 year stags   5 years   2 years   7 years   8 years   6 years

Plate IX B) Red deer recognition by body build (hill)

Behind: Mature stag   V. young
Front: Well developed mature stags (rectangular heads)

Young stags: left: long brows, short
bey and top fork; right: long tines
and good top fork on both sides

Back: Good young (4 years, rectangular head)

Front: Good very young (3 years)

Good mature (6 or 7 years, rectangular head)

Back: Young - medium, all good lower tines, doubtful top fork.
Front: Good shape mature 10 pointer (rectangular head)

Very young (3 years)
Very well developed
Mature - poor top fork
(triangular head)

Antlers

Basic shapes — annual growth — going back

Basically there are three shapes of the general outline of red deer antlers when looked at from the front. They can be described and are known as 'U', 'V' and 'heart' shapes. They are illustrated on Plate X. (page 91).

The 'U' is probably the most classical of all. In appearance the curve of the main beam is like the letter U and if we disregard the tines of the crown, the general tendency is neither to converge nor diverge at the top. Thus, if the antlers grew indefinitely the tops would never meet.

The 'V' shape is that where the main beam is almost straight, showing a general tendency to 'open up' towards the top, so that with the growth of the antler the spread becomes greater.

The 'heart' shape is that where the greatest inside spread falls somewhere between the crown and the trey tine and where above the points of the greatest inside spread, the beams close in towards the top. In the U and heart-shaped antlers, and sometimes in the V shape, there may be an additional guide to age in the shape of the brow tine.

We have said before that in a well-formed stag, the brows start by being short, as compared with the bey or trey. As they grow longer so they show a tendency to curve upwards, and the angle between the line of the direction of the growth of the brow at the base, and the line connecting the base with the tip of the tine is a basis for age judgment. The greater this angle the older the beast. This is not a rule but a guide, applying less to V-shaped heads than the others, mainly because in the former there is more of a tendency for the tines, like the beam, to grow with only slight curves. The exceptions to this are too frequent, however, to make it more than a sometimes useful hint.

The amount of annual growth is, of course, a great variable impossible to assess accurately, specially once a stag has passed the age of four or five years. It is on the growth of additional tines therefore and not on inches of antler length that we must concentrate. In this task the illustrations will be of greater assistance than the written word and it will be enough to say that practically always the general appearance of the antler remains unchanged from year to year as can be seen in the illustrations. Furthermore, the characteristics of the father are so often passed to the sons, that an 'area characteristic' can be developed in time, if feeding and health allow normal development. This is not to imply that the identical antler will be grown by the same stag from year to year, or from father to son, but that certain curvature of antler and the general outline of it will be similar and will repeat themselves.

A good antler at an early age is thick and blunt-tined at the top, and that is the antler with a future, especially if it could be inscribed within a rectangle, whereas an antler which can be fitted into a triangle has no future (See Plate VI). Thus the latter, allowing for the local conditions and the inherent characteristics of the local stock, can be shot without harm to the blood stock.

Fig. 10   Fallow Deer development cycle

	MONTH	IV	V	VI	VII	VIII	IX	X	XI	XII	I	II	III
FIRST	Fawn dropping												
	ANTLER DEVELOPS									K	I		
SECOND	ANTLER DEVELOPS						I						
	ANTLER CLEANING						1st HEAD						
	RUT												
THIRD	ANTLER DEVELOPS						II						
	ANTLER CLEANING						2nd HEAD						
	RUT												
FOURTH	ANTLER DEVELOPS						III						
	ANTLER CLEANING						3rd HEAD						
	RUT												
FIFTH	ANTLER DEVELOPS						IV						
	ANTLER CLEANING						4th HEAD						
	RUT												
SIXTH	ANTLER DEVELOPS						V						
	ANTLER CLEANING						5th HEAD						
	RUT												
SEVENTH	ANTLER DEVELOPS						VI						
	ANTLER CLEANED						6th HEAD						
	RUT												
EIGHTH	ANTLER DEVELOPS						VII						
	ANTLER CLEANING						7th HEAD						
	RUT												
NINTH	ANTLER DEVELOPS						VIII						
	ANTLER CLEANED												
	RUT												

K – Possible formation of knobs I = 1st head ; II = 2nd head etc

Fawns dropped | Antler in velvet | Cleaning of velvet | Antler shedding | Rut

As a guide, it may be said that in endeavours to improve the stock three antler developments can be considered; good, medium and poor (Plate VI) . In this connection all aspects have to be taken into account; form, general characteristic, size, ancestry, feeding conditions, etc; thus local knowledge is indispensable. Of these three antler developments, the good one should be preserved as long as possible even after he has started to go back and deteriorate at the advanced age; the medium should be preserved as long as his value to the stock is a positive asset, in fact until he reaches a standard common to the average stag in the area; the stag with a poor antler development can be got rid of as soon as it has been decided that he represents no value to any herd within the area. The illustrations will again assist in this consideration (Plates VI–VIII).

All deer, without exception, deteriorate with time. Not only does the venison get tough, but the body and antlers deteriorate in size and therefore in quality. Red deer, living in normal wild conditions, exposed to all weathers, and forced to find food throughout the year for themselves, finish their development later, on the average, and possibly therefore the age at which the 'going back' starts is later. The age of nine to eleven years can be said to be the turning point. Park deer, or those fed in the forest, living in comparatively mild climate with abundant food throughout the year, develop quickly and by the age of seven to nine are in their prime. Quite often, after that age they may start deteriorating. Here, as with so many of our considerations, we must look for many exceptions, such as park deer with no sign of going back at the age of eighteen, highland stags at the age of ten well set back; such phenomena are too frequent to permit us to make the ages mentioned more than a very general guide.

Deterioration may be due not only to age but also to lack of food during the antler-forming stage. This type of deterioration, misleading as it may be, will (or at least should) disappear if sufficient food is available in subsequent years and normal development in the following year should take place. After a hard winter, the poor quality of antler will be common and the reason for it obvious, but it may be that owing to some slight upset of the digestive system in the winter months, a wound or illness, a beast has lost the ability to assimilate the required food for the normal antler build-up, and has suffered a set-back as a result. With the improved weather the animal's condition should improve, and given better health in the following winter, providing that the food is available, a normal head will develop.

At the peak of its development the antler will reach the maximum weight, length, number and length of tines, best development of the crown and thickness of the lower and upper beam. The first sign of deterioration is normally the slight curving of the tine tips inwards or outwards, or blunting of the tips. This is the sign of the first year of going back and is followed by the loss of tine-end of the crown or bay-tine. Usually, not more than one or two tines are lost per year, nor does the final going back mean that all tines will disappear, it may be so in rare cases, but normally the going back goes as far as bringing the stag to the basic eight or ten points, all tines being short and stubby, and the beam, having lost its length, will thicken out of all proportion to what it had been at its prime. The burrs which in the red deer are, in comparison to the size of the antler, much smaller than those of the roe, will droop, and form a ring-like extension of the antler, covering the pedicle. In some cases the deterioration of the crown is accompanied by webbing of the tine-ends. In those cases the top fork which remains after the disappearance of the crown will be of a heavy type, with a very thick base slowly narrowing towards the trey down the beam.

Fallow Deer

Antler Development

The calves having been dropped in late May or early June the young buck grow their pedicles under cover of the skin until about early February, when, at the age of nine months, the first heads of antlers start forming. The variation from this rule, to bring the fallow into line with the red and roe deer, where some animals grow a knob-like cap on top of the pedicle between December and February only to shed it in order to allow the growth of the first antler to take place, is very rare indeed. In most cases the pedicles do not finish forming until late January, and by the time they penetrate the covering skin the first head of antlers starts its growth.

The first antler is formed as a single spiked beam, and is velvet-covered until about the end of July to mid-August, when the velvet is cleaned off. The velvet-cleaning time is slightly ahead of the grown-up buck's (see Fig. 10).

The first head (in the second year of life) should be the length of the ears, thick from the base upwards and thinning only in the last inch. Shedding time for the first head is between mid-April and mid-May after the older animals have shed theirs. Cases have been known of the first head being more than single-spiked, where either the brow has already started forming, or a slight palmation occurs on the very top of the antler. These cases are, however, so rare that they can be regarded as the exception which proverbially proves the rule. Unlike the case of red and roe deer, such advanced formation is not necessarily the result of very good feeding conditions or very good blood. It can virtually be said to be a thing which just happens. Judgment of the first head must therefore be based on the length of the spikes and nothing else.

The second head begins to develop within a week or so of the first being shed, to be cleared of velvet between mid-August and mid-September. This is the first head where good parentage and feeding may tell. A good buck at this age (third year of life), by the time he clears the velvet off, should carry an antler consisting of the brow, possibly trey and a palmation marked at least at the flattening of the top of the beam. Cases are known where the palmation was spoon-shaped and some 4 in. high with markings of the tines in the shape of an uneven trailing edge of the palmation. These are, however, very rare. On the average a second head should be over 8 and better 9 in. high, cases of 12 in. high second heads being quite common.

The shedding of the second head takes place about a month before the third birthday, by which day the third head is on its way. This head will normally be cleaned of velvet by early September.

The third head must have the brow and bey developed fully, not just as small knobs sticking forward on the beam. Both these tines should be about 2 in. in length at least. The palmation which was marked on the second head is now developed by having spread upwards and fore-and-aft. Along its back edge there should be a number of rounded-off 'fingers' about ½ in. in length. These are the future tines of the full palmation. Two of these tines should be more pronounced than the others, the spur (the lowest back tine of the palm) , and the top-fore tine of the palmation. Both these should be about 50 per cent longer than the rest of the budding tines, the 'fingers of which are often no more than waves, between these 'waves' there may be a deep depression, a gulf-like division cutting the palmation into two or more parts and running towards the base of the palm. These divisions at that age are quite common and if the antler continues to develop well should gradually fill in with the years. If they remain, the buck will have to be killed, as this type of malformation can be passed on. The division should be all but gone during the following two years.

The third head is shed between mid-April and mid-May and the fourth head starts its development which will last until mid-August–mid-September, by which time it will be cleared of velvet. This head differs quite considerably from the previous one. The beam has thickened by now to support a large palm. Along the back edge of it there should be a number of tines from the spur to the top-fore tine. These two should be pointed and slightly curved, the spur up or downwards and the fore-top forwards, both over 2 in. long. If these two are not developed further than the other tines this does not represent a malformation but such development is desirable. The rest of the tines should be well marked. The depression in the palm if it exists should by now be receding, and the palm filling in.

Should the depression or depressions be of such nature that the palmation does not develop into a flat area, but like a red deer stag's crown consists of a number of tines long and flattish, the buck must be shot before it has a chance of passing on the malformed head.

The fourth head (fifth year of life) is only an advance on the third in the elongation of the tines of the palm and a growing of the head all round, and this process will now follow for three years. The main advancement will probably be seen in the brow and bey, both of which will grow longer and thicker from year to year and after the fifth head should show signs of curving upwards between one-half and three-quarters of their length. The palmation of the fifth head should be a solid body and depressions should not be tolerated unless they are shallow and not too long. Tines should be well defined as single or double (forked) tines at not necessarily regular intervals on the back edge of the palmation, but should be arranged in a more or less symmetrical way on the antlers (see Figs 11, 12 and 13).

The culmination of the development of the head normally takes place in between the eighth and tenth head, after which, setting back commences. There are locations where palmations do not develop, probably as a genetic inheritance; in such locations if antler perfection is of importance, probably the only solution is in introduction of good new blood.

Fig.11   Fallow Deer: bad development of antler

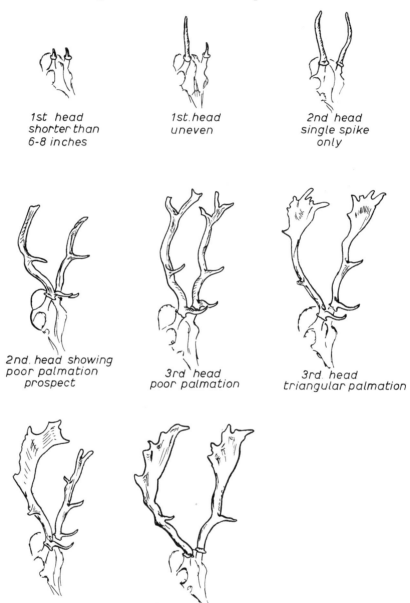

1st head
shorter than
6-8 inches

1st. head
uneven

2nd head
single spike
only

2nd. head showing
poor palmation
prospect

3rd head
poor palmation

3rd. head
triangular palmation

3rd head
uneven formation

3rd head
lacking brows

Fig 12 Fallow Deer: bad development of antler, medium and old buck

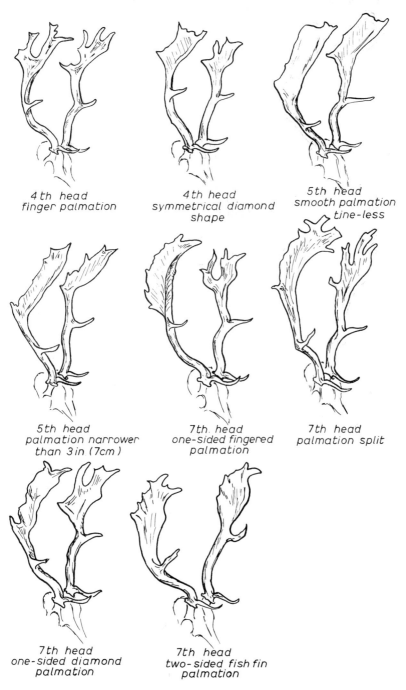

4th head
finger palmation

4th head
symmetrical diamond
shape

5th head
smooth palmation
tine-less

5th head
palmation narrower
than 3in (7cm)

7th head
one-sided fingered
palmation

7th head
palmation split

7th head
one-sided diamond
palmation

7th head
two-sided fish fin
palmation

Fig 13 Fallow Deer: good development of antler

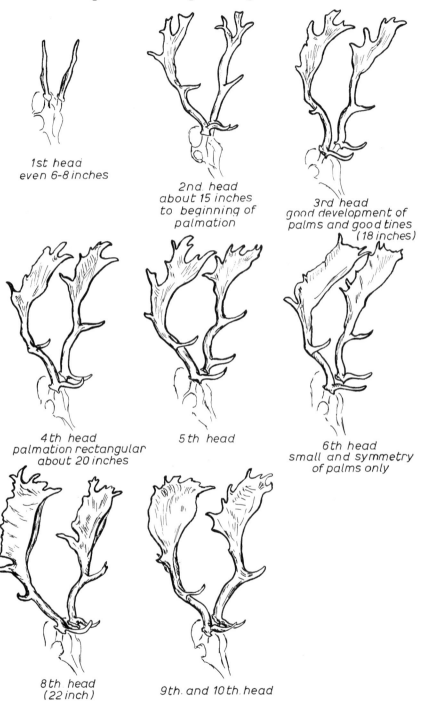

1st head
even 6-8 inches

2nd. head
about 15 inches
to beginning of
palmation

3rd head
good development of
palms and good tines
(18 inches)

4th head
palmation rectangular
about 20 inches

5th head

6th head
small and symmetry
of palms only

8th head
(22 inch)

9th. and 10th. head

Body Development

After a period of about 7.5 month's gestation the young are dropped about May/June, normally a single, sometimes as twin calves. The annual birth rate being about 70 per cent of the stock, the task of maintaining the population at a level figure is quite considerable. Does are capable of producing young from their second year onwards, but the first time the calves are of normal size and capable of developing normally, in the wild, is when produced in the doe's fourth year. The reproductive capacity of fallow deer doe, is by far the greatest of all deer mentioned in this book. A doe is capable of producing a yield every year and can do so for many years.

Einsiedel observed a doe which produced one or two calves every year from her fourth year until her twenty-seventh year of life, and lived for another six years afterwards, but was not able to reproduce any further.[*]

The difference in body build between the young and old animal is not nearly as easy to spot in fallow as it is in red or roe deer.

Calves of one year are easily recognisable because of their size, while their faces are small, pointed and quite unmistakable. The necks, however, are not nearly as slender as they are in red and roe deer, and this remains a characteristic throughout their lives, and thus one of the very best indications of age in red and roe deer is denied us. Until the calf is two years old its face is pointed, with a small muzzle, deep from the top of the skull to the bottom of the lower jaw. In the third year this feature ceases to be so striking as the muzzle thickens and the face elongates. In the fourth year and after the head is unchanged.

The neck thickens slightly with age, but it is not until the sixth year that the neck gives the age away and then it remains of more or less constant thickness. The way the head is carried may provide an indication, but fallow being constantly on the alert, the head is so often carried up, listening, looking out for danger and sniffing, that it is uncommon to find an animal sufficiently at ease to give us a good view of the normal head-holding position. It is thus the antlers on which our recognition of fallow deer's age must depend, the other characteristics being guides only.

Antlers

Basic shapes — going back

The palmation is so striking a characteristic of the antler, that the main concentration in discussing antler shape will be on the palm.

In the search for the ideal and perfect shape, the following outline will have to be followed: The fore edge of the palmation of this antler (when looked at sideways) should be straight or slightly curved forwards or inwards; this edge should form a very wide angle with the main beam and lean forward of it. The height of the palmation should be about 150 per cent of the width, both measured in the widest and highest places, from

[*] E. Ueckerman, *Das Damwild* (Hamburg, P. Parey, 1956).

the forward edge to the deepest depression (gulf) between the tines of the back, and from the base of the palm to the deepest depression between the tines of the top of the palmation respectively.

At the top of the palmation there should be a long top-fore tine and the back and bottom should be armed with a spur, both of which should be curved, one towards the other upwards. The tines should be well defined and not necessarily longer than 1½ inches. The inside of the palmation should be concave, bulging slightly outwards.

The shape of the palm and their grading is shown in the illustrations to this chapter, with explanatory remarks which should provide sufficient information for judgment to be passed.

Roe Deer

Antler Development

As the fawns are dropped, in May or June, it is difficult at sight to distinguish between the male and female.

Very soon after birth the buck starts forming the pedicles on which in the later years the antlers will grow. By August/September the pedicles can be seen as two spiky bulges under the skin of the upper forehead.

From September onwards, the pedicles elongate, and very small knobs of antler may appear on top of them if the skin is pierced. These do not grow upwards, however, and form only a shield over the top of the pedicle. These knobs are lost in February or, if they have not appeared by February, the skin is pierced and the first head of antlers starts growing.

By March or April, when the buck is some 10 months old, antlers are already developing under the coat of velvet. By the time the first head is cleaned of velvet, at the end of June or on occasions even as late as early August, it should be as long as, or longer than, the ears. The antlers should be forked, but a single spiked beam, provided that it is of sufficient length and of good shape, is quite acceptable; shorter antlers of exceptional thickness, however, should be preserved, as these normally develop well in later years.

A head which has not grown longer than the ears and is thin is unlikely to develop well in later years, and such bucks, having due regard to the local conditions, can be shot without loss, in the first year of its life.

At this age (second year, first head) the burrs and the pearling are of comparatively little importance; though the burrs, however small, should be marked.

The clearing of velvet of the first head, in June or later, is an indication of age, as the older beasts clean their velvet off by mid-May. Similarly, the first head, having finished its development later, will be shed later in the year than those of the older animals. The buck in his second year may be seen with his antlers still on in mid-December. The timing of velvet cleaning and antler shedding is, however, affected by climatic conditions.

As soon as the first head is shed, the second starts growing. This head will be clear of velvet a little later than that of a fully grown buck, by about the end of May, but earlier than that of a yearling. The second head (in the third year of life) should be at least a forked one or preferably a full six-pointer, though the tops, and even the front tine, may be short. It is quite likely that where the top fork did not quite develop, a thickening, marking a tendency towards further development, will be found. The burrs should be well marked but they are not expected to be thick and large; they should, however, form a nicely upturned collar. There should be signs of pearling which, though small at this age, should extend well upwards as far as the brow (front) tine.

There is a type of a head which is slow in the initial upward development and which in the first two heads is short (not more than 2–2½ in. by the time the second head is clean), but very thick and well pearled. That head in the later year will provide an excellent trophy and should be saved. Less likely is the head which being slow in the development shoots up (second head over 6 in.) but remains very thin. This head, if it is found, should be saved for another year by which time (the third head) it should be a full six-pointer. Both these abnormal developments are quite pronounced and the only danger is in mistaking the latter for a badly developed older buck's.

Having described the heads which have a reasonable hope for the future it is hardly necessary to say that short knobs somewhere in the region of 1–2 in. spell no good for the future and should, like poorly developed short forked heads in the third year, be shot.

The weaker animals which have insufficient health and strength to build their antlers normally will at that age be very slow in clearing their velvet. It is therefore accepted that a year-old buck, still in velvet by August, and bucks still carrying their second heads by the end of June or early July should be considered weak specimens and be shot at the earliest opportunity.

The second head is normally shed about the time the fully mature buck sheds his, i.e. about the end of the first half of October or on rare occasions early November. This depends on the weather, being accelerated by frost and delayed by a mild autumn and early winter.

The next head (the third, in the fourth year of life) is completely cleared by the time the buck reaches his third birthday and enters his fourth year.

This head is the first which is fully developed in shape and bears the number of tine-ends which will eventually adorn the animal's head. There is no doubt that if a buck's third head is not a six-pointer, after a normal winter when feeding conditions are adequate or at any rate normal, it never will be a six-pointer (see Fig. 14 for antler development cycle).

Here we come up against heredity. There are areas where bucks rarely develop more than a fork and no matter how old will always remain four-pointer. In those areas one cannot expect the impossible in the form of a six-pointer buck except as a freak. New blood is the only solution, as no amount of feeding and care will bring another pair of tines out

To say therefore that a forked head buck must be shot might mean that in some areas all buck would have to be shot. It is necessary to consider local conditions and the average value of the local roe stock before a decision is reached which bucks should be shot. If most of them carry six-pointer heads, then a forked one is not good enough; if most are only four-pointers, then four-pointers fall within the acceptable range, the six-pointer being carefully preserved as blood-stock. Single spiked switches, however, should never be allowed because they are dangerous in fights, their antler being able to penetrate between the tines of their opponent and effect an injury to the opponent's head often resulting in death — hence their name 'murderer buck'.

At the age of four, the burr should be clearly visible and one can expect, in normal feeding and atmospheric conditions, a reasonable pearling to cover the antlers. Both these can be considered therefore as being indispensable requirements for a well-formed third head. There cannot be any expectation of antlers being thick and heavy as yet but they must be proportionately built, the circumference above the burr being about 50 per cent thicker than above the brow tine. As with red deer, the comparative thickness of the upper antler indicates a capacity for the further development in future years, and the distribution of thickness mentioned above implies that the proportions should be not worse than those mentioned.

As far as the length of the antler goes, the third head should be within 10–15 per cent of the average head of the area. This gives us a possibility of assessing our expectations of the future quality of antlers of the present stock of bucks carrying their third head.

This is the first time that the burrs must be well defined, forming a thick rough collar round the base of the antler.

Shedding of the antlers takes place between October 1 and 20 and the new antlers start growing as soon as the old ones have been shed. The next (the fourth head) is cleaned of velvet by mid-May, just before the animal

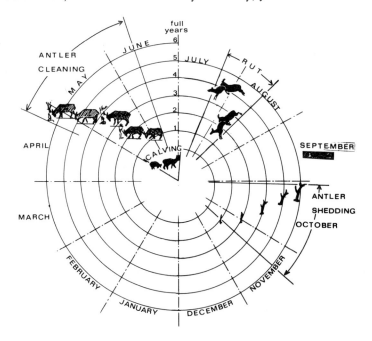

Fig 14 Roe deer development cycle

reaches its fourth birthday. This head will have the full length to which the antler is likely to develop and should have all the attributes of a mature antler except for the thickness. It should be well pearled, have good thick burrs, long tines (six of them) and the main beam should be in good areas 9 to 10 in. and in poor about 7½ in. long. This is the first time that a buck can be graded as a 1A or 1B buck, though it is safer to leave the allocation of buck to the 'old' category until the following year. At any rate, should it be decided to consign the buck in his fifth year of life (carrying the fourth head) to the 'old' category, the good buck should not be shot, under any circumstances, before the rutting season has at least passed its height. In those areas where the good buck are not abundant, it is better to leave the good buck for at least two more years for the purpose of propagation.

From now on, the only changes in the antlers wil be the gradual thickening of antlers from year to year, and thickening and widening of the burrs, until the time comes when the antlers start deteriorating (going back).

A buck who has matured well in the fourth head, should maintain his good characteristics until about the sixth year before the antlers start deteriorating. It is then time to include him in the shooting plan for the current or following year; exceptions, however, of buck going back earlier have been recorded. (For illustrations of typical antlers in various ages see Figs 15A, B, C and Plates XI to XV.)

Body Development as Guide to Age Estimation

In the first year the fawn, like a red deer calf, is strangely like Walt Disney's 'Bambi'. In the roe, however, which is much smaller, the ears are more pronounced and the appearance of the face even more baby-like. The head, the face of which is pointed, with a markedly cupola-like forehead, is small and is borne on a thin, ridiculously long, neck, carried well erect. The body is comparatively short, legs long and appearing unsteady and knock-kneed.

The roe in its second year still has a baby-like facial expression; the body is larger, but the ears are only just too large for the size of the head. The well-developed young buck, by the time he enters his second year of life, should have a smooth summer coat, whereas his older brothers will be still changing theirs. A rough coat, the change of which has not been completed by the beginning of June, is an indication of age if the buck can be considered mature, or of poor development if the animal is young.

The buck in the latter part of the third year of life is about the size of the mature beast and it is difficult to judge it by size alone.The setting of the head on the neck and the shape of the face and neck are a good indication of age. By the winter prior to the third birthday the neck should have filled out and lost its appearance of willow-like slenderness. The face is blunter and the head its normal size, looking blunter than it did in the first two years of life as a result of the thickening of the back of the lower jaw bone.

As about his second birthday the buck was in his new summer coat, so in the third year he may take some days of June to finish changing it. By

Fig 15A Roe deer - good buck, young and old

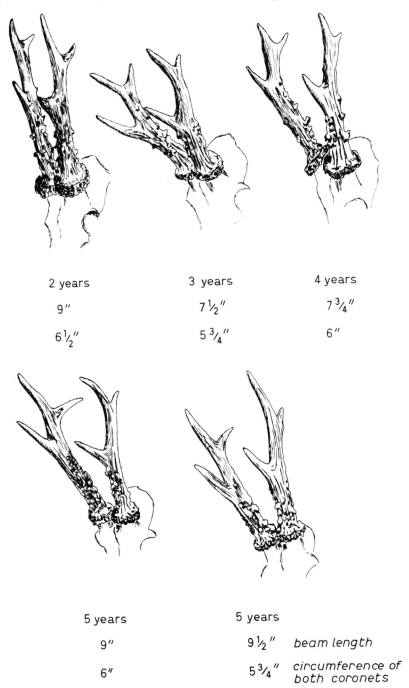

2 years

9″

6½″

3 years

7½″

5¾″

4 years

7¾″

6″

5 years

9″

6″

5 years

9½″   *beam length*

5¾″   *circumference of both coronets*

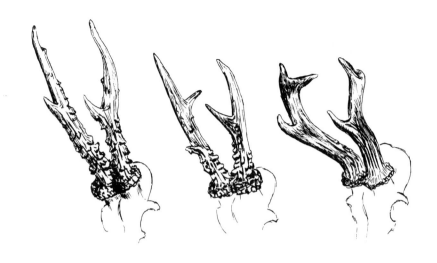

3 years	4 years	4 years
8 ½"	8"	7 ¼"
6"	5"	5 ¾"

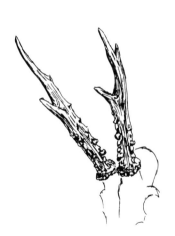 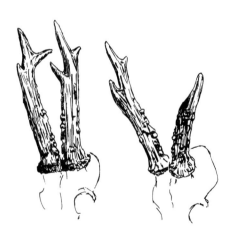

5 years	6 years	6 years
8"	7 ¼"	6"
5 ¼"	5 ¼"	5 ¼"

Fig. 15B   Roe Deer - good future blood stock

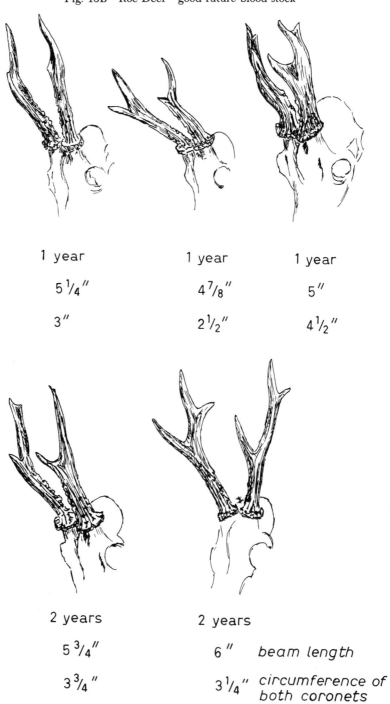

1 year	1 year	1 year
5 1/4 "	4 7/8 "	5 "
3 "	2 1/2 "	4 1/2 "

2 years	2 years	
5 3/4 "	6 "	beam length
3 3/4 "	3 1/4 "	circumference of both coronets

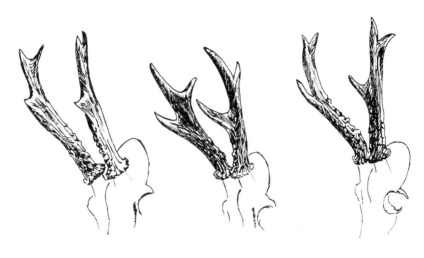

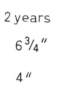

2 years

6 3/4 ''

4 ''

2 years

6 1/2 ''

3 3/4 ''

3 years

7 ''

3 3/4 ''

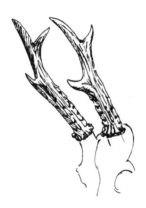

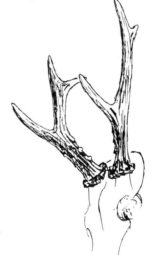

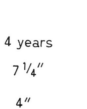

4 years

7 1/4 ''

4 ''

4 years

8 3/4 ''

4 1/2 ''

Fig 15C Roe deer - bad and poor buck, young and medium age

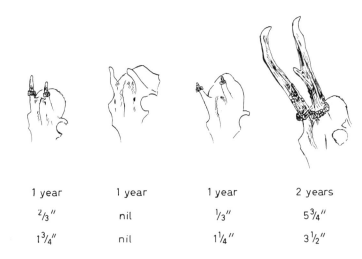

1 year	1 year	1 year	2 years
$2/3''$	nil	$1/3''$	$5\frac{3}{4}''$
$1\frac{3}{4}''$	nil	$1\frac{1}{4}''$	$3\frac{1}{2}''$

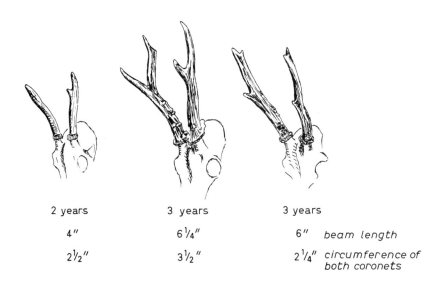

2 years	3 years	3 years	
$4''$	$6\frac{1}{4}''$	$6''$	*beam length*
$2\frac{1}{2}''$	$3\frac{1}{2}''$	$2\frac{1}{4}''$	*circumference of both coronets*

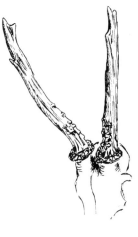

3 years	4 years	4 years
7″	8 1/4 ″	7 1/4 ″
3 3/4 ″	3 1/4 ″	4 1/4 ″

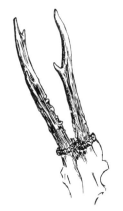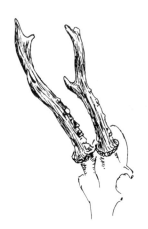

4 years	4 years
7 1/4 ″	7″
4 1/2 ″	4 1/2 ″

the rut, however, all bucks must be clear of the winter coat and any which carry a mangy mixture of winter-grey and summer red must be considered sick and therefore undesirable.

By the time he has reached his fourth birthday the buck is mature. At the time of his birthday he will never be quite red and it may take him well into June to complete the change of coat.

Previously he has carried his head well up and erect on a neck which to start with was long and thin and then by filling out lost its long look. By the fourth birthday the neck is completely filled out and, what is more, seems to be contracting into the body. The head is carried slightly lower, but the marked difference is in the length of the neck From now on the head is carried lower each year, until by the age of 8 or 9 the neck forms a straight line with the back, from the rump to the base of the head. This characteristic is more marked when the buck is walking than when it is running or startled by a disturbance (see Fig. 16).

This stage varies between the park or artificially fed animals and those brought up in the forest, moor or field who have had to cater for themselves. In parks and artificially fed roe signs of ageing follow quickly on full maturity.

Antlers

Basic shapes — annual growth — going back

As with red deer there are three basic forms of roe deer antlers. The 'U' or 'lyre' form, also known as the cup, in which the antler is curved low down and the beams, looked at from the front, grow more or less parallel to one another, increasing the inside spread very slowly towards the top or not increasing it at all above the bottom curve; the 'V' form, known as 'straight', as there is almost no curve in the beam, and from the burr upwards the inside span increases as we reach the top; and the 'heart' shape, in which the antlers first curve slightly inwards then outwards all the way, the greatest inside span being normally below the top fork (see Plates XIII–XV).

Of these three basic forms the 'V' shape is the least popular, and the 'U' and 'heart' shapes the nicest.

The annual growth is slightly easier to describe than with red deer. Normally the first head is between one-third and one-half its normal fully-grown size, the second year up to three-quarters, and the third should be about 85–90 per cent fully grown.

The roe deer's heredity is more marked than that of the red deer. The roe often reproduces faults over two or even three generations, only the fourth generation starting to show a decline in the fault. In the same way as red deer, the same buck, provided that development has not been disturbed by hunger, illness or wounds, will reproduce a head from year to year with the same characteristics (see Plates III, XI and XIV).

The going back in normal circumstances starts in about the sixth to eighth year. The first sign of going back is drooping of the burrs. This takes place first on the outer side of the burr and spreads from year to year, towards the front, between the antlers, the back being the last to droop.

The antler, once it has started going back, loses length, and the tines from year to year 'withdraw' slowly. It is quite common to find a buck which, having developed into a six-pointer at the age of four, with a length of 10 in. by the age of ten, becomes a switch with tineless beams and only 7 or 8 in. length. His antler, under such circumstances, should be very thick, when compared with the thickness at the height of development. The brow tines are normally quicker in disappearing than the back tine of the top fork, which sometimes shows signs of webbing inside the fork (Plate XI).

The tines, before they disappear, become blunt and rounded, with dull surface and without polished-white tine ends; at all times, however, the antler remains strongly built.

Age Estimation by the System of 'Receding Hair' (see Plate XVI — applicable to all deer)

It may have been noted by some, that all male deer have a part of their head covered by long hair which is always located round the pedicles and sometimes spreads over the forehead and down the nose bone towards the muzzle. The hair is sometimes curly, and sometimes darker than on other occasions. In these features lies a system of age definition devised by Vorberg. It applies to deer in their summer coat only, and cannot be said to be 100 per cent fool-proof.

All deer — one year old. Dark hair from the base of the antlers towards the nose even coloured, the longish hair is lying down.

Roe two years — red and fallow three to four. The face is slightly lighter in colour, the long hair from the base of the antlers reaches to between the eyes only, the area is heart-shaped and the hair curled standing up.

Roe three to four — red and fallow five to seven. The area of long curly hair is receding upwards, the previous sharply defined bottom of the heart shape is now wider, almost reaching the eyes and spreading towards the ears.

Roe five to seven years — red and fallow eight to ten. The area of the long hair is now not well defined, it spreads above the line of the eyes and just between the eyes, the long hair is growing greyish and stands up between the antlers.

Roe over seven years — red and fallow over ten. The area of grey hair has receded even higher and in old animals can be very grey, there is no marked line where the long hair ends, the curls are apt to disappear, white hair appearing around the muzzle.

In this method white hair round the muzzle and the grey hair above the upper lip can be used as an indication of age. But in Great Britain, because of the Scottish deer having the grey hair over the upper lip and white patches by their muzzle throughout their life, these indications are misleading. Note: Recent observations suggest this method does not apply in some geographical areas.

Old buck - 9 years or older

Medium aged (4-6 years)

Young buck (2-3 years)

Fig 16 Roe deer body recognition

Plate X Basic red deer antler forms

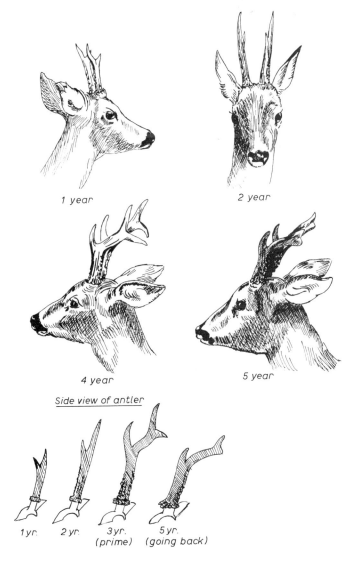

Plate XI   Development of roe antler

Plate XII   Age recognition by antler formations

a) yearling

b) 8 years or older

c) 5-7 years

d) 3-4 years

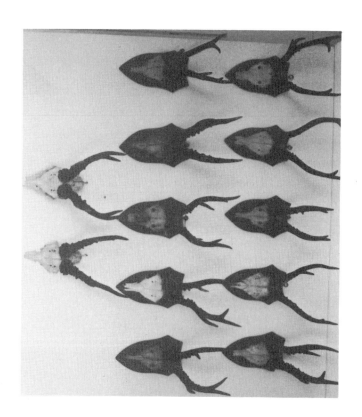

Plate XIII   Types of British roe deer antlers

Plate XIV   Typical development of antlers over years

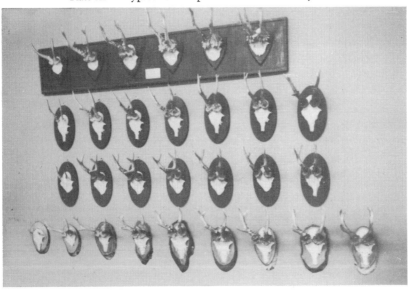

Plate XV   Perfection of roe antlers

a) Irish Co. Sligo (Lissadel)
   12 pointer

b) Scottish head
   (Perthshire). Note
   exceptionally formed
   yearling

c) German (Lower Saxony)

d) Devonshire head

93

Plate XVI
Judging the age by colour and formation of hair of the face (black buck)

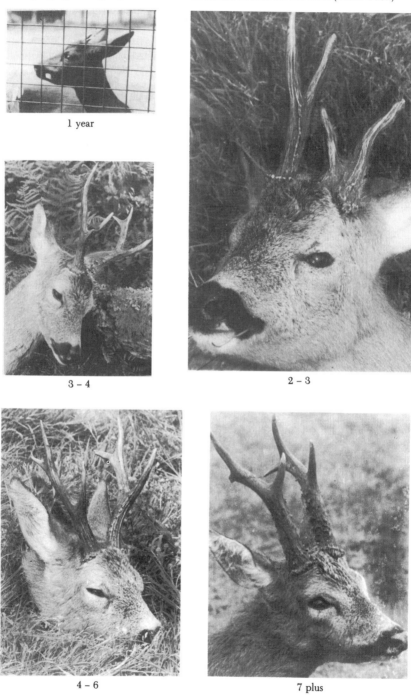

1 year

3 – 4

2 – 3

4 – 6

7 plus

Fig. 17 Red deer development summary

	Jan.	Feb.	Mar.	Apr.	May	Jun.	July	Aug.	Sept.	Oct.	Nov.	Dec.
Calves 0–7 m						Born (coat dappled)				Grows winter coat (loses speckles)		Increases intake of natural food. Male grows knobs.
Calves 8–19 m	Still takes hind's milk	Still takes hind's milk	Knobs grow into spikes			Grows summer coat		Grows winter coat	Cleans velvet (first head)			
Calves 20–24 m				Casts first head	Starts second head / Grows summer coat							
Hinds young				Break-up of hind herds		Calves dropped	Build-up of hind herds with yearling and 2-year stags		2-year-old completes tooth growth / Rut	Rut	Winter coat / Hinds separate from stags	Hinds separate from stags
Hinds mature & old				Grows summer coat		Calves dropped			Rut	Rut	Winter coat	
Stags 2–6 years				Casts 2nd head / Starts summer coat	Summer coat	Antler growth in velvet	Antler growth in velvet	Cleans velvet (2nd head)	Completes perm. tooth growth 2 years / Winter coat	Rut (young last)		Stags separate from hind herds form stag groups after rut.
Stags 7–9 years			Casts 5th/6th head	Casts 5th/6th head	Summer coat	Antler growth		Cleans velvet		Rut (mature) / Grows mane	Winter coat	
Stags old			Casts 8th/9th head / Casts antler		Summer coat	Antler growth		Cleans velvet	Rut (old) / Grows mane / Winter coat			

Fig.18 Roe deer development summary

	Jan.	Feb.	Mar.	Apr.	May	Jun.	July	Aug.	Sept.	Oct.	Nov.	Dec.
Fawns 0–8 m					Born Coat speckled		Fawns with does Start feeding on grass	Coat changes to browny-grey			Young buck grows button antler	
Young 8–12 m	Young buck drops buttons	First head antlers start growing		Coat change to permanent Buck starts seeking own territory	Milk teeth change to permanent							
Does	Growth of embryo begins	Rapid growth of embryo		Coat change to red Family groups fall apart	Young does grow new coat Old does change coat Fawns dropped	Fawns dropped	Rutting time young first	Rutting time	Covered does start dormant gestation Coat change to grey-brown, young first		Family groups forming	Growth of embryo begins
Buck young 1–3 years	Antlers develop; covered in velvet			Antlers being cleaned (youngest last) Coat change	Territorial fraying		Rutting time	Rutting time	Coat change to brown Social groups form	Social groups form	Antler dropping	
Buck old 4 years and older	Antlers develop; covered in velvet			Antlers being cleaned. Buck mark their territories by fraying Coat change		Rutting time	Rutting time				Coat change to grey-brown Antler dropping Social groups forms	
	MOVEMENTS MAINLY TO FOOD AND WATER								SPORADIC INDIVIDUAL AND GROUP MOVEMENTS			

Chapter VI

DEER ANTLERS

What Is A Good Antler?

There has hardly been a page until now on which deer antlers have not been mentioned, and there will be few pages without further mention of them in the forthcoming text. It may therefore be advisable to explain what a good antler is.

Before attempting a description of the antler, it must again be emphasised that antler length, the length of tines and the thickness of the beam depend very much on feeding, quality of blood, weather and health, and it is not always fair therefore to compare any two antlers of, say, red deer, chosen at random, to praise one and condemn the other, without first obtaining accurate information of the conditions under which these two animals have developed. This is of particular importance in Britain, where the bulk of wild red deer comes from Scotland. There, the beasts are never as large as those few which are killed in the more southern part of the British Isles every year, where they can develop under more favourable conditions and as a result grow a more massive and impressive head.

In the last two or three decades, the British roe deer have found their rightful place in considerable numbers, on the pedestal of CIC medals from Gold to Bronze. The distribution of these trophies of the international class is wide, from Southern England to Central and North Scotland. There have also been several CIC class red deer trophies, but these have not come from the wild hill stock in Scotland but from the woodlands.

The fact that 'Nature Provides' should not lead us however to taking with both hands; on the contrary one ought to treat these splendid trophy animals with respect and allow them to propagate for the enjoyment of the future generations of stalkers if not for the benefit of Nature, and only take then out as a part of planned cull when the animals are passed the point of high development.

Red Deer (Mature Beasts other than Park)

Length. The length itself is not all-important. The average antler length for Scotland is 31 to 34 in., but the record length is 45½ in. English heads should be some 2 to 3 in. (at least) longer, and the average would probably show 4 in. (Park deer should measure over 40 in.) A number of heads over 48 in. have been shot on the Continent in the last twenty-five years and there seems to be no reason why similar length should not be achieved in Britain, specially outside the Highlands, provided that deer are given care and attention equivalent to that given to them in many countries of the Continent.

Brow. The brows of a stag should sweep first low over the forehead then upwards and slightly outwards. Ten inches is a good length for the British Isles. Brows should be thick at the base, gradually becoming thinner, and the tine ends should be polished white. The surface should be pearled as far as the white of the tips.

Beys. The bey is not a tine which appears in every stag. The fact that the antler possesses a bey is a good sign, but its lack is insufficient for the antler to be regarded as poor. The bey can be shorter than the brow, but apart from that it should be similar in appearance.

Trey. The length of the trey should be equal or slightly shorter than the brow. Brow and trey of equal length are a sign of perfection in a fully mature beast which has not started going back. The surface should be the same as that of the brow.

Crown. A crown of three on top each side with three other tines on each antler makes a stag a royal (twelve-pointer). The tines of the crowns should be long and slightly curved inwards, or at the worst straight. The only type of the crown where an outward curve is considered acceptable is that of the stag whose crown has more than one double tine, and one or two tines positioned at the back of the crown sweep backwards, apparently to make space for the growth of the tines. The surface of the tines of the crown need not be pearled but the tine ends should be polished white.

Beam. (circumference) 4 to 5 in. is already a fair thickness of the lower beam for Scottish deer. The English heads should be 5 in. upwards. This measurement should be taken between the trey-tine and the next lower tine (brow or brey), in the thinnest place. The upper beam measured in the thinnest place between the trey and the base of the crown, can be somewhere in the region of ½ in. thinner. This measurement, as long as the international system of point scoring is not adopted in Great Britain, is not of importance.

Number of tines. This is a very controversial subject. Generally speaking a twelve pointer is regarded as the lowest form of first class trophy. Many people would much rather have fewer tines (not less than 8) and a heavy massive head with long beam, long tines, well pearled and of a well advanced age, rather than a royal which so often is thin and anything but massive and long tined, often being shot too early in its life.

Tines shorter than 2 cm (0.8 in.) do not normally count. In many circles 1 in. is accepted for simplification. This applies to those tines which, having once been longer, have obviously been broken, as much as to those which have never grown to a better length.

Spread. The inside span measured between the beams from the inside edge of the beam to the inside edge of the other beam, in the widest place. This is an important measurement and should vary between 27 to 31 in. in Scotland and 29 to 34 in. in other parts of the British Isles.

Colour. The colour should be dark brown, nearly black, or very dark grey.

Pearling. (the roughness of the beam and tine surface) should be well marked with deep impressions and sticking out 'pearls', and should be marked in 'veins' (lines of depressions running upwards from the burr, mainly on the inside and outside of the beam).

Burrs. Burrs should be well marked as a rounded off ring around the base of the beam below the brow. They should be pearled, but the pearls can be smoothed off by threshing and fraying.

Fallow Deer (Mature Beasts)

As with red deer, length is not all-important. A good fallow in the British Isles should be 21 to 26 in. long in the antler, but it is quite likely that the park animals will be longer.

Brow. These will be rarely longer than 6 to 7 in. unless exceptionally good conditions prevail.

Trey. Trey should be slightly shorter than the brow. (Bey does not normally grow.)

Palmation. The height of the palmation from its base to the lowest incision between the top tines should be in the region of 12 to 14 in. if the palmation is solid, or at least not less than 7 to 8 in. if it is interrupted by incisions which reach downward. The width of the palmation measured from the forward (leading) edge to the deepest incision (or depression) between the rear tines should be about two-thirds of the height of the palmation.

Circumference of the beams. Lower circumference measured in the thinnest place above the brow is an important measurement in this country. This should be 5 to 6 in. on a good head, but not less than 4 in. on an average one.

Colouring. On the whole the colouring of fallow heads is lighter than that of other deer. Brown-yellow (in the darker shades) is predominant, but dark brown, grey-brown and grey are quite acceptable provided that they are not very light.

Palmation. The palmation must be as solid as possible with a number of tines along the rear edge, spreading from the spur upwards to the top-fore tine. The tines need not be of exceptional length and 2 in. tines are quite reasonable. The palm should be concave like a spoon, bulging outward.

Spread. This should be measured in the widest place from one palm to the other, and should be about 75 per cent of the antler length.

Pearling. The pearling should be fine, and should spread upwards to the top of the palmation. The pearling of the palmation should run in wide veins.

Burrs. Burrs should be in the shape of a ring the cross-section of which should be triangular, one side running down the beam, one horizontally, and one point be at the base of the beam. The burrs should be pearled.

Roe Deer

Length. Length plays an important part in the estimation of the quality of roe antler. The English roe should stand 10 in. depending on area. Some Scottish roe reach 11 in. and more, but these are not very common with 9 in. being a good average.

Spread. Measured from tip to tip, or in the widest place between the beams. The spread should be not less than 30 per cent of the length. This point is not of vital importance.

Number of tines. There are rarely more than three tines on each antler. These should be well formed, long pointed, the tips polished white or light yellow.

Colouring. The colouring should be dark brown or black, but dark grey and yellow-brown (dark) are not bad.

Pearling. In spite of the fact that roe antlers are much smaller than those of red and fallow deer, the pearls are expected to be much larger than those of either of the other two. The pearls should be large, the surface therefore rough. Pearling should spread far upwards, and the further it spreads the better. Ideally it should reach the white polished part of the top tine, but the farther up the pearling reaches the smaller it ought to become.

Burrs. Like the pearls, the burrs of a roe should be better marked, thicker and wider than those of either the red or fallow deer in comparison to size of antler. The burrs should be very rough with pearling all over, meeting or nearly meeting between the antlers. Instead of the circumference of the beams, the circumference of the burrs is measured and the greater this is the better.

Tine ends. The tine ends should be very smooth and white-polished. Dull tine ends are signs of very advanced or very young age. The points should be sharp.

Measuring of Antlers

British System.

Frank Wallace, in the preface to his book *British Deer Heads* (an illustrated record of the exhibition organised by *Country Life* in 1913; published by *Country Life*), describes the system of measurements adopted, and in the case of this particular exhibition carried out by Messrs Rowland Ward, as follows: *Length of horn:* from the bottom edge of the burr (coronet) to the highest tip point, following the outside curve of the horn. *Beam (circumference):* between bez (bey), and trez (trey), that is, between the second and third point; where the bey is absent, between brow and trey. *Inside span:* the greatest width between main beams taken in a straight line.

Since that exhibition the circumference of the coronet in roe deer has been added. In certain cases the width of the palmation in very well formed fallow deer antlers is sometimes given. All the measurements are taken in inches to the nearest $\frac{1}{16}$ in. An allowance of $\frac{1}{8}$ in. is sometimes made in the measurement of red and fallow heads.

The basic difference between the International and the British system is that the British is less accurate, less information being required. Needless to say the International system uses metric measurements. Those few measurements required for the British system are taken between points which are exactly the same for the International — except that in roe measurements the spread is not included, and 'tip to tip' measurement takes its place, and the illustrations which follow the description of the International system will make the British system clear enough.

The International (CIC) System

This system is now universal, and provides an accurate estimation of the value of the trophy. All measurements are taken in cm to an accuracy of 1 mm (0.1 cm), centimal points being rounded off as follows: 0.01 to 0.04 equals 0.00; 0.05 to 0.09 equals 0.1 cm; weights taken to 1 g (0.01 kg accuracy), and volume (for roe deer only) to 1 cc.

Red Deer (Fig. 19)

1. *Beam length*. Measurement from the longest tip of the crown tine to the lower outside edge of the burr. The measurement follows between the tines of the crown (if necessary) following accurately all curvature of the beam along the outside of the beam. The impression formed by the top surface of the burr and the bottom of the beam is excluded from the length measurement.

Formula: $\dfrac{(\text{Length L} + \text{Length R})}{2} = \text{Points}$

2. *Brows:* Measurement of the brow starts at the top of the burr, following the bottom of the beam, along the bottom of the brow, following the curve to the tip.

Formula: $\dfrac{(\text{Brow L} + \text{Brow R})}{2} = \text{Points}$

3. *Trey:* Measured from the bottom of the base of the trey (where its connecting curve with the beam ends) to the tip following all curvature.

Formula: $\dfrac{(\text{Length L} + \text{Length R})}{2} = \text{Points}$

4. *Coronets circumference*. Measured around each of the burrs separately with a well stretched tape overspanning the impressions and unevennesses.

Formula: $\dfrac{(\text{Burr L} + \text{Burr R})}{2} = \text{Points}$

5. *Beam circumference (lower beam)*. Measured with a stretched tape in the thinnest place between the brow — and trey-tine if bey-tine is absent, or bey- and trey-tine.

Formulae:
Circumference R = Points; Circumference L = Points

6. *Beam circumference (upper beam)*. Measured with a stretched tape, in the thinnest place between the trey-tine and the base of the crown (upper fork in absence of the crown).

Formulae:
Circumference R = Points; Circumference L = Points

7. *Number of tine-ends*. All natural tine ends, longer than 2 cm, are counted, each point valued at 1 point.

8. *Weight*. Expressed in kg, with the upper jaws and skull bones (without mounting plaque). With the normal setting (short nose bone) — each 0.5 kg equals 1 point. With the long nose bone uncut and upper jaw bone still in position, up to 0.7 kg may be deducted off the overall weight. When the antlers are mounted on only a small portion of skull bone, an addition of 10 g (0.1 kg) may be allowed (Fig. 23).

$$\text{Formula:} \quad \frac{\text{Net weight}}{2} = \text{Points}$$

9. *Spread*. The measurements of the widest distance between two opposite points of the inner side of the beam (excluding the thickness of the beam), in percentage proportion to the mean average of the length.

$$\text{Formula:} \quad \frac{\text{Spread} \times 100}{\text{Length}} = \text{Percentage}$$

Points allotted: 60 per cent — nil; 70–80 per cent — 2 points; over 80 per cent — 3 points.

10. *Crown.*	*Points*
Simple crowns with a total of five to seven short or poor tines	0.5–1.5
Simple crowns with a total of five to seven good and strong tines	2.0–3.5
Simple crowns with total of six to seven long massive tines or eight to nine short weak tines, or double and quadruple crowns with a total of eight to nine short weak tines	4.0–5.5
Double crowns or quadruple crowns with good strong tines	6.0–7.5
Strong cup or hand formed crowns with long and strong tines at least ten ends	8.0–10

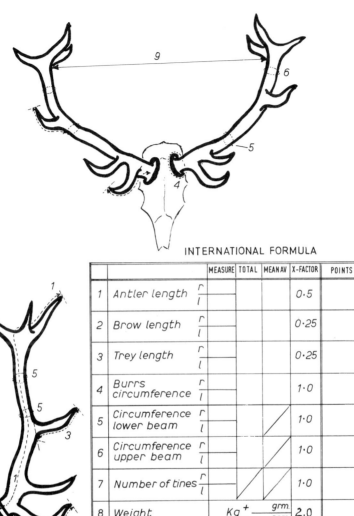

INTERNATIONAL FORMULA

		MEASURE	TOTAL	MEAN AV	X-FACTOR	POINTS
1	Antler length $\frac{r}{l}$				0·5	
2	Brow length $\frac{r}{l}$				0·25	
3	Trey length $\frac{r}{l}$				0·25	
4	Burrs circumference $\frac{r}{l}$				1·0	
5	Circumference lower beam $\frac{r}{l}$				1·0	
6	Circumference upper beam $\frac{r}{l}$				1·0	
7	Number of tines $\frac{r}{l}$				1·0	
8	Weight	Kg $\pm \frac{grm.}{grm.}$			2.0	
9	Spread	$\frac{cm. \times 100}{average length\ cm} = \%$		Max. pts 3		
10	Crowns			Max. pts 10		
11	Bey tines			Max. pts 2		
12	Colour			Max. pts 2		
13	Pearling			Max. pts 2		
14	Tine ends			Max. pts 2		
	Total for 1-14					
15	Deductions			Max. pts 3		
	TOTAL POINTS					

BRITISH MEASUREMENTS

Tines $\frac{r}{l}$	
Length $\frac{r}{l}$	
Beam $\frac{r}{l}$	
Inside span	

Fig. 19 Red deer antler measurement card

103

11. *Bey.*

Disappearing bey or only just marked	0.00
Only one or two weak beys	1.0
Two normally formed beys	2.0

12. *Colouring.*

Light yellow or yellow uneven	0.0
Grey or medium brown.	0.5–1.0
Dark brown or black	1.5–2.0

13. *Pearling.*

Smooth or only weakly pearled	0.0
Normal pearling .	1.0
Very well pearled.	2.0

14. *Tine ends.*

Blunt and dull	0.0
Pointed but dark .	1.0
Pointed and white polished	2.0

15. *Deductions.* All abnormalities, irregularity, lack of symmetry may be penalised with 0.5–3 points (total penal points may not exceed 3).

Note. Serial numbers 10–15 are known as beauty points and on these points scores may de awarded within an accuracy of 0.5.

The chart of red deer antler measurement and the measurement card is contained in this chapter.

Fallow Deer (Fig. 20)

1. *Beam length.* Measure from the outside bottom edge of the burr upwards (missing the depression between the upper surface of the burr and the bottom of the beam, along the outside of the beam following the curvature across the lowest depression between the tines of the upper edge of the palmation).

Formula: $\dfrac{(\text{Length L} + \text{Length R})}{2} = \text{Points}$

2. *Brows.* The measurement of the brow starts at the stop of the burr, following the bottom of the beam along the bottom of the brow following all curvature to the tip.

Formula: $\dfrac{(\text{Brow L} + \text{Brow R})}{2} = \text{Points}$

3. *Palmation height.* Measured from the base of the palmation upwards to the lowest depression between the tines of the upper edge of the palm.

Formula: $\dfrac{(\text{Palmation L} + \text{Palmation R})}{2} = \text{Points}$

4. *Palmation width.* Measured as the circumference of the palmation in the place where the deepest depression or incision between the tines of the back edge is found and can be measured approximately half-way up the palmation, at approximately right angles to its leading edge. On the outside of the palmation the tape follows the curve of the palm, on the inside

overspans the depression. This measurement, divided by 2, equals the width.

Formula: $\dfrac{(\text{Width L} + \text{Width R})}{1.5} = \text{Points}$

5. *Coronets circumference.* Measured around each of the burrs separately with a well stretched tape overspanning all unevennesses.

Formula: $\dfrac{(\text{Burr L} + \text{Burr R})}{2} = \text{Points}$

6. *Beam circumference (upper and lower beams).* Measured in the thinnest places below the trey-tine (lower beam) , and above the trey-tine (upper beam).

Formula: $\dfrac{(\text{Lower L} + \text{Lower R}) + (\text{Upper L} + \text{Upper R})}{2} = \text{Points}$

7. *Weight.* In kilograms with the skull but without the plaque. With the normal (short nose) mounting each 0.5 kg equals 1 point; for mounting with the full nose bone and upper jaw bone up to 0.25 kg may be deducted; for mounting with the full nose bone but without the jaw bone 0.1 kg will be deducted (Fig. 23).

Formula: $\dfrac{(\text{Weight in kg–deductions})}{2} = \text{Points}$

8. *Colouring.*

	Points
Light, yellow or brown	0.0
Medium brown or dark brown	1.0
Dark brown	2.0

9. *Tine ends of the palmation.* These are to be regarded as beauty points and particular attention is paid to the spur-tines and beys (if in existence), as well as to the division of the palm by incisions. Points from 1 to 6 may be awarded.

10. *Impression.* General appearance of the antler, specially in comparison with other trophies (of the year, area, or exhibition). Points 0 to 6 may be awarded.

11. *Spread deductions.* Measured on the inside of the palmations between two opposite-lying and most widely separated points, and as in red deer expressed in percentage proportion to length.

Formula: $\dfrac{\text{Spread} \times 100}{\text{Length}} = \text{Percentage}$

Deduction as follows: 85 per cent — 2 points; 75 per cent — 3 points; 70 per cent — 4 points; 65 per cent — 5 points; 60 per cent — 6 points.

12. *Other deductions.*

	Points
Bad, flat or too bulging formation	0–10
Smooth unpearled surface smooth rear edge	0–2
Irregular or misformed palmation, over-long palmation (in comparison with the width), abnormal form of palm	0–6

FALLOW DEER ANTLER MEASUREMENTS

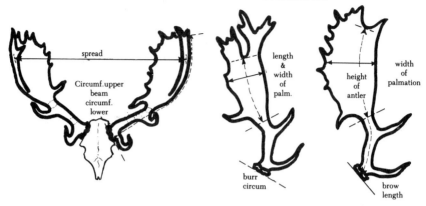

Measurements record card

Serial No.	Measurement of:	Measurement	Total	Mean Average	Mult. by	Point Score
1	Antler length	r. l.			½	
2	Brow length	r. l.			¼	
3	Palmation height	r. l.			1	
4	Palmation width	r. l.			1½	
5	Burrs circumference	r. l.			1	
6	Beam circumf. lower upper	r. l. r. l.			1 1 1 1	
7	Weight				add— deduct—	
8	Colour					
9	Tines					
10	Comparative valuation					
				Total serial 1-10		
11 12	Deductions Additions					
	FINAL SCORE					

Fig. 20   Fallow deer antler measurement card

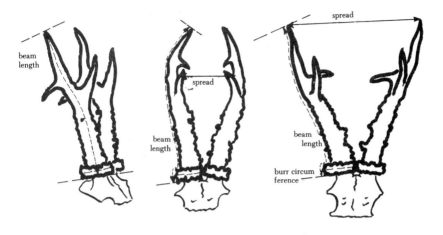

British Measurements

Length Right —— Left ——	Tip to tip ——in.
Circumference of coronet R — L —	Total number of points

International Formula

		Measurement	Total	Mean av.	X-factor	Points
1	Antler length r. l.				0.5	
2	Weight	g	addition ____ deduction ____ g		0.1	
3	Volume	ccm			0.3	
4	Spread	cm x 100 (length average) cm = %			Max.pts. 4	
5	Colour				Max.pts. 4	
6	Pearling				Max.pts. 4	
7	Burrs				Max.pts. 4	
8	Tine ends				Max.pts. 2	
	TOTAL FOR SERIAL 1–8					
9	Additions (for appearance)				Max.pts. 5	
10	Deductions (for appearance)				Max.pts. 5	
	TOTAL SCORE					

Fig. 21   Roe deer antler measurements

107

Roe Deer

1. *Length.* Measured from the outside lower edge of the burr following the outside of the burr and the top surface, to the beam, and then up the beam following all curvature, but overspanning the pearling up to the upper tine tip.

$$\text{Formula:} \quad \frac{(\text{Length L} + \text{Length R})}{2} = \text{Points}$$

2. *Weight.* With the normal mounting of the antlers with the small nose bone only, 0.1 of a point is given for each gram of the weight, where the antler is mounted with the top of the skull bone only, 10–20 g (with 5 g accuracy) may be added to the weight. For skull mounting with the long nose bone but without the upper jaw, or with upper jaw but without the lower jaw-bone, up to 90 g, may be deducted (Fig. 23).

$$\text{Formula:} \quad \frac{\text{Weight (less deductions or plus additions)}}{\text{in g} \times 0.1} = \text{Points}$$

3. *Volume of antlers.* Volume of the antler in cc. The measurement to include the burrs as far as the lower surface so that the liquid in which the measurement is taken does not reach the pedicle.

$$\text{Formula: Volume} \times 0.3 = \text{Points}$$

4. *Spread.* The maximum distance between two opposite points on the inside of the antler, measured in any part of the height of the beam, expressed in percentage proportion to length.

$$\text{Formula:} \quad \frac{\text{Spread} \times 100}{\text{Mean average length}} = \text{Percentage}$$

	Points
30–35 per cent equals	1
35–40 per cent equals	2
40–45 per cent equals	3
45–70 per cent equals	4
Less than 30 and more than 70 per cent equals	nil

The following serial numbers 5–8 are regarded as beauty points, and points with the accuracy to 0.5 may be awarded as follows:

5. *Colouring.*	*Points*
Light yellow or bleached	0
Yellow, light-grey or brownish.	1
Medium-brown or grey .	2
Dark brown	3
Black	4

6. *Pearling.*	*Points*
Smooth surface	0
Poorly pearled	1
Medium pearl, few pearls	2
Well pearled	3
Very well pearled.	4

7. *Burrs.*

Poorly marked, small, weak	0
Medium, poorly pearled	1
Ring or drooping	2
Well pearled drooping	3
Very good strong	4

8. *Tine ends.*

Porous, dull, blunt colourless	0
Pointed, dull, weak	1
Sharp, white, well polished	2

9. *Additions.* On each assessment of the antler, an addition of up to 5 points may be added or deducted as follows:

	Points
(a) For normal, good or very good long form	0–2
(b) For exceptional form or regularity	2–5

(Maximum addition, 5 points total).

10. *Deductions.*

For one-sided or both sided malformation	1
For lack of tines or short tines	2
For irregular form, unnatural build, etc.	3

(Maximum deduction, 5 points total).

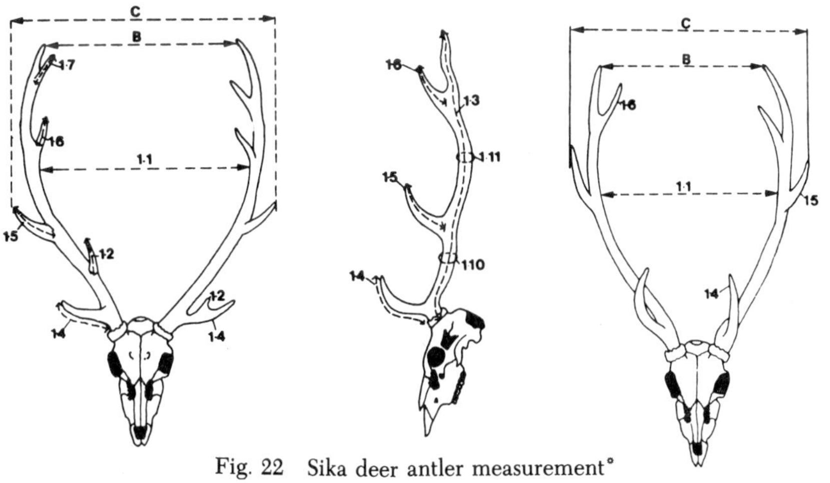

Fig. 22   Sika deer antler measurement°

Supplementary data

A. Number of tines on each antler: to be counted a tine, a projection must be at least 2.0 cm in length and its length must exceed the length of its base.

B. Tip to tip measurement: measure distance between uppermost tips of main beams.

C. Greatest spread: Measured at widest spread of antlers.

Score Data

1.1 Inside span: measured at widest distance between the normal second and third tines on the main beam. If the latter is missing, the measurement is taken at the widest inside span mid-distance between the normal 2nd tine and tip of the antler. Any span measurement in excess of the length of the longer antler will be entered in column 4.

° Based on *The Game Trophies of the World*, International Council for Game and Wildlife Conservation (P. Parey Verlag, Hamburg, 1981).

Supplementary Data	Left	Right
A. Number of tines		
B. Tip to tip		
C. Greatest Spread		

Score Data	1 Span Credit	2 Left	3 Right	4 Difference
1.1 Inside span				
1.2 Total length of all abnormal tines between brown and the third tine on both antlers (enter Col 4)				
1.3 Length of the main beam				
1.4 Length of brow				
1.5 Length of middle tine				
1.6 Length of the third tine				
1.7 Length of the first extra crown tine**				
1.8 Length of the second extra crown tine**				
1.9 Length of the third extra crown tine**				
1.10 Circumference of the lower beam between the brow and middle tine				
1.11 Circumference of the upper beam between the second and inner tine				
Total				
Cols 1+2+3	Less Col 4	SCORE		
Score Total				

* Based on The Game Trophies of the World, P. Parey Hamburg 1980

** If these extra tines are present

1.2   Total lengths of all abnormal tines placed between brow (1.4) and third tine (1.6) : this figure is entered in column 4 — Difference. Although 8 tines (4 + 4) is the usual full complement of tines on a Sika stag, additional tines are in order if the form distinct tines of the crown area. Tines or small jags located between brow and third tine must be considered abnormal. These include any tines erupting from the posterior (back) side of beam. Every individual tine must be measured as at 1.6.

1.3   Length of main beam: follow outside curve from lower edge of coronet to tip.

1.4   Length of brow tine: measure from upper edge of coronet along the lower edge of brow tine to its extremity. If the brow sprouts from main beam 5 cm or more above coronet, brow length will be taken from point of eruption.

1.5   Length of second (middle) tine: measure along the outer edge of the tine of each antler from the spot where it starts to emerge from the main beam.

1.6   Length of third (inner) tine: measure along the outer edge of the tine of each antler from the spot where it starts to emerge from the main beam.

1.7   Length of first (1.7), second (1.8) and third (1.9) extra crown tines (if present): measure exactly as for inner top tine (1.6).

1.10   Circumference of lower beam: measure circumference of main beam at thinnest place between brow (1.4) and middle tine (1.5).

1.11   Circumference of upper beam: measure circumference of main beam at thinnest place between middle tine (1.5) and upper fork tine (1.6) — if present. If not, then at half distance between middle tine (1.5) and tip of antler.

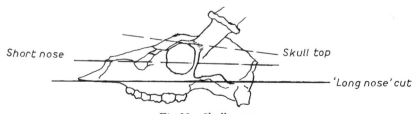

Fig.23   Skull cutting

Chapter VII

MALFORMATION OF ANTLERS

There is not much definitely known about the malformation of deer antlers. It has been the subject of much discussion and study in many countries and certain theories have been developed; but they are theories only, and this applies just as much to the cause of malformation as to the likelihood of their being passed on in the male or female line, in the latter case coming to light when the daughter has a young male fawn or calf.

It is known that in normal circumstances a good buck should pass his good qualities to his sons, specially if the doe with which he has mated comes 'from a good family'. It does, however, happen that this almost obvious assumption is upset by a doe producing a poor specimen of a buck for no apparent reason, having mated with a good buck during the previous year's rut. In the same way, cases have been known of a poor buck fathering sons who grew good six-pointer heads, in spite of the fact that the father buck with monotonous regularity reproduced poor heads, completely malformed, from year to year. Admittedly these cases are not common, or at least not commonly observed, since there are few places where anyone can state with any accuracy which doe (or hind) has mated with which buck (or stag), and what the result of the mating has been. The theories now available are based therefore on the observations made by the members of such organisations as the Goettingen Forestry Academy, the staff of certain experimental deer parks and forests on the Continent, and the staff of some deer parks in Britain, where deer are under meticulous observation throughout the year.

Having elaborated on the exceptions which make the rules, one must underline the other side of the case. Observe a deer forest or deer park where the deer live under good conditions, and where the blood-stock on the whole is good. It will soon be noted that such similarity exists between the antlers of certain deer that in some cases one could call them twins, triplets, etc. There are cases of remarkable similarity in such items as the shape of the antler, the shape and formation of the crowns, the position of the bey and trey tine in red deer and the curvature, length, etc. It may equally well be observed, especially in places where the shed antlers are available for inspection, that the same type of antler is normally developed from year to year. Why then this odd, inexplicable fact of 'outcasts', who by some freak of nature reproduce their species with heads which do not resemble those of their ancestors?

The fact of similarity in reproductive strength in deer is based on an examination of numerous cases. In certain forests, where deer have been introduced in the last fifty years (mainly on the Continent) and where the male and female have come from the same place, and are of very good stock, one can see immediately the striking resemblance between the antlers of deer of the same age groups.

Much has already been said about the influence of feeding and blood-stock on the quality of antlers, and this subject therefore requires no more elaboration here, but it cannot be ignored when consideration is being given to malformation of antlers.

A review of the entire range of malformed antlers of all types of deer suggests that there are two, possibly three groups of malformations of antlers.

The first of these groups, possibly the easiest to deal with, is malformation due to 'self-inflicted injury' to the antler or the pedicle.

The second, slightly more complicated, is where the malformations are due to injuries to body or antler attributable to 'outside causes', here we have to deal with two sub-groups — injuries due to natural causes such as frostbite, and injuries by a 'third person' under which heading come gun wounds, and would resulting from fights between the animals.

Finally, there is the group where we are all very much in the dark, consisting of malformations which are the result of illness and other, unknown, causes; here in the main, mere suggestive theories can be framed.

Let us consider each group separately and arrive at some conclusion, which will assist our efforts to produce pure blood-stock, and thus improve the quality of deer.

Self-Inflicted Mechanical Injury

We know that the antler, at the period when it is forming, from the time following the shedding of one year's growth to the time when the new growth is mature and ready for cleaning, consists of soft living tissue, and is therefore susceptible to injury.

During that time deer avoid thickets and endeavour to survive in those parts of the forest where there is no danger of antlers being damaged by collision with solid obstacles. Needless to say, from time to time deer have to take cover — it may be from their enemy, human or otherwise, it may be in very inclement weather. They may be running away after being startled by something or somebody, and inadvertently run into a solid or semi-solid obstacle. The soft formation of their antler in velvet suffers damage. The damage thus sustained may be only superficial, resulting in a slight deformation such as a slight bending of the antler, or loss of a tine; it may be, however, that more serious damage is suffered.

In the first place it is possible that a foreign body may have become lodged underneath the velvet. In such a case, around that foreign body a pocket of blood and pus is formed. As the antler hardens towards the end of its development the pocket or capsule, of liquid is encased, forming a bulge in the antler (Plate XVII). Furthermore, it is quite possible, for example, in the case of an animal's running into a tree trunk, a fence or other similar obstacle, that both antlers may be nearly destroyed, squashed almost flat, without any injury being inflicted on the pedicle through which the antler-building stuffs and bodies are delivered to the forming antler.

The squashed antler substance will continue to form, but the injury sustained will remain in the form of malformation, e.g. odd misshapen tines, if one can call them that, growing in an unusual manner until the antler is hard and cleaned (see Plate XVIII).

These malformations are not lasting, the antler-building 'permanent' parts of the beast (permanent, that is, as opposed to the antlers themselves, which being shed every year are of a temporary nature) remaining unharmed.

Such an injury may also be of deeper penetration (specially when sustained in the very early stages of the antler-forming period, when the antler is very short and very soft) and may injure the pedicle. Here the result is quite different: If such injury is only slight, it is possible that the antler will grow, but the form may not be normal, inasmuch as it may be thinner, may have fewer or no tines, may also grow additional tines or even additional beam. The variety of possible malformations is infinite in shape and size. It will depend on the extent of damage whether such malformation will be recurring from year to year but whichever it is, it is unlikely to be passed on to the offspring. It is also possible that, having run into an obstacle the pedicle may be not only damaged but completely broken off. If this happens late in the year, just before the antlers become completely hard, the antler will survive as a 'pendulum' attached to the head by skin, but otherwise almost normally developed; if it has happened early in the development phase, the pendulum will harden as soon as the flow of blood caused by the breakage stops and only a knob or spike beam will remain (Plates XVIIIA and XIX).

Plate XVII   Antler malformation through breaking when in velvet

b) X-ray shows congealed blood in the 'pocket' formed (white areas within the broken tine)

a) Antler thickened in the location of breakage

Plate XVIIIA Malfunctions due to damaged pedicle

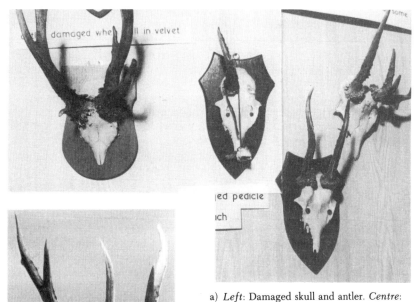

a) *Left*: Damaged skull and antler. *Centre*: Broken pedicle (note the antler and upper pedicle hanging loose on pendulum) *Right upper*: Damaged pedicle and antler. *Right lower*: Damaged pedicle of right antler rehealed, allowing almost normal antler growth.

b) Damaged pedicle may, under some circumstances, cause a multi-antlered head

c) Fallow deer damaged right antler and pedicle

d) Result of damaged pedicle causing deformation of right antler

e) Damaged antler and pedicle

This antler will most likely drop off sometime during the year, quite often by the animal itself tearing it off with its legs or rubbing it against a solid object, such as a stone or a tree. Cases have, however, occurred when the pedicle has been broken but a part of it remains in contact with the base, and the two parts have regrown at an odd angle. In these cases the subsequent growth of the antler will always be at an unusual angle. It is even possible that the upper part of the pedicle has regrown with the lower, but the lower part in the act of healing has redeveloped a 'false' pedicle. In these cases a three-antlered head is possible (Plate XVIIIA). Normally, however, the two antlers growing on the fractured pedicle side will be smaller than the antler growing on the healthy pedicle.

Ultimately a broken pedicle may not regrow, the healed bone having lost its antler-forming qualities. Here the beast will remain a one-antlered animal.

It needs little more evidence, then, to make it clear that in cases where the pedicle is undamaged, the antler malformation is not a lasting one, and that as soon as the damaged antler has been shed, a normal growth of

Plate XVIIIB   Malfunctions due to damaged antler

a)

b

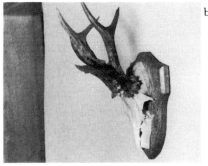

c) Damaged antler and skull. Note the hole in the skull 'A' and malformed tines especially of left antler. It is possible that the damage was caused in a fight with a murderer-type buck.

a) and b) Damaged antler showing the crack of breakage of the brow tine. The broken tine is black due to congealed blood and proportion of uncleaned velvet. The broken part is dead from time of breakage, has ceased to continue normal development.

c)

115

Plate XIX   Malformation of red deer heads due to mechanical damage

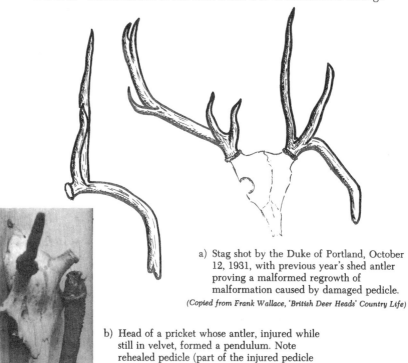

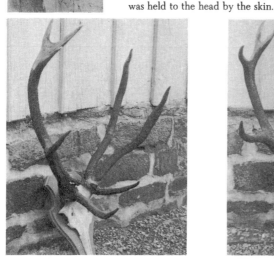

a) Stag shot by the Duke of Portland, October
12, 1931, with previous year's shed antler
proving a malformed regrowth of
malformation caused by damaged pedicle.
(Copied from Frank Wallace, 'British Deer Heads' Country Life)

b) Head of a pricket whose antler, injured while
still in velvet, formed a pendulum. Note
rehealed pedicle (part of the injured pedicle
is visible attached to the antler). the pendulum
was held to the head by the skin.

c) and d) Injury sustained when antler in velvet, showing clearly
the location of the injury. The penetration having been
shallow, not reaching the pedicle, the antler continued
growing. These heads are often wrongly called 'three-antlered
heads'. The chances are that the head would regrow normally
after shedding.

antler will follow, which is not so in cases of damaged or broken pedicle. With a broken pedicle the malformations are normally lasting ones; in the damaged ones they may be of a lasting nature but, this is not always and necessarily so; here a possibility exists of the malformation being of hereditary nature, but the reason for it is not established.

It will thus be seen that a self-inflicted injury may result in such malformation as multi-tined head, multi-antlered head, pendulum antler, and, finally, complete disappearance of one antler or both (Plates XVIIIA and XIX).

Malformations Due to Injuries by Outside Causes

Let us deal first with injuries suffered by deer from wounds inflicted by inaccurate shooting, or shotgun shooting. The bulk of the latter are of minor consequence as the pellets will not normally penetrate far enough to inflict heavy or lasting injuries. Needless to say, wounds affecting the head, like those described above, will have identical results and the likelihood of the pellets embedding themselves in the soft antler, and thus causing a bulge, is much greater than with a similar type of injury being sustained in any other way. Unless shot, with a shotgun, from a very close range, the pedicle is unlikely to be damaged by being broken or shot off completely.

The bulk of wounds suffered by deer are in the legs and in the body. An injury in the legs, when the flesh only is damaged, is without consequences as far as the antlers are concerned, but breakage of the leg bones normally results in a malformation of the antler, on the opposite side to that of the leg which was wounded, normally formed as a 'kink'. Thus damage to the right fore or hind leg will result in a kink of the left antler and vice versa. Instances of these malformations have proved the point beyond doubt. Such malformation is a lasting one, but will be more noticeable at the time when the bone is healing than in the subsequent years. Not all 'kinks' in the antler are due to this cause.

Leg breakages other than those due to wounds by shooting, have the same effect. The 'kinks' normally takes the direction opposite to the side on which the leg bone was wounded. Thus when the right leg is wounded, not only will the left antler be malformed, but the 'kink' also will be to the left.

Wounds to other parts of the body have different effects, and in most cases affect both antlers to the same extent or neither of them, depending on the location and degree of wounding.

The result of an injury to lungs, stomach and other internal organs is the same as it is in a case of disease or parasitic activity in those organs, and can be found in Table 15 at the close of this chapter.

There are not many ways in which a deer can lose its sex organs; they can be lost as a result of attack by other animals such as dogs, foxes, or wild cats, especially where young deer are concerned, and man may destroy them by accident when shooting or, as in the older days, sometimes on purpose. The degree and timing of injury to the sex organs results in different malformations. Complete removal of the sex organs (castration) of a young buck or stag may result in complete disappearance of the antlers and complete inability to form them (see Plate XX). It is possible that the damage to the sex organs is not of such a type as to make the animal impotent, and its lack of horns may then be transmitted to its young. Thus, rare as it may be, a hummel may be a hereditary malformation but at the same time there are reliable records which prove that a hummel can father a normal antlered offspring.

Damage to the sex organs of a fully mature male deer, be he buck or stag, may cause lasting upset of the system of sex hormones without destruction of sex organs, and manifests itself in a malformation not of the antler but of the pearling and velvet. The first growth after the injury is sustained is quite normal, but the antlers are not as firmly placed on the pedicles as they normally are, and it is possible that in the act of cleaning the velvet, they will be shed. However, once the antler is cleaned, the danger of losing it passes, and what is more, the beast cannot shed it when the shedding time comes. As a result, the following year's growth superimposes itself upon the existing antler.By February the mass of velvet-like substance, hard inside where the previous year's antler forms its basis, and semi-hard underneath the velvet covering, is well established and quite likely to obliterate the burrs of the lower antler. (In stag and fallow buck this phenomenon starts about the time of their antler shedding and the beginning of the formation of the new antlers.) The size of this growth will depend upon the age at which the sex organs were injured or hormonal upsets due to other causes occurred. The speed at which growth progresses depends possibly upon the degree of injury. When the upset takes place at the time of the first growth of antlers, i.e. between the time of the shedding and the beginning of the hardening up process, it may result in the formations remaining soft forever. (See Plate XXI (c).)

Cases have been known of clearing the formation ('perruque') described above. In many known cases the beasts had recovered from the upset, and having shed the antlers on which the perruque has formed, regrew a normal antler. However, the cases where the perruque has formed on one antler, the other being perfectly formed, are still unexplained at the present day and endanger the nearly proved theory expounded above.

A case has been recorded where, as a result of upset in the sex-hormonal system, the antler was malformed by the burrs being built of bone and the normal division between bone and horn which is found at the top of the pedicle in the shape of a gristle-like layer, was found in that particular case above the bone-built burrs. Unfortunately the buck was killed accidently and it cannot be conjectured what further progress the antler growth might have made.

Upset of the sex-hormonal system in does (roe) and hinds may result in the growth of antlers (see Plate XXI) which are rarely normal in shape, and sometimes form a perruque which is dropped from time to time. In those cases where normal antlers are grown they are normally shed immediately before or just after the fawn dropping time. Cases of antlered does are described by Ferdinand von Raesefeld in his book *Das Rehwild* (The Roe Deer). One of those described was found to possess normal female sex organs on one side of the body and male organs on the other.

Plate XX   A Hummel Stag

(Photo: G Kenneth Whitehead)

Antlerless stag - caused normally by damage to sex organs. In some cases possibly inherited.

Plate XXI   Various malformations

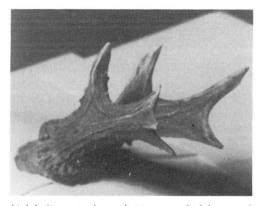

b) left: 'Luxurious' growth. Note very thick beam and heavy short tines, small by comparison burrs (sometimes lacking altogether)

a) Unknown malformation of young buck

c) Perruque (wig) heads

119

Plate XXII   Malformations due to various causes

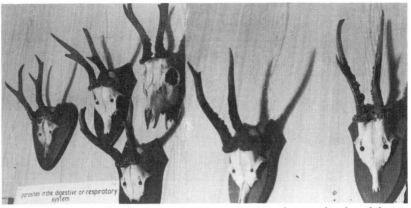

a) Parasites in the digestive and respiratory systems. Note the curved antlers of the specimens on the left and 'murderer' type tineless antler on the right.

b) Frost bite incurred in winter during the early stage of antler formation.

c) Porous antler possibly caused by frost bite in late spring.

Plate XXIII   Corkscrew heads

a) roe deer

b) red deer

Double antlers are not common phenomena. The possibility of such growth due to damaged pedicles has already been described; there is, however, another possible way in which such growth can come about. This is when the animal is unable to cast its antlers and as a result the new antler, forming underneath the old one, forces the old growth to shift without severing it off the pedicle. These cases are very rare, however, and it is impossible to say what would follow such an occurrence, whether the old and new antlers would be shed at a later time, or would both stay on, or whether one or the other would be shed. In red deer, inability to throw off the antlers is more likely to result in an extraordinary build-up, of the normally small pearls, which form a massive heavy and rough surface, as well as in general thickening and ultimate malformation of the entire antler, rather than in the multi-antlered head described above. It is suspected that inability to shed the antler has a connection with an upset of the sex-hormonal system, but little is known of it as yet.

The last instance to be noted in this group is the case of frostbite of the antler when in velvet (see Plate XXII).

Because of the time of year when the antler is grown, this concerns only roe in Britain and observation of other deer's antlers when frost-bitten is not possible on the continent of Europe either, owing to climatic conditions.

These cases again are rare, since the amount of blood circulating inside the building antler, and its coverage with the velvet should enable it to combat frost. It is possible that proof will be found that the malformation described below is due to some influence other than frostbite. In the meantime, frostbite is the accepted cause.

Depending on the stage in the annual development of the antler, at which the frostbite has taken place, so will the final antler be long or short. The theory is that after frostbite the antler ceases to grow, and a part of it, if not all, breaks off, including the tines (if these were already forming). The frostbitten antler is for the rest of the year brittle, dull in appearance and often porous. It will often be cleaned before the other buck clean theirs! Growth in the following year is not affected and normal development should take place.

Illnesses and Other Causes

A table of various illnesses and mainly parasitic influences (Fig. 24) and their reflection in the antler formation is presented at the end of this chapter. This table is based on the research carried out by Dr Werther Rieck (*Jagd und Hege in Aller Welt*, Collective work published for the D.J.V. by Heinzwolf Kolzig), von Raesefeld *Das Rewhild*, and Kerschagel *Rehabschuss*.

Among the various rare malformations, the causes of which are unknown, two are quoted below:

Tulip Growth

This may be the result of a sudden inability to propagate further. How it happens and why, and whether it is a temporary failure applying to the sex activities, or is limited to the inability further to reproduce the stuffs required for the build-up of antlers, is not known. The antler is wide in circumference of upper beam, and appears to start multi-tine growth.

Luxurious Growth

The cause of this growth are unknown. There are not many recorded examples which without doubt can be ascribed to this type of malformation, it is difficult to say. This antler grows very much thicker and heavier than the normal, and appears without the burrs. The circumference of the beam is equivalent to that of the burrs had they existed, i.e. the beam grows up from the burrs. Part of the tine length is engulfed in the beam thickness, thus only short tines protrude from the beam normally.

Luxurious growth can take one of two forms; one is unpearled, short, exceptionally thick and normally more than six tined; the other slightly slimmer more normally built but multi-tined (see Plate XXI).

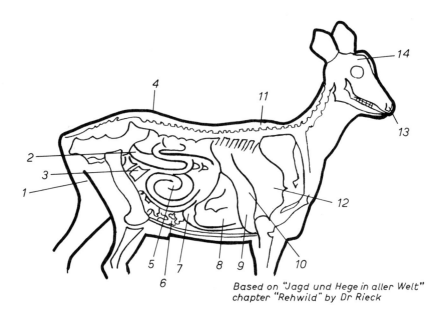

Based on "Jagd und Hege in aller Welt" chapter "Rehwild" by Dr Rieck

Fig 24 Malformations due to parasitic influences and illness.

TABLE 15 Chart of Malformations
(To be used in connection with Fig. 24)

Serial no.	Parasite	Location	Influence on antlers
1	Common tick	Skin with little hair growth	No known influence
2	Tapeworm	Appendix	No known influence
3	Bilharzia worm	Reticle (plexus) and liver°	°Disappearance of tines to the extent of tineless switch head developing after a time, possible disappearance of burrs and early setting back (Plate XXIII)
4	Maggot of stag louse	Hair	No known influence
5	Trichin (ulcerative colitis – *Trichnis chabertia*)	Colon	No known influence on antlers but loss of weight of the body
6	Tapeworm	Small intestine°	°Disappearance of tines and retraction of the beam to the extent of knobs only being left.
7	Ascarides (roundworm)	Small intestine°	Sometimes inability to clear velvet. Decrease in body weight.
8	Stomach worm	Rennet bag°	°Freak formation such as goat-head antlers bent outwards and down, or inwards and over the face. (Plate XXIII)
9	Small liver leech	Biliary duct°	°The influence of these parasites on the antler formation is uncertain, some specimens have shown
10	Large liver leech	Biliary duct	similar effects to those mentioned under Serial nos. 6 and 7
11	*Hypoderma boris*	Underskin	No known influence on antlers
12	Lung worm and TB	Lungs°	°Most of the diseased animals were found to be corkscrew heads (Plate XXIVA and B), but some have had goat and other freak formations listed under serial no. 8
13	Larva of pharynx gad-fly	Nasal passages°	°None definitely established; some animals have shown corkscrew formation possibly as a result of the ultimate influence of the parasite on the breathing system affecting ultimately the lungs (see Serial no. 12)
14	Tapeworm (cyst)	Brain and nerve canals of the head	No known influence on the antlers, but deterioration in body, and ultimate death

Note °Also applies to malformations due to wounds and damage to organs.

Chapter VIII

AGE CALCULATION BY TEETH AND BONE FORMATION

The ability to estimate age by outward visible signs may be of assistance when out deer stalking or establishing the shoot-ability of deer; indeed, it is indispensible if the plan is to succeed and to result in correct apportioning of animals to age groups. Regardless of our experience this is a far from infallible system, and mistakes happen even among the most experienced stalkers. It is, however, possible to judge the age of a *grassed* beast in three other ways. The first of them is by wear on the teeth; the second by the centre seam of the skull bones, running from the back of the pedicles to the top of the nose bones; the third by the shape of the bone formation of the pedicle.

Of these three, only the teeth enable us to judge the age accurately, the others allowing an approximation which may be useful when looking at a head which has had teeth smashed with a bullet, or is hanging on a wall, the teeth not being available.

It is for this reason that a system of tooth wear as well as aquaintance with other systems of age estimation, is important to the deer stalker.

Tooth wear varies in different species of deer of equal ages. In roe, whose life is shorter then that of red deer, wear is faster. The tooth wear of fallow and red deer, both living longer than the roe, is slower and between these two so nearly identical, that he who knows one can assume that he knows both, allowing fallow about one year quicker wear. Allowance must, however, be made for the type of feeding the animal finds in its area. This has a double aspect, the hardness of teeth caused by the mineral content of food found and the hardness of the food itself.

Early tooth growth in the first three months consists of the four front and three cheek teeth on each side of the lower jaw, all milk teeth of the primary growth. The upper jaw contains only three cheek teeth. These teeth are similar in all three species of deer.

For the purpose of age calculation, we will interest ourselves particularly in the cheek teeth of the lower jaw. The front teeth do show age, but they differ so considerably from area to area, depending on the type of food which is available to deer, that an all-round knowledge of them is insufficient without an intimate knowledge of the particular locality even sometimes of one particular block of the forest. This chapter is designed to give the reader a knowledge applicable generally, and so the front teeth will not enter into our deliberations.

The cheek teeth of the lower jaw are divided into premolars (the first three) and molars (the last three). Of these the three premolars are the first to appear (Fig. 25 and Plates XXIV and XXV).

The first molar is the first permenant tooth to grow, and as the jawbone elongates with the animal's development so the other two molars follow in due time when space is available for them. The second and third molars appear when the premolars are still milk teeth. In roe deer, the three molars are grown by the time the animal is about twelve months old, though the growth of the third may be delayed sometimes by two months. In red and fallow deer the third often does not appear before the eighteenth month.

The secondary premolars appear after all three, or at least two, of the molars are grown.

In the primary (milk) growth the second and third premolars are different from the permanent. The second and third look as if they consisted of more than one tooth, and this is particularly marked in the third premolar. The second milk premolar may appear to consist of two teeth, the third often of three. The division in the first often does not appear except in the root.

Permanent premolars are more solid in appearance, the first is and looks single, so does the second, while the third looks as if it consisted of one large and one small tooth.

A full set of permanent teeth in roe deer is completed sometime between the twelfth and the fourteenth month, in red and fallow deer often as late as the thirtieth

All teeth are subject to wear but it is on the central part of the jaw affecting the third premolar and first and second molars that most of our age estimating is based, as their wear is gradual and continues practically to complete destruction.

With advancing age the saw-like edge of the biting surfaces is worn down. The saw-edge line of the inside of the teeth remains sharp for some time but the length of the teeth decreases and the chewing surfaces from being rough in youth become smooth and hollow ground. From the age of four in roe deer and eight in red deer the saw-edge on the premolars almost vanishes; the rounding off of the molars comes four years later in both species (see Fig. 25 and Plates XXIV and XXV).

Skull Bones

The first sign of age appears in the centre seam of the skull. This seam is well defined in the young head and in a dried skull-bone a certain amount of movement between the two skull cupolae may be felt. With age, however, the cupolae grow together along the seam until at an advanced age (seven to nine years in roe and fourteen to seventeen in red

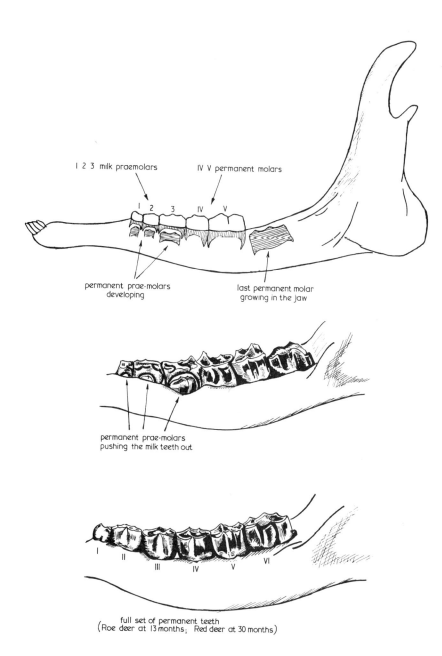

I 2 3 milk praemolars   IV V permanent molars

permanent prae-molars
developing

last permanent molar
growing in the jaw

permanent prae-molars
pushing the milk teeth out

full set of permanent teeth
(Roe deer at 13 months; Red deer at 30 months)

Fig 25   Development of teeth

126

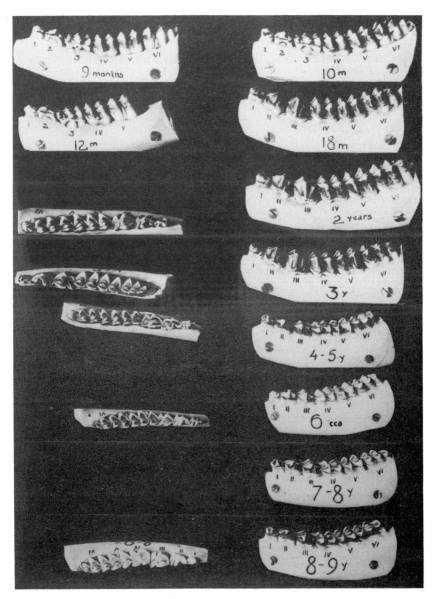

Plate XXIV Judging age by teeth - roe deer

Plate XXV   Judging age by teeth - red deer

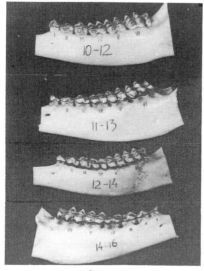 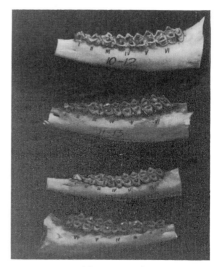

Side views

Oblique views

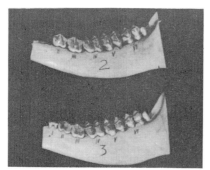 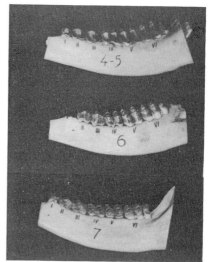

Above and right: Side view ages 2-7 yrs.

Vertical view: 2, 3, 4 and 6 yrs.

and fallow deer) the seam almost disappears, the two halves virtually growing together.

Calculation of age by means of the skull pedicles is based on the fact that at an early age these are thin and their extensions running down toward the eye sockets are well defined. The pedicles on the inside of the antlers form with the skull a well-defined groove, the bisection through which appears in the shape of the letter V, slightly sloping inwards, so that one arm (the inside of the pedicle) is about vertical, the skull seam falling where two oblique arms of the V's cross. From the age of three in roe, and four to five in red deer, these well-defined parts of the pedicles start to disappear. The extension running towards the eye-socket increases its circumference and thus flattens and ceases to stand out from the skull-bone.

The inner parts of the pedicles 'grow-in' into the skull, the base spreading until the two pedicles between them form a letter U the centre of which rests on the centre seam.

Neither of the systems is sufficiently accurate to allow exact age estimation.

General note

It is not an uncommon occurrence in the areas where the deer are short of minerals, for the stage normally attributed to the age of twelve onwards in red and fallow deer, and ten onwards in roe, to be accelerated, and the general decay of teeth takes place. This can be normally recognised by the fact that all teeth are being worn down and the deterioration, which is normally more advanced in the third premolar (III) and the first molar (IV) is almost equalled in the other teeth, possibly with the exception of the first premolar (I) or the first two premolars (I, II). Animals feeding mainly on the field and other 'soft' crops, retain their teeth longer than those of the forest; it follows also that the wear of the teeth differs. This difference can be quite marked, the tooth of the field animal being, at the age of ten years, less advanced by two years than that of the forest one.

Much research on antler development and age estimation by the shape of the pedicle is quoted by Bubenik[*] who quotes mathematical models for age estimation, based on the diameter and length of the pedicles.

Another system developed by Eidman[**] is based on the wear of the crown, and the angle, of the incissors. The crown is worn down and at the same time there is a marked paradentoza (the roots of each tooth are slowly forced out of the jaw-bone). As a result, the angle of the incissors increases gradually from about 40° (from horizontal) at the age of three, to more than 70° at the age of ten (Fig. 26).

[*] Dr A. B. Bubenik, *Das Geweih* (Paul Parey Verlag, Hamburg, 1966).
[**] H. Eidman, *Untersuchungen am Gebiss des Rothirsches* (Hanover, 1939, Forstwirtschaft und Forstwissenschaft).

TABLE 16 Comparisons of the Wear on the Teeth in Roe and Red/Fallow Deer
with Advancing Age
(Fig.25 and Plates XXIV and XXV)

Red deer	Roe deer

0–4 months   0–3 months
Three milk premolars (marked 1, 2, 3) only. The third appears as a treble tooth; the first and second as single and double respectively.

8th month   4–6 months
The first permanent tooth (first molar marked IV) has grown and is a definitely double tooth.

8–10 months   6–7 months
The first and second permanent molars (marked IV and V) have both appeared as double teeth.

12 months–2 years   12–15 months
A full complement of teeth. The first three (premolars) in red and fallow are still milk teeth (marked 1, 2, 3), with roe the development is more advanced and by the end of the 15th month the premolars are all permanent (marked (I, II, III). Red deer grow their permanent premolars slower and thus the first permanent premolar (I) should appear about the 14th month, together with the last molar (VI), and the second and third premolar (II and III) in about the 18th and 23rd month. These times cannot be considered as very definite, and especially in the last four teeth they may vary by as much as four months. From this age onwards the toothwear appears, and will serve as the age-defining guide.

2½ years   1½ years
On the backsloping chewing surfaces of the first and second premolars the wear has reached the dentine which appears there as a smooth yellowy brown line. In roe, the chewing edges extend above the chewing surfaces by about $\frac{1}{6}$ in., in red and fallow deer $\frac{1}{4}$ in.

3 years   2 years
The backsloping chewing surfaces of the first premolar shows sign of wear and the brown dentine starts appearing, the wear on the second premolar is considerable more than it was 6 months previously, the back of the third premolar shows a lot more wear and the dentine shows through the front of this tooth. The saw edge is still sharp but extends only $\frac{1}{8}$ in. above the chewing surfaces in roe, and $\frac{1}{6}$ in. in red and fallow deer.

4 years   3 years
The first three premolars are losing their sharpness.

6 years   4 years
The surfaces of the neighbouring teeth form an extension of one another in a clean unbroken platform, which undulates, the depressions falling where two teeth meet. In roe the saw edge is getting blunt, in red and fallow deer the chewing surfaces are wearing by far more on the cheek side than on the chewing edge. The roe are showing a rounding of the chewing edge; the chewing edge and the chewing surfaces are almost on the same level now, especially in the first molar (IV).

8–10 years   5 years
Heavy wear on the front part of the first molar where the hitherto well-defined longitudinal dividing line of white glazing has given place to a large

patch of brown dentine which is extending to the edges of the tooth. The surfaces of all premolars are smooth and almost flat, the back of the third premolar (III) and front of the first molar (IV) are showing more wear than any other teeth. The red deer's saw still stands out; the chewing surfaces are now considerably lower.

9–12 years   6–7 years

The premolars on the chewing surface are now all brown, except for the edge of each tooth, the dentine showing all over the area; the surfaces are very much polished down. The red deer's saw, hitherto preserved on the second and third molars, is getting blunt and the edges are rounded; all the cutting and chewing surfaces are lowering.

10–14 years   8–9 years

The first molar is barely above the gum. All surfaces are very smooth, dentine covers large areas on all teeth.

14–16 years   10–12 years

The second molar is now as bad as the first and a general decay of dentine may be found. The teeth are obviously hardly capable of performing their task properly.

18 years and over   12 years and over

The first molar is so worn that the front root is divided and virtually no upper tooth is left. The jaw-bone below the tooth decays, all teeth form a roller-like surface; teeth start falling out.

General note

It is not an uncommon occurrence in the areas where the deer are short of minerals, for the stage normally attributed to the age of twelve onwards in red and fallow deer, and ten onwards in roe, to be accelerated, and the general decay of teeth takes place. This can be normally recognised by the fact that all teeth are being worn down and the deterioration, which is normally more advanced in the third premolar (III) and the first molar (IV), is almost equalled in the other teeth, possibly with the exception of the first premolar (I) or the first two premolars (I, II). Animals feeding mainly on the field and other 'soft' crops, retain their teeth longer than those of the forest; it follows also that the wear of the teeth differs. This difference can be quite marked, the tooth of the field animal being, at the age of ten years, less advanced by two years than that of the forest one.

Fig 26   Age estimation by incisors

Many experts place great emphasis on the wear of the third molar (the last tooth at the back of the bottom jaw), which is of a treble build. The last section of it is high and narrow. This tooth is fully developed when the red deer is thirty months old (roe deer about eighteen months). From this age onwards the high and narrow section is subject to gradual, regular and continuous wear, thus giving a good indication of age (Fig. 27).

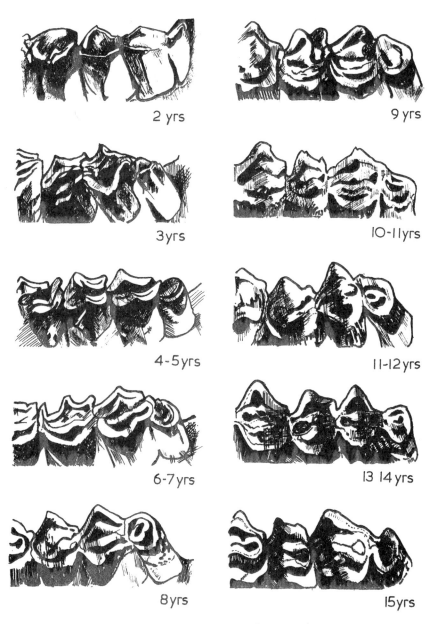

2 yrs

3yrs

4-5yrs

6-7yrs

8yrs

9 yrs

10-11yrs

11-12yrs

13 14yrs

15yrs

Fig 27   Last molar

All these methods are valid, but all have to be used with some care; ideally every indication should be considered, and this is why, when attempting to estimate the age the entire jaw bone (both sides) should be used. Occasionally access to the upper bone may reveal reasons for unusual wear in some teeth.

In Britain, work on the applicability of various methods of age estimation to Scottish deer, using material from deer of known age began in late 1950s (Mitchell, 1963, 1967; Lowe, 1967). The outcome was the development of a method based on growth layers in dental cement which grows around the roots of all teeth, but also forms a thick pad below the crowns on each molar (Plate XXVI). Although these layers are a little easier to expose and interpret than those of dentine, either method is convenient for routine management purposes. The main values of this technique are in research or in checking other methods of age estimation. Interestingly these works confirm the applicability of the various methods to deer not only in Scotland but also to other deer elsewhere.

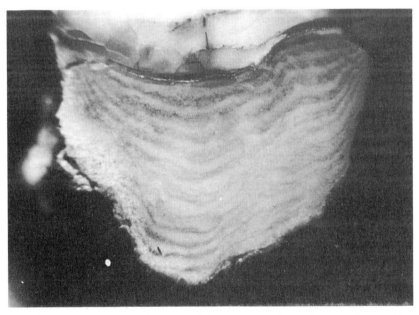

Plate XXVI Magnified section of the cement pad on a lower molar tooth°

Finally in an attempt to summarise the tooth wear as means of estimating age, it is necessary to draw attention to different tooth hardnesses. This has been made in Table 17 which also differentiates between red deer and roe deer.

° *Red Deer Management, Red Deer Commission* (Dr B. Mitchell) (HMSO, 1981).

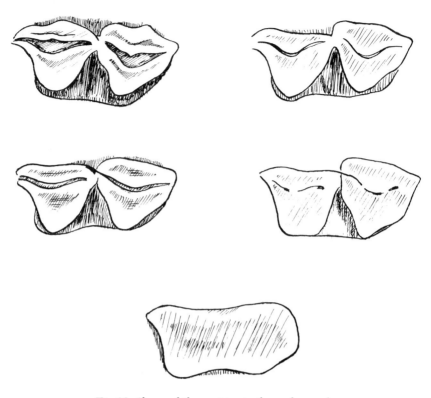

Fig 28 Shape of the register in the molar teeth

TABLE 17 Changes in tooth formation related to age (roe and red deer)

2nd Premolar Registers	3rd Premolar Registers	1st molar Register	1st molar Dentine	2nd molar Register	2nd molar Dentine	3rd molar Register	3rd molar Dentine	Roe Yellow (soft dentine)	Roe Brown	Roe Black (hard dentine)	Red Yellow (soft dentine)	Red Brown	Red Black (hard dentine)
Newly developed	Newly developed	wide open	line	wide open	line		Newly developed	c	c	i	c	c	c
		open	narrow rhomb			wide open	line	c	i	2	2½ years (30 m)	2½ years (30 m)	2½ years (30 m)
wide open	very thin	narrow (closing)	rhomb	open	rhomb	open	narrow rhomb	i	2	3	3	4	4
open	open	open	narrow rhomb					2	3	3/4	4	5	5/6
narrow (closing)	thin	narrow (closing)	rhomb	narrow (closing)	rhomb	narrow	rhomb	3	3/4	4/5	5	6/7	7/8
narrow	narrow	very narrow (nearly closed)	oval					3/4	4/5	5/7	6/7	8	10
very narrow (nearly closed)	wide	dis-appearing	oval	very narrow (nearly closed)	oval	very narrow (nearly closed)	oval	4/5	5/7	7/9	8/9	9/10	11/12
dis-appearing	very wide	minimal (traces only)	whole area	dis-appearing	oval	dis-appearing	oval	5/7	7/9	9/12	10	12	14
traces only	whole area	vanished	whole area	traces only	whole area	traces only	whole area	7/9	10+	11+	12	14	16
vanished	whole area			vanished	whole area	vanished	whole area	10+	12+	13+	13/15		18
teeth worn to the roots, some falling out	teeth worn to the roots												

135

Chapter IX

SPOORING AND TRACKING

One of the more important skills for a stalker, keeper or 'deer watcher' to acquire is the ability to find, and follow the track of an animal he has recognised. In itself, the art of tracking is possibly limited to patience and good eyesight; the spooring and tracking, however, in the sense used here are not limited solely to the ability to find a track of any deer, and to be able to follow it until it is too dark to see, or until one hits the march line or until finally the track gets lost, but to be able to recognise the track of a particular animal and, having identified it, interpret the creature's movements and intentions, and find it. Whether the animal, once found, is shot or photographed or just watched is immaterial, the object is to find *the* beast, and not *a* beast.

The first requirement is, therefore, to be able to distinguish the spoor of male species from the female, the general characteristics of which are common to all species, but in detail they differ, not only as regards size, but also in the outline and such points as weight distribution, curvature of the toes, etc. The differing details are overemphasised in the drawings so as to make them stand out more prominently than they sometimes do in the actual imprints which we are likely to find. For this reason the drawings are not absolutely accurate.

In all deer, the male is heavier than the female of the species, and so, given the same consistency of soil or other spoor-bearing material, the spoor of the male is deeper and slightly larger than that of the female (the difference in size is that of about one-sixth to one-eighth).

The pace length of the female is about one-fifth to one-sixth shorter than that of the male. The pace measurement for this purpose must be only applied to the animal walking, and measurement must cover imprints of all four legs, thus incorporating the complete movement cycle. The deer in trot, or more so in gallop, change pace frequently and it is impossible to judge the pace length in the fast movement for that reason.

Whether walking or running, the spread between the spoor of the left and right legs, fore and aft, is an excellent guide as to sex. In the female this is so narrow that the insides of the spoor of the left and right legs make a straight line, whereas in the male the spread, particularly when walking, is fairly wide. The width spread is difficult to define, but it is approximately that of the length of the hoof when walking, and about half that distance when running. That is a characteristic common to all deer, though more marked in roe and red deer than in fallow deer; the latter, especially when running, have a very narrow spoor which is nearly identical in both sexes.

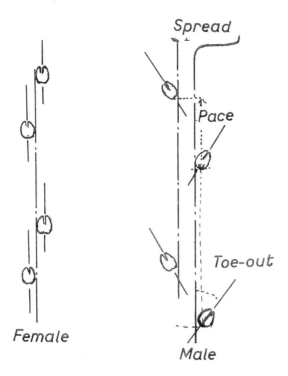

Fig 29 Tracks

The imprint of the hoof itself, its shape and distribution of weight is well marked and is therefore of great assistance.

It will be noted that the male leaves a heavy imprint all round, walking so to speak on the whole foot. For that reason the 'instep curve' is well marked in the imprint. The ball (the rear part) of the foot leaves a more pronounced impression in the male than in the female, the female walking more 'on her toes'.

The imprint of the male reminds one more of a flat-footed person as not only does it walk on the whole hoof but also with the toes pointing well out, whereas the female's hoof points straight ahead. This is more marked when walking or trotting slowly than in running, when the female's imprint makes about half the 'toe out' angle of the male. The balls of the hoof of the male are larger in size and more heart-shaped than those of the female.

The toes of the hoof of a stag are more rounded than the female's and the toe-tips more crescent-shaped, with one toe often longer than the other.

By the difference in length of the toes and also by the depth of the crescent curve age can be judged in stags and other male deer, as the crescent deepens with age. Another sign of age is the spread of the tips of the toes in the spoor of running deer, or in old male deer when walking. Here the dew claws, which have been slowly declining over the last two or three thousand years, provide an additonal guide to age. In male deer at a very advanced age the joint at the back of which these claws are located becomes weak and the animal when walking touches the ground with them, leaving a faint mark shaped like an inverted V. In walking, the front toes of the hoof are not splayed, thus when a spoor of a walking male deer is found with the dew claws marked it means an old animal. The width between the claws in the running animal when, owing to the impetus of the run, the joint gives sufficiently to cause them to leave an imprint, is indicative of age: the wider it is the older the animal. No formula can however be provided as to the width/age ratio. It has to be learned the hard way.

It may easily happen that the ground on which we find ourselves is such that tracking by spoor is impossible or at least impracticable. It may be that the ground is very hard and no tracks are left, or that mossy or grassy underlay obliterates the imprints; furthermore we may be in forest where fallen leaves or needles form a thick carpet where detail of the spoor is impossible to trace. In these cases we must resort to the next best means of tracking, not nearly so accurate as following the imprint of feet. We must look for other signs the deer will leave behind.

There are often indications of animals' presence, which a keen eye can pick up with careful observation and practice.

All animals leave behind them a trail of marks, but most human eyes, unaccustomed to reading these marks, miss them and therefore learn very little from them. In this respect we Europeans could learn a great deal from the Africans who can follow tracks of big and small animals almost subconsciously. Unfortunately, because they do it by instinct, they find it difficult to explain the finer points in this art which they posses.

Some indications are described below.

The easiest to pick up is the track which an animal leaves behind in dewy grass or low undergrowth; there, specially when viewed against the sun one can easily spot the line of movement, which the dew drops have been brushed off by the moving animal or animals. In dew-less conditions, grass and other soft undergrowth, is bent by the moving animal, in the direction of animals movement, the dry track of this sort often appears a shade darker because of the different angle that the light is deflected by the surfaces of the undergrowth's leaves or blades.

Droppings are an easy indication and a good tell-tale of the animals' presence but they are not often deposited along the path of movement but tend to be concentrated in chosen locations; when fresh, they look glossy-wet.

Finding the established deer paths is comparatively easy, but reading the path for recent movement is not easy specially in dry weather. Even the light-footed deer has to step on fresh or dry leaves, twigs or small stones. Where these have been disturbed, the recently uncovered soil looks a little darker because it is more moist; furthermore broken leaves and twigs tend to stick upwards for a time, until they fall back either helped by a puff of wind, or forced down by their own even slight weight.

When the animal browses as it moves, one can sometime find parts of leaves or twigs that have fallen from it's mouth, the shapes of the incissors showing on one side of the leaf or twig and the tearing by the tooth-less upper gum on the other.

Red Deer

Plate XXVII Red deer slots

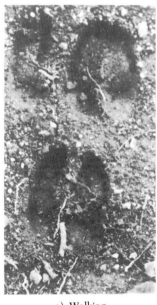

a) Walking   b) Running

The presence of red deer will be ascertained by the 'couches', the impressions their bodies make in the grass, dry leaves, etc. when the beasts are lying down to sleep or to chew their cud. The couches are normally found only in the driest of places, and where the sun will warm the deer after a frosty or wet night. Red deer warm themselves lying in the sun. To and from the couch will lead a track on which the hoof-print is left, in the soft carpet of dried leaves or needles, looking like a sequence or holes, the depth of them and the length of pace only giving us some idea what animal has been there.

It is quite possible that in following the tracks we will come across places where the deer have been either scratching the ground in search of food such as beech-nuts or acorns or, as is the habit of the male, scratching under tree trunks as a mark of their presence (this habit is more common in roe and red than in fallow). Finally the droppings may provide a guide. The faeces of a stag are barely distinguishable from those of a hind but

HIND

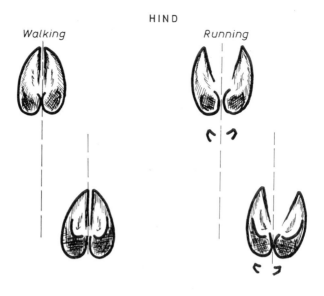

STAG

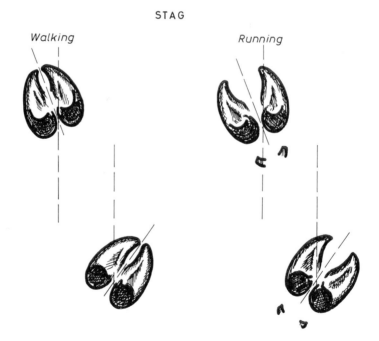

Fig 30   Red deer slots

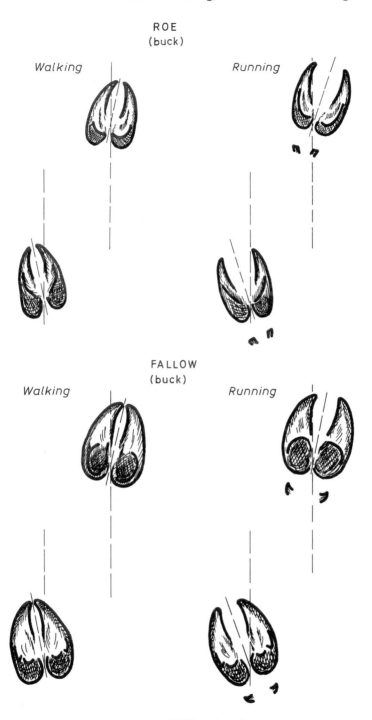

Fig 31 Roe and fallow deer slots

they are slightly larger, and whereas those of a hind are oval-shaped the stag's are almost round. This is a point easier to observe in winter when the droppings, owing to the preponderance of dry food consumed, are dry and fall apart in smallish oval egg-shaped particles. In summer the faeces are soft and often their shape is indistinguishable, but then freshness will give us a clue as to the time lag between our arrival and the deer's departure.

During the warm season in areas where flies infest the forest and deer cannot escape to fly-free areas, muddy ponds, depressions in the terrain where water accumulates after rain, will form mud-baths frequented by deer, particularly by stags. The misconception of black red-deer has come from these baths, for after indulging in a bath, covered with mud all over, stags do look black until the mud dries and peels off or turns into powder and is dusted off the body. The presence of deer in the area of these mud baths will be easily revealed by the tracks round them and also by considerable numbers of patches of mud left in the grass by stags rolling about between one mud bath and the next. The freshness of the tracks and of the mud left on the grass will give us some idea of the presence of deer, and the length of time since their departure.

In areas where deer are not fed, and where during the winter there is a shortage of natural food, the infallible mark of red deer is stripping of young trees of five to ten years, and of branches. Whereas the first may not be seen if the mineral content of the ground is high and natural salts are abundant, the second are always present to a smaller or greater extent. In forests where deer are fed during the winter the number of trees thus marked is so small that it bears no relation to the number of deer and may therefore give a false impression of numbers. Furthermore it must be remembered that it is mainly the females who strip trees with their teeth, and rarely the males.

In areas where deer are not fed artificially, but where there is an abundance of food to be found in the fields, damage in the forest may provide little information to the tracker.

Red deer, and in particular stags, can also be recognised and located by smell and sound during the rutting season. The smell of a stag is difficult to describe, but it is a strong odour which remains for some time after the stag has visited a place and even without a dog one is normally able to follow the beast without much hesitation. The stag's roar is, of course, during the rut, infallible proof of his presence.

Fallow Deer

The spoor of fallow deer is slightly smaller than that of red deer and there is a slight difference between the general characteristics of the fallow doe and other female deer in the way she walks. The fallow doe leaves a foot imprint less marked in the toe, by virtue of the fact that she walks more 'flat-footed' (the 'toe out' characteristic not being present) than other female deer (see Fig. 31).

The couches of fallow are far more difficult to find than those of red deer as they will be located in very thick undergrowth. When found however, they will be comparatively more numerous, for fallow, being less restful, move throughout the day from one place to another giving the impression that a larger number of animals is present in the area, than the actual total.

The principles of finding and following fallow are the same as those described for red deer, and an additional guide to their presence is afforded by the trees on which during the coat changing time they have been rubbing and attempting to rid themselves of the outfalling hair, thus loosening the bark and leaving the hair of the old coat on the rough surfaces. Fallow will always come back to the same tree to rub, and so, having found one, the stalker is advised to remain in its vicinity if looking for fallow during the coat changing time. Fresh rubbing marks mean that the animals are not far, and will come back.

During the rut the presence of fallow can be established by their barking, which takes the place of the red deer's roar. The bark is guttural and does not carry a great distance.

Roe Deer

The imprint of the roe hoof is similar to that of red deer but about one-third of the size. The mode of moving and shape of the trail are also very similar (see Fig. 31).

The couches, allowing for size, are identical with those of red deer, but they are to be found in places where the search for warmth or sun, rather than for dryness as with red deer, has reached satisfactory conclusions. When sunning, the roe is just as likely to stand exposing his back to the sun as to lie down and sun his sides.

The buck marks his domain march by browsing, fraying and scratching the ground with his hoof. The scratchings are normally found under and by bushes and tree trunks. These signs are normally concentrated on the fringes of the covert and thickets.

The faeces are the shape of small bobbins, not unlike those of a hare and rabbit, longer in does and shorter in buck, and differing between summer and winter like those of red deer.

The noise is a bark; that of a buck, sharp, short and deep; that of a doe, more drawn out and higher pitched. The older the buck the deeper his voice is normally and the more difficult it is to make him bark unless he has been frightened.

Chapter X

FOREST AND DEER

Business Considerations

For far too many years now, a feud has existed in Britain between the two factions of 'forestry' and 'deer and game'. Both have been at loggerheads really because of the deer themselves, and the time has now come when the two sides should, and can, be brought together.

That the damage-producing activities of deer should have brought them into disrepute is not surprising: nor is it surprising that the forestry element must defend itself against that damage. Many millions of pounds could have been saved over the years had there been no need to protect the woodlands from deer and, equally, many millions of pounds have been lost where the animals have either broken into a protected forest, or where the forest had not been protected at all. One cannot lose sight of the fact that forestry is a long-term and extremely expensive investment, and that even a small loss of trees, evaluated and discounted over the period of forest maturation, can then be translated into a huge financial loss. The converse approach is, however, also possible: the potential revenue from deer and game at the moment is not optimised although–discounted over the period of maturation of the trees–it can also add up to a very considerable sum.

With foresight, a forest could be planned in such a manner wherby damage by deer is reduced drastically, income from deer and game is realised, and both would be considered as viable, and important, by-products of the business of forestry to produce income.

Planning a forest is, both financially and in terms of silviculture, a complex exercise. Capital of appreciable size is invested over a very long period and the risks, especially those connected to the vagaries of climate and also those linked to the changes in technology, are considerable.

Perhaps at the present, fast changes in technology and the market have both been instrumental in a new approach to afforestation programmes, where hardwoods have become more popular. Ironically enough, this in itself is a great potential advantage to deer and game.

Because the investment in a forest is expensive and long term, it may be appropriate to reconsider the financial benefits which can in fact be derived from deer and game within that forest; the basic requirements for the benefit of deer and game can be itemised as follows:

144

(a) wider planting of trees to replace the present system of close-planting;
(b) more rides and glades to provide feeding areas, with underplanting of suitable grasses, shrubs and bushes for the animals to browse on;
(c) mixing deciduous varieties with conifers;
(d) soil dressing where the soil is too poor to encourage fast tree growth;
(e) the provision of deer leaps and 'down-falls'.

At first sight, this might all seem to be in direct opposition to the forestry interest but in fact is not so. Wider planting not only allows for a healthier development of trees, but also saves the number of trees needed to cover a given area. The planting distances need to be increased by 10–15%, hence the decrease in the number of trees which then have to be thinned is proportional.

Rides and glades should cover some 5% of the area. These also provide long-term benefits in that they furnish better and easier access together with areas for the storage of maturing timber at the time of cropping. They are also an insurance against a spread of fire.

Admittedly these considerations imply a reduction in the ultimate tree crop but, in the present system of forest planning there is already a loss allowance of some 15–20% of trees, which can be accounted for in a variety of ways — from downright failure of saplings to infections and infestations, weather problems, and damage by animals. If one accepts that this level of loss will be reduced perhaps by half, with a healthier subsequent development of trees and a lower level of damage, plus a lower cost in provision of plants, then the total value of the timber crop is not being reduced by a vast percentage. Added to this, easier retrieval of the crop and cheaper fire insurance are benefits, as is the saving on fencing after the trees have reached a 'safe' age of 10 years or so.

The overall benefits to the forest as a whole do make the total picture vastly more acceptable to the forester, provided that deer and game are not just an accidental element but a planned diversification.

The first important consideration is the density of deer, for this is the controlling factor: provided that the number of deer to be allowed within the forest is carefully planned and maintained at an appropriate level, the damage they may inflict is not excessive and is well within certain limits. After all, the damage through browsing declines after a few years (during which the saplings have been protected anyway) when the trees' leading shoots are beyond the 1.80 m (6 ft) mark. It is at this stage that the forest can be opened up to the deer. Provided that some suitable shrubs and bushes are added along the rides and glades, to provide a natural source of food and also of antler-cleaning material, both threshing and stripping of bark within the forest decrease appreciably.

In terms of income, the revenue from stalking lets and from shooting lets, plus the sale of venison and game, can be quite considerable. Evaluation at current prices is not difficult but forecasting the future is difficult as the market fluctuates and changes according to such a variety of reasons as the leisure time available to the adult population, the level of expenditure on leisure, the level of demand for venison and game, the demand for stalking, etc. This applies not only to the United Kingdom but also to the Continent.

Added to this, there is the question of potential improvement to the quality of antler — the main attraction to many Continental stalking clients — and the value of the venison, itself an increasingly attractive commodity in the present days when lean and high-protein meat is in high demand. The market changes in the recent years have been considerable: stalking fees have soared from £25 per head in 1974 to £140 and over in 1985, and at this price is cheap: venison has gone from 15 p per pound to 70 p: there is now the possibility that under woodland conditions, stags might so improve in antler quality as to reach the level required by the Conseil International de la Chasse for its medals, and therefore that the present fees of $3,000 per head, current market price for a 'good' or bronze medal head on the Continent today, could also be a realistic possibility in this country in the future.

Forestry Considerations

These can be divided into 5 stages:
1. area planning;
2. planting;
3. protection;
4. access by deer to the forest, and to deer in the forest;
5. culling the deer.

Area Planning

Many areas intended for large-scale afforestation are to a certain extent hilly and therefore inevitably contain within them valleys and gullies which are difficult to plant: ideally these should be drained and left unplanted.

Rides, of about 20 metres wide, should be provided, and planned in such a manner that they cross each other at right angles — some running along the contours of the terrain and some as downfalls into the valleys.

Additionally there should be some glades left unplanted especially on the south-facing slopes, probably amongst the naturally awkward areas like gullies or rocky outcrops where planting is anyway difficult.

If the area of afforestation is large, and runs across or cuts off the high hill from the lower ground where the deer winter or feed, there should be some fenced downfalls located more or less along the deers' natural paths. This will encourage them away from the fenced area of the forest and will also prevent any attempt to break the fence in order to get at their usual feeding ground; likewise the forest is protected when for instance a sudden change in the weather makes the animals seek the sort of shelter often provided on the lee side of the woods.

The planning of rides must include provision of rides along the fence; this is vital for such rides prevent the build-up of snow drifts (which can bury parts of the fence and allow deer to leap over in search of food and shelter); they also deny shelter in the lee of high trees near the fence and therefore prevent the deer from congregating and pressuring the fence; and lastly they prevent fallen trees from damaging the fence and, once again, providing access to the deer. It is also important to provide deer leaps, located usually at the end of rides and in fence corners, and later perhaps additionally placed there where the established deer paths emerge from the woodland opposite the fence.

In area planning, a provision is usually made for crop rotation after the trees have been felled. From the point of view of preventing deer damage, both planting and rotation crops should be effected in such a way that there is a gradual age distribution block after block – not a chequer-board effect where small block of old trees stand next to small blocks of new plantations: if this happens, the old trees provide harbour and shelter for deer while the young trees provide potential feeding areas, thus causing the need for large-scale fencing and increased expense.

Planting

The need to increase the distance between young trees has already been mentioned. When practicable, the sowing of seeds rather than the planting of saplings is preferable, as seeding is done in rows and then the young trees thinned out. At the time of planting it is useful to include shrubs and bushes to provide future browsing areas for the deer and so form the feeding areas, which should be along the rides and glades. These glades should include a range of grasses and cereals high in protein. It is now becoming increasingly popular in poor soil areas to dress the soil within the tree plantations, and such dressing needs to be extended to rides and glades to improve and enhance ground growth of a wide variety.

In areas already inhabited by deer, and therefore probably in forests due for rotational replanting, the cleaning up of areas planted or due for planting should be carefully considered. This is done in two stages: the first is aimed at giving young plants better conditions for development and here, clearing the ground completely allows the deer easy access to neatly exposed food as a replacement for their natural browse. Where ground clearing is necessary, it is better confined to the immediate surrounds of new plants, leaving the natural browse to flourish. Better still, were it practicable, would be the freeing out of the tops of young plants, for as long as they are surrounded by natural vegetation, deer will mainly feed on ground growth and only partially on young plants.

The second stage of clearing comes when the trees need thinning out or brashing: in areas where bark stripping by deer is anticipated or evident, bundles of thinnings left on the ground will not only provide browsing material for the deer but will also provide cover for other game as well.

If it is intended to underplant the afforested areas (be it to add variety, to replace blown or cropped trees, or as a future browse for deer) it is necessary to provide individual protection for the plants and, even more importantly, never to plant those trees singly which are 'unusual' for the area: if planting solely to provide future food for deer, much cost and effort can be spared by simply sticking cuttings from shrubs and trees into the ground: these which root easily and be fairly quick to develop, and should be of a variety which will attract the deer.

Access and Protection

As previously mentioned, there is protection from damage by fencing and the individual protection of trees; there are chemical and other deterrents; there is also the fact that additional feeding, and feeding additives, can be used as protective measures for young trees; by no means least, there is the question of controlling the density of the deer themselves.

What perhaps needs examining, however, is the question of when such protective measures can be relaxed; this is important for not only does it mark the beginning of the revenue inflow from the deer, but also saves the need for fence maintenance — and is therefore a saving in terms of capital.

The forester's main fear is damage by browsing by most deer, and threshing by red deer. (Fraying, where there are too many roe deer, can also be extremely costly.) The danger of browsing is that which affects the leading shoots of the plants but, once these grow to a height of about 1.80 m, or 6 ft, they are no longer vulnerable and, as far as red deer are concerned, are more or less 'browse-proof'.

Threshing is more difficult to prevent, other than giving the deer plenty of room to move around in, as threshing is usually a manifestation of frustration or of over-crowding in given areas. This can be prevented by providing shrub and bush underplant in areas which will be, from the foresters' point of view, harmless.

On the whole, the current practice seems to be to overprotect, unnecessarily in those areas which have ceased to be vulnerable — such as mature woodland — by maintaining fences, and yet on the other hand not to pay sufficient attention to such factors as the actual density of the deer, and deer control.

It is also necessary to mention here the question of access to the deer by those who are to exercise deer control. Rides and glades will provide the areas where deer will be in evidence but, both for the efficacy and the safety of this operation, it is necessary to provide high seats from which observation of larger areas is possible, and the culling be effected more efficiently and accurately.

Cropping

However undemanding the 'deer for venison' policy may be in terms of the expertise needed to run it, it is one not really suited to forest areas. The risk involved in possible under-culling of hinds, and the subsequent possibility of a population explosion, are too great; at the same time it must be said that the advantages of aiming towards antler development and general quality improvement as a potential source of increased income from deer in the woodland are too great to be disregarded.

It goes without saying that if 'quality' of deer is the ultimate aim, a high level of selection needs to be applied. It may be useful here to consider the cropping of deer in terms of a 60 year investment, so that it can be compared with forest cropping which is also a 60 year investment.

It is not difficult to calculate how a proportion of revenue from deer, and invested over a period of 60 years could offset the possible losses due to damage.

For the purpose of this exercise the following basic parameters are set up:

TABLE 18   'Value' of deer

	Red deer	Roe deer
Rate of investment 8%		
Prices:	*Red deer*	*Roe deer*
Stag (buck), stalking per head	£ 150	£ 50
Venison per lb	.80p	0.80p
Weight–market male	140 lb	30 lb
female	110 lb	25 lb
From the proceeds, one-animal equivalent per year invested over a period of 60 years		
Stalking	£ 180,323	£ 60,107
Venison–male	134,641	28,851
female	105,789	24,043
Proceeds from investment of revenue from one each male one female per year	£320,753	£113,002

It is interesting to compare these sums with the possible value of damage that one animal of each sex could create over 60 years.

Chapter XI

DEER STALKING

A lthough the general term 'deer stalking' is used to describe the pursuit of deer, as opposed to deer hunting, it covers only one of the possible ways in which deer shooting can be conducted. Before approaching the problem of deer stalking, let us consider what equipment is required.

Clothing. Any old clothing including a hat or cap, of a colour blending well with the background to provide camouflage. Few people realise that the face, in many cases, specially on a sunny day or in twilight, is visible a long way, and that when the rest of the body is well camouflaged, the face gives them away. Comfortable footwear, with rubber soles where possible. Other types of footwear make a considerable noise and, like the unshaded face, give away the presence of the stalker.

Telescope or binoculars. The choice between the two depends upon the type of stalking. For stalking in Scotland, in the Highlands, when a need exists for spying an area of as much as three or four miles away, a telescope is invaluable; in the afforested country, for comparatively short-range work, binoculars are better and easier to use. Both should be of a type giving good magnification and a good light-power, especially binoculars, so as to allow work in the early morning and late evening inside the forest where the light is normally poor.

Rifle and telescopic sight. It is almost as difficult to give advice on choice of the rifle–ammunition–telescopic sight system as it is to advise on what car to buy, or what woman to marry. Like car or wife, the rifle must be suitable. Suitable?

In the first place it must suit the law; England, Scotland, or abroad. In the second place it must suit the purpose for which it is to be used; just roe deer, roe and red deer, bigger game outside Britain?

In the third place it must suit the person who is to use it; a slight person should avoid a rifle with a heavy recoil (lightweight rifle with heavy-load ammunition); an old person who wants to stalk on foot, should avoid a heavyweight rifle, for carrying it will be tiring and will reduce the shooting accuracy.

The safe bet is to shop around the gunsmiths who know about rifles and not buy the first rifle one sees but look for a rifle that suits you, and try it out on the range before buying.

Telescopic sight. Today, only a few people use open sights for stalking, and the choice of a telescope is an important factor. To a degree it is a matter of one's eye-sight specially if one has to wear glasses. Graticule in the sight is important, personally I do not like crossed wires, or anything that obliterates the actual aiming point and prefer graticules of a vertical and two horizontal posts, with either a silver wire, or the sharp edge of the posts silvered, so that is shows clearly in twilight, each post being pointed, the vertical one indicating the point of aim. The graticule must be adjustable and the adjustment capable of being safely secured. The telescope should be water-proofed, but not made of plastic or very soft metal, for these crack or dent too easily.

The standard 4 magnification with object lens of 32 mm is a good compromise between the field of vision and light power. I am not sold on zoom lenses; they are only one more thing that can go wrong! The mounts must hold the telescope rigid and therefore must not only be solidly and accurately made but well fitted by a well practised gunsmith.

Finally, one should not try and save cash on the telescope; there are many telescopes made for air and other low recoil rifles, these are not suitable for sporting rifles.

There is no point in giving advice to stalkers with camera. They are normally very experienced photographers with the benefit of years of photographic experience behind them, who choose the camera they like and obtain good results. To the budding amateur photographer, however, one piece of advice is offered. A telescopic lens is not the only requirement. Wild animal photography is quite as difficult as stalking with a rifle, if not more so, and hours of patient waiting lie ahead of those of you who wish to secure a good photograph.

In areas where flies and mosquito are known to be, it is advisable to have some repellent with you. Once you are within sight of deer any movement not carefully concealed means time wasted on stalking, as deer are very quick on picking up any movement, and the flick of a hand chasing away the worrying fly or biting mosquito will send the deer bounding away.

Now we come to the actual art of finding and stalking deer.

There are many methods. The selection of that one of them which we intend to use will depend on the terrain we are working on, our knowledge of the area and perhaps last, but not by any manner least, the type of deer we are after, and the time of year.

As most stalking of red deer in the British Isles is done in Scotland, let us first look at the Scottish way of deer stalking (Fig. 32).

Stalking in Scotland

The countryside on which we stalk is mainly open, or at least very little afforested. This has its advantages and its drawbacks. Armed with a telescope one can see a long way; on the other hand the approach is difficult as the beast can easily see the stalker unless he is well concealed.

You are out early in the morning, making for a good spying point. The selection of this is normally left to the stalker who accompanies the rifle and knows where deer are or should be, and knows the terrain and the winds. You reach the spying point, often after a hard climb, and look round

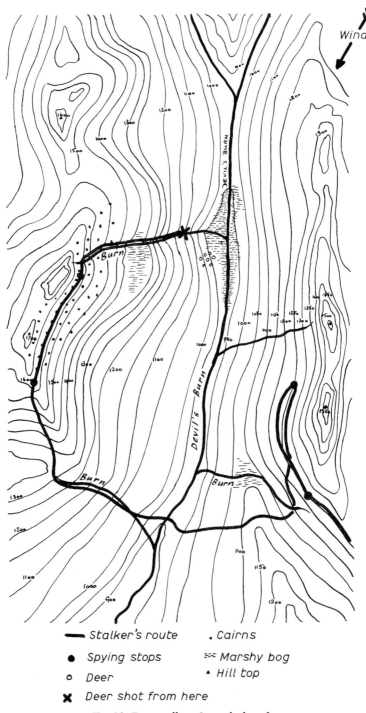

Fig 32 Deer stalk in Scottish deer forest

through the telescope. You find a herd here, another there, one is perhaps two miles away and the other even further; but the nearer one is down wind. Admittedly, from the present range the deer show no sign of knowing of your presence, but once you get down the slope and within a mile up-wind of them they will soon move away.

The down-wind herd has a stag within it and you know you would like him as your quarry for he is old and well shaped, whereas the other has two stags, one too young, and the other worth keeping for the future.

The stalker explains the land. You learn that by going back, hidden in the depression, you can get to the bottom of the hollow where the deer are. Then behind the shoulder on the other side of the valley you can get on to the other side of the deer and they will be up-wind from you. There is a burn running down the slope and the deer are not far away; on the upper reaches of the slope there are large boulders (cairns) which should provide adequate cover until you reach the burn. The only risky move will be the crossing of the valley unless you go about two miles away where it turns.

You get up, and following the stalker retrace your steps. After a while you are at the bottom of the valley. You sit down and have another spy. The herd has not moved at all; you can continue with the prepared plan.

Taking advantage of the high grass and one or two small depressions, you cross the three hundred yards of valley and make for the far side of the shoulder which is to hide you from the deer. You have been out now for more than four hours, and you know it will be another two before you are in a position, if you are lucky, to look at the deer from a reasonable distance.

You make your way uphill until after some time you reach the level of the boulders. Now, hiding behind them, you work over the shoulder and have another spy. There they are at the bottom of the slope by the burn (at least you think it must be by the burn which at the moment is not to be seen). Crouched down, and sometimes on all fours, you make for the top of the burn. The sun is now quite warm and you are sweating.

Finally you arrive. The burn is in front, the deer in the valley not more than 800 yards away. You look for your stag. He is up, nearest of all the herd to you, feeding quietly.

The stalker bids you to go forward. The burn is very shallow and does not allow you to stand up. You can tell that even when you are crouched your back will show, so you must crawl. Never mind the cold water which will soak you, provided that the rifle and the telescope remain dry.

With the stalker just ahead of you carrying the rifle and the telescope, you make your way over the stone-covered bed and sides of the burn. After 100 yards you are out of breath. The excitement and the strain of this unusual way of moving are having their effect.

Another fifty yards and you find that the burn is flowing over a ledge of peaty soil where everything is soft and marshy. You can see where the stags have been having their mud-bath from the many trails and mud slopped over the moss and grass. The ledge allows you to stretch, and you are keen to have a little rest and straighten your limbs. The stalker however looks at the sky and whispers something in your ear.

Breathing heavily you cannot hear him and ask him to repeat.

He tells you that the wind will change soon and any change of the wind now means disaster as it will be deflected by the valley and the slopes and the deer are bound to smell us then. So you get on all fours and reach the place where the burn disappears over the ledge.

Here the burn flows deeper in the ground being on less rocky soil. You can just move crouching down, but the stalker will not allow this, he thinks it is not safe. So down on all fours you go again.

Fifty yards lower down you feel a touch on your arm. It is the stalker. He motions you to stop, and himself getting the telescope out of its cover gets on the edge of the burn by a rock and cautiously looks down. He is back beside you in a flash to tell you that the stag is only 150 yards away, so that in another 50 yards you can shoot. Very carefully you move forward. You can see the place 50 yards forward where the banks will provide you with a good rest for the rifle. Minutes seem hours.

You have been so busy crawling that you had forgotten the stalker, and having arrived at your chosen place you look back. He is some yards away, getting the rifle out of its cover, checking the ammunition in the chamber and the safety catch.

It takes him only a minute or two to reach you. The cold steel of the rifle gives you confidence again in this moment of excitement when both of you look over the edge of the burn.

There they are, barely 100 yards away, but the stag is lying down. You can see his antlers and the top of his head.

The stalker motions you to get ready and he himself slips back into the burn.

As soon as he is there he whistles gently. You look for a reaction among the deer. Nothing.

He whistles a little louder. The hind which was lying near the stag looks your way and stands up, then another hind stands up. Your finger on the safety catch and you are ready as soon as the stag gives you a chance.

Then the stag lifts himself onto his hind legs, then slowly onto his fore-legs.

He presents you with an almost full broadside. Your heart is beating like a pneumatic drill.

You hold your breath, take the final adjustment on the aim, and pull the trigger.

At the crack of the shot the stalker leaps on the edge of the burn.

You watch the stag. He throws his head high, then takes a few paces forward. . . . He seems to be lying down gently, so as not to hurt himself, his legs sag, then he rolls over onto his side.

The rest of the herd run away. You and your stalker make for the stag. He is dead.

The gralloch, performed with the speed of the expert, takes the stalker only a little while; and pleased with the old beast as your trophy, you make for home.

From the description above it will be seen that stalking in Scotland is an art. It requires an infinite knowledge of the land not so much from the point of view of finding cover, but because of the changing winds in the mountainous country. The wind blowing up the slope on one side of the mountain may also be blowing up the face on the other. The wind blowing along the ridge may have the effect of sending the scent down the slope instead of along it as could be expected. Furthermore, blowing up or down the valley the wind, when it reaches another valley which is an offshoot of the first one, may be blowing in a completely different direction depending on the configuration of the terrain. It is not impossible when in the mountains, to find such apparently miraculous happenings as the wind on the ground, where we are, blowing in the opposite direction to the direction of the lower strata of the clouds!

The weather, too, must be studied as a factor affecting the stalk. To know what deer will do under certain weather conditions is an art which can only be acquired by long experience of the countryside.

Generally speaking, tracking is not needed in Scotland, mainly because its place is taken by the long-distance spying, and the stalk is done by visual contact

It is because stalking is so complex an art, that the stalker is almost indispensable; but it is also the stalker who does all the work, it is he who is the tactician in the stalking operation while the rifle is no more than the 'soldier of the line', doing no more than pulling the trigger at a target presented to him by the stalker. And rightly so. For what would happen if a person completely unacquainted with the countryside was let loose in the Highlands? Deer would be disturbed, he himself would be quite likely lost, and if he did get back, it would be most likely without a stag to boast of as trophy. With experience of the locality, more and more freedom will be given to the sportsman by the stalker, until a day may come when, recognising the sportsman's ability, the stalker will himself fall into the background and the sportsman will be the tactician, the stalker his assistant. Then and only then will it be the rifle who can say 'I have stalked and killed a stag'.

So much for stalking in Scotland.

Stalking Red Deer in Forest Areas (Fig. 33)

The forest restricts our field of vision. Most of the stalking must therefore be by means other than visual contact.

The first and foremost requirements is therefore to find the whereabouts of the deer with some accuracy, and to assure ourselves that the deer we have located is one which can be shot, or should be shot. Most of this can be done by spooring and tracking.

Having found and studied the spoor and track, we should be able to make an appreciation of the number of deer and of their sex. Following the spoor we shall sooner or later find a path — a path made in the undergrowth by the deer moving along the same route day in and day out.

We know now that a herd we have found follows a certain line of movement and we should know at least approximately what the herd consists of — as yet, however, we know nothing more about it.

Early morning and last light are probably the times at which we stand the best chance of seeing something. Thus, well before dawn we are out looking for the herd. The place where we found the path reveals none of its secrets, so we follow the path, not walking on it but keeping it within sight. We find the couch of a few deer: one is deeper than the others, possibly that of a stag (this being mid-September it is quite likely that a stag has already joined the hinds for the rut).

The path crosses a fire line and a forest road and ends in a clearing where the grass looks fresh and good. A few self-seeded oaks show signs of browsing.

The evening finds us at the far end of the clearing. A fresh wind is blowing from the side where in the morning we found signs of deer. We sit under a tree and wait. Half an hour before sunset a hind shows her head among the bushes. She is absolutely motionless, only her ears are working. You can see from this distance how she turns her head from side to side listening and spotting. You stand up behind the tree to watch through the glasses.

Satisfied that she will not be disturbed she looks back and then slowly as if picking her way in the grass so as not to step on her feeding-stuff, she comes out, followed by another. A little while later two more hinds appear followed by a young stag. The deliberate way in which he left the cover without caution is enough to make you realise that he is a youngster, and a quick scrutiny of his head and body prove your suspicion; he is a stag not two years old who has probably not left his mother yet. Absorbed by these happenings, you have missed something at the spot from where the first hind appeared. A number of white spots can be clearly seen which you are certain were not there before.

The spots are perfectly motionless, and then suddenly something flicks, and now the jig-saw fills in quickly. The flick was that of an ear and the white spots are the polished tines of a stag's antlers. You can make out his antlers and his head just projecting above the bush. He surveys the scene carefully, then comes slowly out. From time to time he lifts his head as if to roar, but no roar comes as yet. It is too early.

He is a good stag and only just in his prime, so you decide that he is not for shooting this year. Slowly and quietly, so as not to upset the herd, you withdraw to the ride which is a few yards behind you, and walk on.

At last light, a herd breaks across the ride. You can see that there were six or seven animals in it, but it was too dark to see what they were; so you make a mental note to return to this place next day to check the spoor.

Next day, you find the spoor with ease, and observation of the tracks reveals to you that one stag and five hinds were in the herd. By its spoor the stag could be an old one. You follow the track, which within a few yards joins another ride, and follows it, disappearing on the short grass and the baked earth. You move into the forest a few yard off the ride and look for signs of deer breaking away into the thick stuff. After some three hundred yards you find nothing. You cross the ride and work back on the other side. Soon you find the tracks of seven (you think) animals. You are not quite certain of the accurate number as the tracks in the pine needles are not well defined, just holes in the thick pile carpet. Some yards into the forest the tracks join a deer path. Here the needles are not so thick and in the shadows of the trees the earth is moist and shows the spoor reasonably well. You find a track of a stag. You note that one of his hoof-toes is slightly broken at the tip.

Keeping down-wind of the deer path you follow it, only to find that it leads into a very thick plantation of oaks and beeches. The plantation is only ten years old and the trees are too close together to allow you inside. You skirt the plantation and find that a deer path comes out at the other side. You follow this path and find a pool of mud, which at a glance shows you that the path had not been used for some time. The deer must be inside unless they left some other way.

It is late afternoon and you decide to wait until the evening and hope that they come out the way they went in. You settle down, camouflaged by a few bushes. The sun is nice and warm and you are not sorry to be having a rest.

The sunset is about half an hour off when you feel that you have seen a movement somewhere and, indeed, in the deer path, on the edge of the oaks, stands a hind. She has a good look round and then crosses the ride, after her a pricket and some more hinds. After the fifth hind there seems to be a gap. You know those gaps which normally precede the appearance of the stag. You watch carefully with the glasses on the place from where the beasts appeared. You wait patiently.

There is a movement, and a stag, a ripe old beast, shows his head, looks both sides and slowly comes out from the cover, his head low down on a thick-maned neck. He crosses the ride unhurriedly. If you were out to shoot you could have had him with ease, but you have wisely decided to wait till the forthcoming rut. He may still cover the hind and have a good offspring who will throw a good head. Good heads are not too plentiful, and there are not too many stags to your liking. The old one is only a ten-pointer, but the thickness of his antlers and the heavy tines, apart from his shape of the body indicate that he was once a better animal, now going back.

This system of deer stalking in the forest, where it is up to the stalking sportsman to find his beast, is perhaps the most exciting of all. When on the track of the stag, one is never sure, whether the old wily one is not watching us from a well-camouflaged place, only to break when he knows that the main danger has passed. Throughout the time when we are out there is a chance that suddenly, quite unexpectedly, we shall come across the beast, or *a* beast. In the first case, a quick confirmation that this is *the* beast we have stumbled upon may be sufficient to allow us to shoot; in the second case, a split second recognition and a decision which, if false, will haunt us for some time. Many a time an unexperienced stalker, having grassed the wrong animal, has had to blush for many stalking seasons; many times an experienced stalker has let an uncertain stag go to avoid a blemish on his reputation.

Better be safe than sorry.

And now to the third possible way of deer shooting: the sitting up (Fig. 33).

Fig 33   Sitting up on ground or high seat

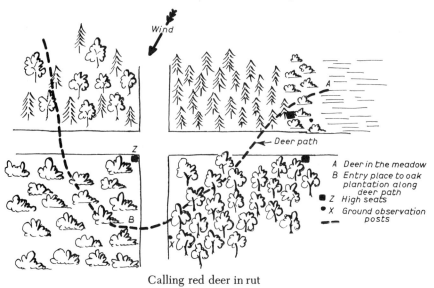

A Deer in the meadow
B Entry place to oak plantation along deer path
Z High seats
X Ground observation posts

Calling red deer in rut

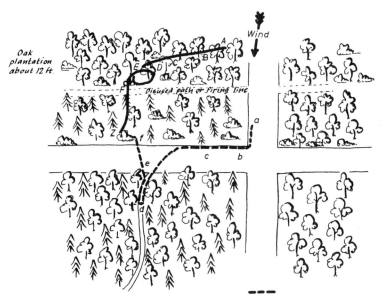

A - Position of the stag when rifle at 'a'.

B - Stag moves inside the plantation called by rifle from location 'b'.

C - Stag roars, called by rifle at 'c'.

D - Stag grunts and appears to be lying down. Rifle moves to 'd' and calls threshing a branch.

e - Rifle moves back to fire line and calls. Stag breaks cover for the first time at 'E' roaring.

F - Stag comes out roaring, rifle ready to fire, hidden at 'f'

Z - Stag shot from position 'f'

This is a method common on the continent of Europe, and now well accepted in the British Isles. It involves the building of a high seat near a place which is known to be frequented by deer. In the seat sits the rifle, alone or accompanied, surveying the movement of the beasts in his vicinity. The seat twelve or more feet up, positioned so as to allow the best possible field of vision, is so situated in relation to the surrounding trees that the occupier is in the upper parts of the crowns of the trees. As a result, the human smell is carried above the trees instead of down below and the beasts cannot detect the presence of a human being except from the scent which is left behind on the path of approach. The seat is the best way of observing life in or out of the shooting season, specially when positioned near a young plantation which from the ground level the human eye cannot penetrate; from above, inspection, albeit limited, is possible.

The high seat method has another advantage and that is safety of the shot. The shot being fired at an angle converging with the ground, there is no danger of the bullet, even if it misses the beast, careering into the unknown. It buries itself a few feet from the target.

In itself the method of shooting from the high seat is a simple one, provided that the seat is sited for the purpose of sporting shooting, allows a comfortable shot, and easy recognition of the quarry. On the other hand seats erected for the purpose of observing the animals in off-season time, or for the purpose of culling the does or hinds, and the unwanted young buck and stags, can be and should be positioned so as to allow the optimum field of vision, unobstructed and over a wide area.

The fourth method, which may be considered by some as as unsporting one, but which requires the maximum of skill, is that of calling (Fig. 33). Where red deer are concerned, the carrying out of deer shooting by this method, unassisted by another person and without the use of artificially made calls, may be considered the *finesse of the stalking art in the forest*.

The method is purely dependent upon the rifle's ability to imitate the roar of the stag in the mating season, and upon applying this ability at the right time and from the right place, in order to lure the stag into the open, by making him think that the rifle is another stag wanting to fight for the ground or herd.

In the forest, this method is often the only way to bag an old stag who will not normally emerge from the thick cover except during the hours of complete darkness, there to return before dawn. These stags are often the greatest damage makers, and spoilers of the rut. They will gather a harem of hinds, but are too old to cover them, yet they will keep the younger and weaker stags at bay.

The roar must be produced from the lungs through the open throat and muffled with the hands cupped together.

You enter the forest where you hear an old stag roar. You know that he is an old one by his voice, and by listening to the direction of his voice you realise that he is in the thick of a plantation. You get close to him but he is safe inside, where nothing can penetrate save by making as much noise as an armoured division crashing through the trees. From time to time you can hear him threshing a young tree or a sapling, and then roaring again.

You calculate his position in relation to the wind. The wind is from him to you and you are some fifty yards from the edge of the plantation. Fifty yards inside he must be. You are in a ride or a forest road where you can move freely.

When you are opposite that stag you put your cupped hands to your mouth and from the depth of your lungs let out a roar, followed by a cough, modulated as nearly to the stag's note as you can manage.

You wait for a reaction.

The stag is silent. You try again.

This time your roar is answered with a threshing of a tree and a grunt.

You roar again, and the stag inside answers with a roar.

You now wait for him to start a challenge. He does.

In a slightly deeper voice than his, you answer, imitating the same roar, the same pauses and coughs as his.

The stag gets angry and threshes another tree. As soon as he has attacked it, and beaten it with his antlers to his satisfaction, he roars.

You answer.

He now moves along the plantation, but without giving you a chance of seeing him. You think he is going forward, so you move forward along the ride as noiselessly as you can. Each time he roars, you roar back.

After a while the roaring ceases, though there is a definite sound of threshing. This probably means that the stag is getting ready for his morning rest — the worst thing that can happen now. Your roaring is only occasionally answered with a grunt, and even the threshing ceases. You grab the nearest sapling or branch and imitate the sound of threshing by hitting it with the butt of your rifle, or your boot. The stag gets angry again and gives a series of short, very deep roars. You answer.

If he is quiet you run (without bothering much about noise, very short paces to sound like four feet hitting the ground in a trot), away from the stag, for some thirty yards, your hand catching and letting go of branches you meet on the way, as if the antlers were catching them. As you run, you grunt aloud; then, having stopped, you turn towards your beast, thrash another tree good and hard, and roar again.

He answers. To his roar you roar back, and now quietly return as near as possible to the place where you feel he must be. Thinking that his opponent has given way, the stag should be making for the edge of the plantation. He will do so grunting, and as soon as he reaches the edge of the thicket he will stop and roar. You should be in a position from which you can observe him, to make sure what sort of a beast he is, and if you decide that he is shootable, you should lure him further out before you attempt to shoot. When he emerges he will most likely be standing looking in your direction, affording only a poor head-on shot.

Now the real duel starts.

You must muffle your voice so as to sound some distance away and roar preferably from cover of a tree or a bush. You should avoid being caught uncovered, as that means you probably cannot move at all without being spotted. If your roaring is well muffled, the stag will come forward slowly, roaring at you. If a stag comes out to fight, his hind will normally come out behind him to see what is going on; the stag, however, is not normally well disposed to any spectators when he is coming out to meet his opponent. The reason is that it may be comparatively easy for a hind to slip away between the trees unnoticed and be taken possession of by another stag. Guarding his hinds is therefore another occupation for the stag and this forces him to come towards his opponent zig-zagging, looking back toward them. Sometimes he will turn and chase then back into the cover, only to come out again. In one of those movements he is bound, once he has come out, to give a nice broadside for a shot.

There is one other reason why, when calling stags, one should be under good cover, and that is that stags have been known, during the rut, to charge a human, and a charge is done quickly and head on, so that a shot is very difficult. A cover in the event of this worst happening, will provide a shield against such a charge.

The calling can also be done with a large 'humming' star-shell. This, however, must be suitably drilled, otherwise the vibration of the shell produces a roar which is unnatural. Bark of a silver birch, fresh and carefully taken off, and rolled into a trumpet, is a good calling medium; but its use requires great skill.

Finally, manufactured deer calls can be used, but these are rarely true in tone, and do not allow changes in intonation

Calling by two people, one being the rifle and the other the 'caller', is much easier, though it does not provide the same thrill. The caller should always be positioned so as to keep the rifle between himself and the stag.He should start calling immediately behind the rifle and then work his way slowly back as soon as the stag starts answering — this prevents the stag developing any idea of going to sleep; but should the stag start grunting, the rifle, being nearer, should thrash a tree or two to tease the beast.

Fallow Deer

The stalking of fallow deer is carried out in very much the same way as the stalking of red deer in the forest. Because of the fallow's habit of changing their hiding-places frequently one is quite likely to stumble across a herd at any time of the day. Their movements during the day are, however, quite unpredictable, whereas in the mornings and evenings they can be found in their deer paths on the way to or from the feeding grounds. Thus the time for stalking is first and last light. Fallow's acute eyesight, sense of smell and hearing make the stalk extremely difficult and it is quite imperative when one spots fallow deer, single or in a herd, to remain absolutely motionless.

Owing to slow-developing antlers, which do not adopt their final form until the buck is in middle age, as has already been described, recognition of fallow and assessment of their shootability is much easier and this to a certain extent offsets the drawback of their alertness.

Other than stalking at first and last light on or near their feeding grounds, possibly the best way of shooting fallow is from a high seat well positioned for the purpose.

Calling fallow deer during the rut is impracticable. They do not develop a call like red deer and are quite unwilling to react to a call, possibly because the herds never have a virtual master buck as a herd of red deer has a master stag; nor do they appropriate ground and conduct their mating within its perimeter like roe; being of a more wandering nature and not opposed to competition from other buck they are less eager to fight for their herd or ground. It is their fighting spirit which with the other two species is the basis for this type of deer shooting.

Roe Deer Stalking

The fascination which roe stalking undoubtedly has, though few recognise it, is difficult to explain or prove to those who have not tried it.

Whether it is because of their unsurpassed beauty and the fact that their form is the only one amongst deer which has not changed since prehistoric days, or because, agile and quick as they are, they present a quarry which avoids the rifle for days on end is difficult to say. The fact is that once bitten by the bug of roe stalking one will always return to it somehow or other.

Roe are shy animals and being small are not easy to spot, and thus present a difficult object for stalking; patience and experience however will with time, achieve results.

Most of the roe deer live in the forests, and some on the Scottish moors; it is in forest or moor therefore that the bulk of roe deer stalking is done. Let us then consider the difficulties which the stalker will always experience, so that this chapter may prove of real assistance to him.

One can never sufficiently stress the importance of wind. Wind is the chief enemy of the stalker, specially when stalking roe in the forest where the wind wavers and changes, almost as dangerously as it does in the mountains. It is important that we keep the wind specially in mind the whole time during the stalk. One should always attempt to stalk into the wind. Even stalking across the wind is dangerous as the cross-wind may always turn into a back-wind and blow from the stalker towards the deer. If a large area is to be covered in the stalk one must remember that the part of the forest down-wind of the ground already covered must be considered as having been disturbed, so that a zig-zag movement, working slowly into the wind, is the only solution. Returning down-wind in order to cover another belt of the forest is not advised unless the belt can be considered as one which has not been contaminated by the smell which the stalker had left behind.

Roe like thick bushes, ferns and brambles and even nettles are not their enemy as they are the stalker's; and they like soft ground. What, then will one do when stalking roe in high thick undergrowth?

The answer is, be patient.

There are always places where roe are bound to come into the open, crossing rides, coming out into meadows, walking along the fire lines and eating the grass there, coming out to sun themselves, dozing standing between the bushes where their red coats contrast with the green leaves.

You enter the forest and look for deer paths used by roe. It is morning — mid-morning — and you know that by now only a chance encounter will give you an opportunity. But you do not know the forest, and you know that your first need is to find out something about it, to find the deer paths, roe's hiding-and feeding-places, and what is more, to get to know the average quality of roe in the area.

It is June, and does are about with the young. As you work into the wind up a lane you see a doe walking slowly with her fawn. You stop within the shadow of a tree to let her move off into the cover again; otherwise she will stir everything for some distance, if she sees you and starts barking with fear, so you watch patiently and wait, following the two with you binoculars. Bambi looks as if he had stepped out of the Walt Disney film. They are not far and you could all but take a photograph if you had a camera. Still, there is the thought!

After a while the doe and fawn are in the bushes and you carry on knowing that even if you pass her within a few yards, once she is under cover and knows she cannot be seen she is not likely to make a noise and bark a warning to all other roe.

You look at the ground carefully, especially where she has disappeared, and there it is — the first roe path.

You observe the tracks, and study the slots. The soil is soft and sandy and takes a good impression of foot-prints. There are the slots of the doe and the fawn. You marvel at the tiny cloven hoof of the youngster. But wait, what is that. A track of curved and blunted toes which has been here for some time, a day perhaps, for the edges of the imprint are quite dry. You are sure it is a buck's trail. And the moon-like shape indicates that he is not a young buck.

A little farther on you find another roe path. Here the only track is that of a buck. This is fresh and you are sure it is a buck's spoor, possibly the same beast's.

You return to the same place in the late afternoon and having positioned yourself down-wind of the two deer paths you wait for evening. This is the only place where you have found deer tracks in this part of the forest and you hopefully wait for some signs of movement. Not to be tempted, you left your rifle behind, but you have your glasses. As evening approaches, the wind is dropping, which means that it may waver, change direction and play tricks. Your watch tells you that it is over half an hour to sunset.

A bush moves and a doe, a lonely doe, crosses the ride. She is almost across when a fawn follows her and disappears in the bush even before she does. You wonder whether they are your acquaintances from the morning.

You wait longer.

The wind has dropped completely. The birds are singing, a woodpecker drums against an old tree behind you.

All of a sudden, as if sprung from the earth's surface, a roe has appeared in the middle of the ride — you never saw it break cover. It is a hundred yards ahead and you think it's a buck. You place your glasses on it. Yes, a buck. Quite a good one, six points, and he must be an old animal. The burrs are difficult to see but the tines are thick and blunt and not very long, and you think there are signs of webbing between the top fork — at any rate the beam is thick all the way as far as the forks. He stands there motionless now looking in your direction.

A mosquito bites the back of your neck. Surreptitiously you move one hand from the glasses to flick it away. Before your hand has reached even half way up to your neck the buck jumps into cover. You can hear him running and he gives a slight bark when he is some way away.

Yes, he had seen you. You must choose in the future between chasing mosquitos and watching deer.

During your wanderings in the forenoon you found a small meadow. You had not found any trace of roe there, but you are not quite sure that there were no tracks. The meadow looked quite attractive, so you make your way there.

The luscious grass is high, just about high enough to cover roe specially if, head down, they were feeding or what is more likely, lying down chewing.

There is a tallish tree stump under an oak and you climb onto it. You are in the shadow with a good background and there is not much chance of your being seen, provided you move carefully, if you have to move at all. You are on the stump, and with the naked eye you see nothing.

Up with the glasses and you sweep the meadow regularly from one side to the other, starting at the near end. No, there is nothing there.

But it is pointless looking for roe in the forest now. In ten minutes it will be dark everywhere, so you decide to stay put, just in case.

Your glasses are working overtime.

You decide to make a last sweep through the glasses, and then give up.

In the very centre, not fifty yards from you, stands a buck, and further down the meadow another, and the grass is not nearly as high as you thought it was. You look left — there is a doe with a fawn; and two more does just by the forest at the far end. Where did they come from?

Just like roe; they appear from nowhere. They may have been sleeping in the quiet meadow; maybe there is a ditch and they worked up it till they reached their present position. The first possibility is the more likely. Within ten minutes, just as it is getting dark, two, no three more, appear at the edge of the meadow.

Very quietly you retrace your steps so as not to upset them. You will be back in the morning with the rifle. The buck near you was an old, easily shootable one with antlers very much gone back, thick and heavy, short and only a four-pointer.

On returning you share your observations with your host and he agrees: shoot the old one.

It is still dark when you return to the woods, making for the meadow.

With difficulty you locate your tree stump, but this time you stand behind it. The very slight breeze is blowing straight from the meadow and you welcome it.

First light is breaking, and you can just make out the far end of the meadow. Your glasses go to work. There is nothing there. You watch the meadow for half an hour — not a suggestion of a living creature. The morning is cold and the first rays of sunshine are reflected in the dew.

Even with the naked eye you can see everything, nothing can escape you.

But in the middle of the meadow stands a buck; the old buck, looking at you. You could swear he was not there a second ago and yet he is there now. He is over a hundred and fifty yards from you and you know it is too far for you to shoot.

Back you go and see if you can stalk him along the side of the meadow; for then, the distance from the edge of the wood will be less than a hundred yards.

You crouch between the bushes alongside the meadow.From time to time you stop to look. He is feeding now, and another buck is in the meadow, too. You look at the other; he is a younger one and in the prime of life — a taboo.

In your keenness you forget that to reach the place from which you were hoping to get a shot you have to cross where the doe and the fawn appeared from on the previous evening. Without thinking you pass it, and you have gone barely twenty yards when a doe barks behind you. Startled you look back to see a rump disappearing into the bushes. The doe was just coming out. You look at the meadow. Nothing there.

Oh, the wind!

Like red deer during the rut, so the roe in the rutting season can be a source of vast amusement and good sport.

During the rut, roe are quite unpredictable. They can be found miles from their usual habitat, they may appear sometimes fearless and inquisitive to the degree of being reckless, and they are on the move day and night.

Just as there are places where throughout the year roe can be found without fail, so during the rut the usual rutting places are a safe bet. It has been said elsewhere that buck will run after a doe and the doe will circle, or describe a figure of eight with a bush or a tree as centre. The vicinity of these rings will always provide an opportunity for sighting if not shooting roe.

Calling a buck is quite a skill, and it can be achieved with wetted lips, a piece of thick grass, a fresh beech leaf, or with artificial calls, by imitating the bleating tone, which the doe, when chased by a buck or when calling the young, or a buck when chasing a doe or in a state of unfulfilled sexual excitement, produces. All three bleats are similar, and their pitch hardly distinguishable by a human ear even with experience.

The bleat is something approaching a very drawn 'fieep' noise, which has to be arranged in a succession of bleats described later.

The most successful and probably the easiest method is by the use of a beech leaf or grass, of medium hardness, and a flat uncorrugated edge. The lead should be held with both hands, pressed one on each side of the main stem. Bring the leaf to the closed mouth, and blow at it between the lips exhausting the air under slight pressure so as to set the other edge of the leaf into vibrating motion which must produce a tone. With experience this tone can be controlled so as to give the right volume and the right note.

Calling roe is very much a matter of luck, more so than with red deer, for if it so happens that we call in an area where the buck is with a doe we shall get no reaction from him at all. Reaction from a buck, is comparatively easier to obtain where the proportion of buck to doe is about 1: 1; in those areas where the number of does exceeds that of the buck by a large number, the calling is difficult and often not successful (Fig. 34).

It is early morning in the latter part of July.

The previous day a buck was seen chasing a doe in front of a number of workmen in the wood. The rut is on.

Out at the crack of dawn and into the woods. From the experience of the previous year you know where the rings are and you make for that part of the forest. You know the beginning of the rut is the time to get an old buck who will have spent himself by the middle of the rutting time, so that wild horses will not drag him out of the thickets before the latter part of August.

The morning is cool and windless, the stars are still shining on the pink-shot morning sky.

Very slowly you make your way along the wood lane. As it gets lighter so a slight breeze springs up and blows into your face. The wind is all right.

Not far away there is a clearing where a few old trees felled a few years before provide a suitable place for roe rings. Furthermore, roe were seen there last year during rutting time.

A suitable place for waiting is soon found opposite a clump of self-seeded beech which in the middle of the clearing provides roe with good cover (see Fig. 34).

You wait for the light to improve, hidden behind an old oak on the very edge of the clearing.

The light is now improving very quickly and you know you could shoot.

Just as you have come to that conclusion a doe runs out of the clump ahead and a buck, his head stretched forward like a setter sniffing the air, goes after her without a care as to who can see him or where. You know that at any other time of the year a buck will never break cover in this manner, nor will a doe run out from cover without first looking round to ensure that she is safe unless chased by something or someone. There is no mistaking it, the rut is on; you have just seen the proof.

Unfortunately the speed of the two lovers was too great to make sure of the buck's antlers, age and other important information you know you must have before you can even dream of lifting the rifle.

You wait a little while in case the two come back. But it is not to be, they are away.

From the nearby beech bush you pick a leaf, place it against your lips and pressing your hands on your mouth you blow:

Fieep-pee-pee, in a high pitch

After a second or two, but not more.

Pee-pee-pee.

Then you wait for not less than ten and not more than twenty seconds.

No reaction. You try again, four times, pause, three times.

Now wait a long time, some minutes perhaps (they seem hours), but ready for a buck who may appear from anywhere.

Still no reaction. You have made one set of calls; you may make another from the same place.

Four calls, pause, three calls; long pause; four calls, pause, three.

You have barely finished the last 'pee' when a red body flashes between

Fig 34   Roe stalking to a call during the rut

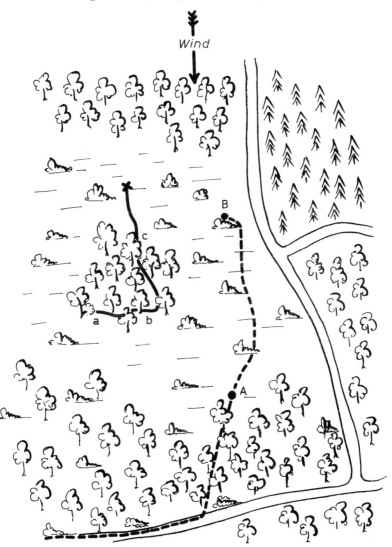

----- *Stalker's movements*

------ *Buck's movement*

A   *Stalker's first call*
a   *Buck first sighted*
b   *Buck first breaks cover to call but
      breaks back*
B   *Stalker moves parallel to buck's path*
c   *Buck breaks breaks cover and is recognised*
X   *Buck shot from B*

some branches in the clump.

You watch carefully.Nothing stirs.

Your four minutes between calls are up and there is still complete silence. You must call again. Normally no more than two calls should be made without a change of location, but having had some reaction you may have the third call.

Another leaf and a 'four pee', short pause, 'three pee'. You have just finished when a buck breaks cover ahead. He is fifty yards away and has not located you very well, as he is looking at a spot some way away from you. You watch him through the glasses. He is a very good old animal and you think that his age is sufficiently advanced for him to be killed.

Slowly you lower the glasses and get the rifle up.

But the buck has spotted the movement and is now looking straight at you. You must freeze in your movement and wait. The buck is not happy, and turning very fast on his hind legs, gets under cover.

You can hear him moving now inside the cover; he does not run away so you know he is not unduly worried, and probably sensed danger rather than knew that it was a human in front of him; so working on that assumption you decide to get to the other side of the clump, since you know that there is a good chance that the buck, who has not been scared away, will walk leisurely through the cover and come out on the other side in a few minutes time. You move along the edge of the clearing till you are past the clump and cross the clearing. The wind is not too bad, so there is a hope of you making contact.

You find cover and wait. The buck, if he does come out, will be not more than fifty yards away — not a long shot, but most likely he will be walking.

You have your glasses ready, for you must make sure that when the buck comes out, he is the buck you have seen and not another one which ought not to be shot.

You have worked it out by now, that the buck walking at a slow pace and nibbling odd blades of grass and shoots, should just about be out.

The tension mounts. It is now or never.

There he is, walking out now. Up with the glasses.The buck does not suspect that he is being observed, but having broken cover he quickens his pace. It is the same buck, you are quite certain, but you are not happy shooting him on the move knowing that during the rut these are, like all deer, more difficult to kill than at other times of the year.

Down with the glasses, up with the rifle. You follow him with the sights. He is now sixty yards or so off, still moving. You decide to take desperate action to stop him for just long enough to take the final adjustment of aim and press the trigger.

You have shot a buck when someone else who accompanied you tried to stop the animal, even when running. A whistle, a sharp high-pitched short whistle, not loud, did the trick, giving you that second, perhaps even less, to steady yourself. Now you are alone and you must try yourself.

A sharp, high-pitched whistle.

The buck stops in his tracks and looks in your direction. You are quite ready and he has given you just the time you needed.

A split second later he is beating the ground in convulsions.

This was a lucky occasion. The buck did exactly what he was meant to do.

If, after the third set of calls, the buck does not appear, the location is spoilt for calling for three or four days. The reason for this is difficult to explain. It follows no rule of nature, but it is a fact based on experience, that having unsuccessfully called in one place, it is futile trying to call there again for the following three or four days.

The first call should be slightly louder than the subsequent ones, the last 'pee' of the last call quiet and gentle.If during your blowing the wrong note slips out in a harsh unharmonious manner you may just as well give up; if the error was a slight one it is worth waiting as roe are by nature curious, and occasionally a wrong note may bring them out faster than the right one, provided that the tone was not too harsh or too human!

Calling a buck who is already with a doe is pointless even if outward appearances indicate that they are not interested in one another.

If we spot a buck at a distance and he does not even lift his head after the first series of calls either he is not interested or he has a doe near him hidden or resting (possibly lying hidden in the grass). In such circumstances persistent calling will have no effect other than general disturbance.

The calling must be done from a place where we are hidden from view, as the slightest suspicion, without even a sight of a human being, will send a buck bounding away if he is searching for a doe.

Most of the cunning old buck that have been shot we shot in this manner and apart from a chance encounter no other method would have secured them as trophies as they rarely appear outside cover.

And finally to close this 'roe calling' saga, calling should never be attempted from other than ground level. The call sounds quite different from a height and will always give the game away instead of bringing the animal out.

There only remains now the stalking of roe on the moors.

First let us consider what type of moor is likely to carry roe. A completely open one, with acres of heather-covered undulating land and no cover from trees and bushes is not a likely place. Roe prefer some cover, and only those moors where there is some cover from trees or young plantations of trees, etc. are likely to hold them.

The roe of the moors travels a great deal more than that of the wood and forest and to stalk one is almost impossible as the quarry will move at a faster pace than the stalker, specially as the matter must keep under cover. It is therefore by far the better plan to attempt to cut the animal off. This often means that we can move more freely until we reach the point where the anticipated close range contact is likely to be established. To do this it is important to know the lie of the land and the direction of the roe's movements. It is not sufficient when a buck is spotted to run ahead of him and wait for him a few hundred yards on. Knowledge of the terrain should tell us where he is making for, and we are better off waiting for him at his destination than trying to cut him off too early on.

Chapter XII

HIGH SEATS — USE AND LOCATION

In the last three decades high seats have found their place in the stalking circles of Britain specially in woodland stalking. The increasing need to control deer in the forestry, the need to cull deer on flat land where shooting from the ground level gives no margin of safety, or in few year-old plantations where young trees obliterate the view, have made high seats indispensible.

Not surprising therefore that not only has the construction of do-it-yourself high seats been helped by the sharing of information or purchase of designs from the large users like the Forestry Commission, but also a variety of high seats have appeared on the market, from heavy semi-permanent ones made of steel, to sophisticated lightweight collapsible ones, easy to carry and easy to erect wherever they are wanted.

Needless to say, there is little sport in shooting deer from a high seat, and stalking on foot will always remain a challenge, but at the same time one has to admit, that for most, a shot from a high seat is likely to be more accurate, more humane, than one taken standing, kneeling or sitting even with a stalking stick, or using a tree as a rest for the rifle.

For the purpose of spotting deer and preparing the shooting plan prior to the commencement of the season, a high seat is almost indispensable in an afforested area. It can be imagined that it is necessary to watch the deer prior to the shooting plan being drawn up, to ensure the whereabouts of the deer and, what is even more important, to mark the deer which are to be shot. From the ground level this is often very difficult, especially in the thick plantations.

Imagine yourself looking for a roe on a plantation of three to four foot high trees planted close to one another, the chance of seeing something is negligible, whereas at a height of a few feet, in a high seat you can look between the trees, and although the whole of the beast's body may not be visible, it will be posible from the view of its antlers, head, neck, etc. to establish its shootability. Admittedly, often the beast will be lying down, and so will remain invisible even to observation from a high seat, but after a few days' observation in the same location one can assume that one has

Fig 35 Permanent high seat

Plate XXVIII Modern portable high seats

seen most, if not all, of the animals which come out to feed or sun themselves in that place.

In a similar way the observations of deer in lanes, rides and fire-breaks is much improved from a high seat. Admittedly it is possible to move along the edge of the wide fire line and watch from there the movements of deer. The width of some fire lines and even of the lanes is sufficient to allow the spotting and observation of deer with the aid of binoculars, before the beasts realise that they have been observed. This, in narrow lanes, is often not possible, and the observations carried out there are, more often than not, inaccurate. Quite often, the deer will observe us by the time it has reached half-way across the fire break, or lane, and jumping into cover will allow us only a cursory glimpse of itself.

The value of the high seat will, of course, be wholly dependent on its siting, taking into consideration the principal uses of it, i.e. for observation in the preparation of the shooting plan, and as a shooting stand for carrying out the plan specially where doe and young animals are concerned, and as a shooting stand from which to give the 'shooter' a sporting shot, that is to say requiring one skill in deer recognition which has to precede the shooting.

In itself the high seat offers one enormous advantage if well sited: if it is located at the correct height the human scent will be carried above the crowns of the trees and thus almost regardless of wind direction the deer will not discover the observer's or rifle's presence by smell. Also, deer do not make a habit of looking upwards, and even when poorly concealed, it is unlikely that our presence in the seat will be discovered short of acting in such a manner as to attract the animals' attention.

It may well be for these very considerations which in themselves are to our great advantage that many people think the use of high seats unsporting. Of course, here again much of the British opinion on the subject of deer shooting derives solely from experience of stalking deer in Scotland where the two controversial methods of deer shooting, i.e. calling deer in the rut, and shooting from high seats, would be of advantage only in the forested areas.

The location of the high seat is the most important factor affecting success. The following points must be considered before a decision on permanent siting of the high seat is taken:

1. *The prevailing wind.* In spite of the fact that the scent is normally carried from a well-adjusted seat into the crowns of the trees wind strength and other atmospheric conditions may cause 'dropping of the scent'. Furthermore, continuous growth of trees will, with time, cause the seat to find itself below, instead of among, or even slightly above, the tree crowns. The scent will then be arrested underneath the crowns and will travel downwards very quickly. Thus the seat should be sited so that prevailing wind will carry the scent away from the principal observation area.

2. *Siting.* There is only a little skill and a little imagination needed in siting of high seats.

From the point of view of the occupant it must give an unobstructed view of the arc of fire or observation it is important therefore that one tries to envisage the development and growth of the neighbouring and overhanging trees and bushes.

The occupant must be camouflaged from deers' view, so he (and the seat itself) should not be silhouetted against the sky line; to conceal the movements within the seat, the seat should either be surrounded by a wall or a curtain of camouflaged netting, hessian, or even fresh branches with leaves. The seat should be approachable within cover and quietly, so a stalking path to it is advisable.

3. *Height*. There are at least two requirements that the seat needs to satisfy: if it is to be used for shooting, it must be high enough, to allow a downward shot at an angle of no less than 8° to the ground (to minimise the risk of ricochet) . If it is to allow a view into a plantation, or a corn field, it must be high enough to give a view as clear and unobstructed by ground cover as is possible.

4. *Supported high seats*. If the seat is of a type which needs to be supported by a tree, a tree chosen as a support must be firm enough not to heave in the wind. Nails should not be used to secure the seat to the tree; ropes or galvanised wire are much kinder to the tree.

5. *Locations in mountainous country*. In the mountains, where the wind can deflect from its main direction by more than 90°, it is important to have knowledge of the locality, especially of local wind directions, before giving consideration to the siting of the seats.

It is often found in siting high seats in a valley that the only practical location is across the valley, so that the slope used by the deer is opposite the seat; in these cases the seat should be used only if the field of fire is within the normal shooting range. In the valley, where distance is very deceptive, the rifle should be well briefed as to the range of possible fire so as to avoid unnecessary wounding of animals.

Where the high seats are erected for the first time, it is advisable in the first place to produce an easily transportable seat of the ladder type, the moving of which offers little difficulty, and use it for one season, adjusting its location to suit the terrain and movement of deer. Only when one has ensured that the particular place is the most advantageous one, having in view its purpose, should the permanent structure be erected.

The ideal time to erect permanent seats is late autumn after the end of the deer shooting season, so as to give the deer a chance to get used to the presence of the new structures by the time we are likely to use them in the following year. It is advisable to use weathered timber and to weather-proof it. Creosote proofing is probably the most efficient, but one must remember that tar is a deer repellent and creosoting therefore should be carried out before the timber is brought to the site. If it must be done, on site, the use of the treated high seat should not be contemplated for two to four months after treatment.

The drawing within this chapter (Fig. 35) and the photographs (Plate XXVIII) will give some idea of the structure of the seats.

An important factor in the 'construction' of the seat is the question of planking of the flooring and seating. Both should be made of solid materials so as to avoid their creaking when one moves in the seat. It is also important that both should be easily drainable, by either being slotted, or built on the slant. By efficient drainage, rotting will be prevented. As far as the seat is concerned, the best method is to make it detachable so that it can be stood against the wall of the box, tipping up, or even sprung.

Seats located for shooting animals which are sporting quarries as opposed to shooting unwanted animals should be so sited as to present an opportunity to recognition rather than for the actual act of shooting. Recognition of the animal is the factor that makes deer shooting so attractive a sport; the act of shooting itself has very little sport attached to it in the full meaning of the word.

The shooting of unwanted animals must be carried out. On the efficiency and promptness of it the future of the deer may depend. It is our duty to make certain this is carried out with the least suffering to the animals, and with maximum efficiency in time and expenditure.

If we fail in the carrying out of the shooting plan the effects of it will not only mean a loss of revenue to the shooting tenant, and thus upset his financial calculations, but will also increase the incidence of damage caused by deer in the fields. Deer damage to agricultural crops is normally followed quickly by deer drives and the consequent 'peppering' of deer with shotguns. If shooting from the high seat is not ethical, the shooting of deer with shotgun is even less so, as it creates untold suffering and rarely meets its object of killing the deer.

Our sporting shooting of trophy-bearing animals, being based on selective shooting, will always mean days spent on the seat before a shootable animal comes in front of our sights, or at any rate comes out at a time when a shot is possible. The sport will thus consist of the patient waiting for the opportunity and the throwing away any number of chances of shooting an animal which is not *the animal*.

Needless to say even when a number of high seats have been erected stalking on foot will not be eliminated, and often stalk and an hour in the high seat together may provide an evening's or morning's amusement.

Chapter XIII

THE BEHAVIOUR OF DEER ON BEING SHOT

It is quite a common occurrence for deer when shot not to drop immediately but to take a few paces or to jump forward even if the shot has been well and carefully placed. In open country such as the open deer forests of Scotland this behaviour causes little anxiety as the deer can be watched without hindrance; but in woods or forests, if a deer does not drop immediately it is shot or very soon after one must be able to interpret the movements and behaviour of deer at the moment of impact, and what is equally important, interpret the signs which can normally be found at the spot where the deer stood when it was hit.

Before we attempt to describe the signs left by deer it is important that the rifle knows exactly what action should be taken when firing and immediately after.

First of all it is absolutely imperative that the location, the absolutely acurate location, of the deer shot at is memorised. It is sometimes impossible once one has moved to retain the mental picture of where the deer was standing at the moment of firing. Many experts advise therefore that as soon as the shot has been fired, if there is some doubt as to whether the deer has been killed outright, a line be drawn on the ground in the shape of an arrow indicating the direction, or, if drawing on the ground is impossible, two sticks are thrust in the ground making a line the extension of which carries to the location of the deer. A branch with twigs in the shape of an arrow will also meet this purpose, provided that when laid on the ground it is not immediately lost in the brushwood. Two such lines will at their intersection give the exact position of the deer.

The next thing to remember is the direction the deer was facing and, if it moved off after the shot, the direction of its movement and the location of it at the moment of disappearing from sight.

In searching for a wounded animal it is important to know whether the beast is stunned and likely to recover and carry on; whether wounded slightly and as soon as the shock passes likely to get up and run for cover, where after recovery from the wound it will live; whether paralysed and unable to move it requires the *coup de grâce;* whether it is dead and in its last convulsion, or about to die after having moved a few yards only.

175

It would be folly, to say that any absolute deduction can be drawn from watching an animal's behaviour at the moment of shot. Animals will behave differently if hit when running and when standing still, and their reactions and powers of survival during the rutting season are different from, and much stronger than, those during the rest of the year. This is particularly applicable to deer. Nevertheless, a useful guide can be found from observation of the animal, and this together with the marks found at the place where the beast stood at the moment of impact will give a picture from which certain deductions can usefully be made.

We must realise that the number of deer shot at but not killed (though seriously wounded) is smaller than that missed or only superficially wounded. What we are doing therefore is, ensuring that a provision is made for the basis of the equivalent of a 'pick-up', after a day of partridge or pheasant shooting, and preparing ourselves for that 'pick-up' to be done quickly and efficiently. This is the more important as in the British Isles not many dogs, trained or capable of tracking wounded deer, are available.

Let us first consider, then, how the deer react to being hit.

First of all the accurate, mortal shot in the heart is normally marked either by a jump forward, and a noisy, senseless run through the undergrowth for a matter of a dozen or two paces, or by a jump on the spot with the fore-legs lifted higher than the back ones. The run is with the head and neck stretched out, forming a straight line with the back, and the pace is very fast. It also happens that a shot in the heart, especially with a heavy bullet, causes sufficient shock for the animal to remain standing still for some seconds, before sagging slowly, fore-legs first. The former reaction is quite common in a rutting stag or buck, the latter is the more normal reaction during the rest of the year.

Care must be taken, however, when the animals drop immediately on being shot as it is possible that the hit was scored in the head bones without breaking any, in the neck without mortal damage to spine, arteries or windpipe, or in the upper extremes of the spine along the back, when a strong but non-lasting paralysis may result. In all these cases the beast will get up after a few seconds and will run away. In the instances quoted, the beast drops immediately and remains very still on the ground until it regains consciousness.

The next easily distinguishable sign is when at the impact of the bullet the animal jumps up on four legs with the head low down and kicks back with the hind-legs. This is normally the sign of a hit low in the stomach and too far back. Where there is a possibility that a low shot will send up a spray of stones, the reaction immediately upon the shot being fired will be so similar that it may be indistinguishable from a case of stomach wound, but whereas the former is followed by a get-away in a trot, the latter is followed by an all-out gallop.

A hit in the liver or kidney may be difficult to recognise by the animal's reaction, since the animal simply shudders as if a shiver were running through its body.

The most deceptive sign is given when the beast is shot through the muscle of the upper leg. This shot, provided that the bones or arteries are not damaged, is not fatal and the injury not serious, the wounds healing quickly; at the moment of shot, however, the animal drops immediately through the shock to the muscular and nerve system, only to get up almost immediately and run away, possibly with a slight limp.

A nod of the head is a sign of a very near miss, where the bullet has scarely jarred the body, possibly just cutting the skin without doing any damage whatsoever.

A hit in the antlers has the effect of completely paralysing the animal for a short space of time. The signs are very deceptive as paralysed animal's legs give, on occasions, very slowly and the animal may show signs of having been hit in the heart; however, it is soon up and away. It is enough to scrape the antler with the bullet to produce the same effect, but there the control of muscles is completely lost to the animal and the beast drops immediately and may remain paralysed for some minutes, specially if the antler or antlers are shattered by the bullet.

It will be seen that the first signs can tell us a lot. In addition we have the amount of blood and its colour, the possible finding of shattered bone splinters, the tissue of intestine, lung or liver, and cut hair from the location of the bullet impact or from its immediate vicinity to serve as additional indications. Depending on the signs, the search may have to be postponed or may have to be undertaken immediately, or finally abandoned.

Consider an animal which is mortally wounded but has run away to die quietly in the nearest cover. If disturbed by searchers it will move on, in agony; whereas if left for several minutes it will die peacefully. Surely the latter is the kinder and more humane action? (See Fig. 36).

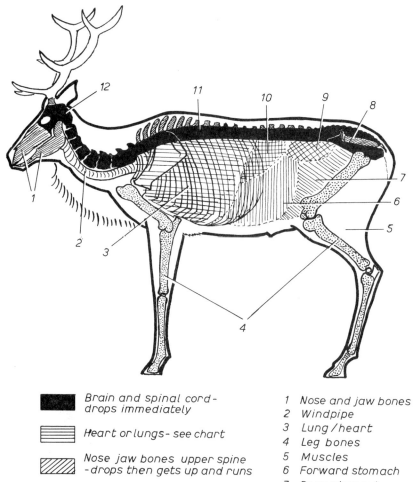

Brain and spinal cord-
drops immediately

Heart or lungs- see chart

Nose jaw bones upper spine
-drops then gets up and runs

Forward stomach - see chart

Rear stomach - see chart

Kidney - see chart

Liver - see chart

Leg bones - see chart

Muscle - see chart

1 Nose and jaw bones
2 Windpipe
3 Lung / heart
4 Leg bones
5 Muscles
6 Forward stomach
7 Rear stomach
8 Pelvis
9 Kidney
10 Liver
11 Backbone
12 Skull

Fig 36 Location of wounds and injuries

Based on Schulze 'Der Waidgeredite Jager' P Pavey, Hamburg 1955

TABLE 19 Marking by Roe Deer after Shot (when wounded)*
(To be used in connection with Fig. 36)

Behaviour after shot	Distance	Blood Colour	Hair cut off by the bullet and other marks	Moves after shot (paces)	Search after	Location of wound
Slight jump, fore-legs up high, getaway loud through undergrowth	In loco or after 3–5 paces	Light red, with air bubbles in numbers	Short, light in colour, stiff	20–50	Immediately	High heart or lung cavity
Slight shudder and shiver of body, delicate shaking	In loco	Dark red-brown	Short, light in colour	40–80	15 mins	Liver
Drops immediately, cannot get up	Nil	Nil	Nil	Nil	Immediately	High spine
Drops immediately, gets up, runs limping (possibly in a curve)	In loco	Very light, and little	None, but bone splinters	Can run immediately a long way	Search with dog, normally inconclusive	Leg bone
Drops immediately, but in convulsions, gets up, runs	Nil	Nil	Nil	Can run indefinitely	Pointless	Antler or skull bone. No penetration. (Skull penetration mortal)
Drops immediately, kicks with legs upwards, gets up, runs away	In loco	Very little, with red saliva	Nil	Can run indefinitely	Immediately	Shattered jaw bones
Jumps up on all four legs with head low down	15–20 paces	Light red, with contents of stomach	Short, grey-yellow, woolly texture	100–200 paces	One hour, very carefully, better with dog	Stomach intestines
Drops immediately, kicks, gets up and runs	In loco	Little red	Light yellowy	Can run indefinitely	Normally pointless	Muscle shot without broken bones or arteries
Slight shudder	In loco	Little blood, dark	Mixed	—	Pointless	Cut skin superficial

Note:
* Based on von Raesefeld, *Das Rehwild* (Hamburg, P. Parey, 1956) and H. Dziegielewski, *Przewodnik Informator Lowiecki* (PWRL-L, Warsaw, 1970).

TABLE 20 Marking by Red Deer after Shot (when wounded).*
(To be used in connection with Fig. 36)

Behaviour after shot	Blood		Hair cut off by the bullet and other marks	Moves after shot (paces)	Search after	Location of wound
	Distance	Colour				
Rockets forward; head, neck and back in line	After 10–30 paces	Light red to orange with air bubbles	Thin, straight wool-less	15–100	15 mins	Central or high lung
Head low, rockets forward, runs	In loco	Red, many air bubbles, much blood	Thin, straight, wool-less	30–70	15 mins	Low lung, and/or heart
Rockets forward, low and stretched, antlers lying upon back	15–20 paces	Red-brown large drops, if rubbed leave sand	Thick, flat, wool-less	100–150, more possibly	1 hour	Liver
Drops immediately, cannot get up	Nil	Nil	Nil	Nil	Immediately to give *coup de grâce*	Spinal bone
Drops immediately, rolls on the ground kicks, with legs upwards, gets up, runs	In loco	Medium amount, light in colour, sprayed	Thin woolly	Runs a long way	Search usually pointless	Upper spine ridge. (Momentary paralysis)
Drops slowly, front or back legs first; gets up, runs limping	In loco	Light, plentiful, sprayed sideways. Bone splinters	Thin, short, wool-less	Can run miles	After 2–3 hours, should be with dog	Lower or upper leg with bones shattered
Drops, immediately, gets up, runs. Signs of momentary paralysis	None	None	None	Can run miles	Search pointless	Skull bone and or antlers. No penetration. (Penetration is mortal)
Drops immediately, gets up, runs	Very little	Red with saliva	None	Can run miles	Search normally with no result	Jaw-bones
Kicks with back legs, appears to sag; but recovers, runs	20–40 paces	Light in colour with green contents of stomach	Medium thick, grey-white	2–10	2–4 hours very carefully	Stomach or intestines

Note
With a slight stomach wound, the blood contains no stomach residue and the animal will find, and remain in lair until it recovers from the wounds.

Behaviour after shot	Blood		Hair cut off by the bullet and other marks	Moves after shot (paces)	Search after	Location of wound
Nod of the head	10–40 paces	Light, plentiful, both sides of tracks	Very long thin, grey	Can run miles	1 hour	Low neck wound
Slight shudder of whole body	10–100 paces	Irregular, dark red	Mixed	Can run miles	Pointless	Slight flesh wound

Notes
* Based on von Raesefeld, *Das Rehwild* (Hamburg, P. Parey, 1956), and H. Dziegielewski, *Przewodnik Informator Łowiecki* (PWR-L, Warsaw, 1970).
1. When shot through the leg, a stag drops immediately. 2. When shot through the windpipe or the arteries of the neck, he normally drops after a few paces (in the latter instance the blood will be in profusion); then dies. 3. If animal is not found within 100 yards with wounds other than suspected liver, stomach, or lung wound, the wound is not likely to have been serious and the animal is most likely to recover. In this case the finding of the blooded lair (couch) is tantamount to finding the animal, which was most likely disturbed by our approach.

Chapter XIV

FEMALE AND YOUNG IN THE SHOOTING PLAN

T he graph contained in the chapter on the shooting plan shows that a proportion of hinds, does, fawns and calves must be shot yearly if our general aim of maintaining the deer population at a certain level controlled by the size of the area and its feeding capacity is to be effectively enforced.

The shooting of the male deer, both by virtue of their carrying antlers and of certain outward signs which can with practice be recognised and provide adequate guidance, should present comparatively little difficulty. Furthermore the shooting of diseased bucks and stags is comparatively easy as the disease is normally reflected in the antler formation or, indeed, in the general appearance. What then of the female?

The question of hinds and does in the cull plan ought to be closer to the heart of the owners, professional and sporting stalkers and sportsmen, than it often is, for it is through the control of the females that the numerical control of deer is achieved; additionally it is through the females, and not only males, that the imperfections of quality can be passed on.

Undershoot the females for a year or two, and within a short time the numbers will explode. Hence, numerical control of the females, in an environment which is vulnerable to damage, is paramount.

The second important issue in culling the females is its timing. The cull season covers winter months. The actual dates are not important and of course can be changed by legislation, but what is important is the fact that it happens in winter. This is the time of food shortage, the time when the pregnant female needs food, and in it's absence quickly loses condition. Hence the aim is to cull early in the season in order to optimise the return from venison.

There is a belief in some places that a female which has no calf is barren; nothing can be further from truth unless the female is an old one. In most instances a female has a rest or two from calf bearing during her fertility life, producing a strong calf after a year's rest; hence these females should only be shot when they are old or obviously unwell. Nor should a calfless leading hind be shot unless very old, or, unless it is intended to split a very large herd of hinds into smaller units, when the shooting of leading hind usually results in a split-up. Socially, in the life of the herd, the leading hind is as important to that herd as a good caring mother is to her family.

It is difficult to provide a clear selection of guide lines for the cull of female deer. First in the order of priority should be those in poor condition; the condition is more marked early in the season when healthy females can be easily distinguished from unhealthy ones. Those that need culling look thin, often dirty and untidy sometimes hollow-sided; they often keep well away from the others, or at least are not within the herd group but some distance away as if they were not welcome.

These qualifications apart, the cull has to be carried out diligently and often good females have to be shot in order to complete it. Clearly if a mothering female is shot, the calf should also be shot; often the calf returns to the place where the mother had been shot sometimes within half an hour, sometimes the following day.

The young are not always by their mother's foot, and it is quite normal for the mother to come out into the open to ensure that there is no danger before allowing her young to appear from cover — hence the danger of shooting unaccompanied females. Furthermore, a number of young are lost yearly to predators, death in winter, etc. whose mothers may well be fully capable of producing generations of good healthy offspring; indeed perhaps the pride of the forest may come from one of them.

It is necessary therefore to learn the 'personality' of female deer.

In most cases it may be truly said that the quality of the female deer and therefore her value to the stock is depicted in her young ones, and in many cases therefore the offspring must be our guide.

In the late autumn when all other deer have changed their coats, an old barren female who has worn down her teeth and thus finds assimilation of food difficult and slow, will show signs of the red summer coat and will thus stand out among the others. Furthermore, most such female deer will have their outwardly visible reproductive organs swollen. Both these features are certain signs of age, the latter being peculiar to old barren female deer — they can quite easily be spotted in a chance encounter and suffice as a reason for the deer being shot.

A normally developed female deer with full reproductive ability will show through her long winter coat nipples which at this time of year will appear slightly puffed up. Such a female deer, provided that the description of barren deer above does not apply to her should be preserved. The doe or hind however which can be assessed by size as being fully mature but is slightly thinner than normal and whose nipples are covered under the winter coat, so as to render her indistinguishable — in that part of her body — from the male, can be accepted as a weak and underdeveloped specimen and shot.

Here it must be borne in mind that the hinds younger than four, fallow does younger than three and roe does younger than two may not be sexually mature, and their nipples will not and should not be fully developed. These females can, however, be distinguished by their comparatively young appearance, and are slightly smaller than the fully grown mature animals.

Lastly, the shooting of calves and fawns.

Here the size of the animal is the safest and indeed almost the only guide alongside the health of the mother.

It is unlikely that a sick and diseased female deer will produce normal healthy offspring. Thus both mother and young can be shot with a fair degree of safety.

When twins are born (and this applies even more to the uncommon triplets) one of the young is always larger than the other(s). The smaller one is always the weaker and more helpless and requires more motherly attention than the stronger. The smaller one is thus unwanted by us and should be shot, preferably before the beginning of the rigorous winter, when not only is it unlikely to survive but is quite likely to cause the death of the mother.

The weak young ones will normally be noticed as being the last to follow the mother.

With red and fallow deer there is the additional possibility of weak calves being born of mothers who, though they have fully developed sex organs come on heat late with the consequence that the young are born late; the young will look undernourished and weak compared with others of their generation. The mother of such young will often leave them as soon as the feeding conditions deteriorate and they will die, or, if she allows them to suck, she herself is unlikely to survive the winter. Females coming on heat late, and the late born young are better shot regardless of their age.

In cases where weak young survive, their development will be slow even at a more advanced age having been retarded in their early life, and their offsprings will also be weak.

Chapter XV

LEGISLATION

The legislation covering the British Isles is outlined below. The information is current at the time of writing. Anyone wishing to shoot deer should ensure that he or she is fully conversant with all aspects of legislation; lack of knowledge or appreciation of legislation are not an excuse acceptable in the courts of law!

TABLE 21   Statutory close season for deer in the British Isles (all dates inclusive)°

Species	Sex	England & Wales	Scotland	Northern Ireland	Eire
Red deer	Stags	1 May–31 July	21 Oct.–30 June	1 May–31 July	1 Mar.–31 Aug.
	Hinds	1 Mar.–31 Oct.	16 Feb.–20 Oct.	1 Mar.–31 Oct.	1 Mar.–31 Oct.
Sika deer	Stags	1 May–31 July	21 Oct.–30 June	1 May–31 July	1 Mar.–31 Aug.
	Hinds	1 Mar.–31 Oct.	16 Feb.–20 Oct.	1 Mar.–31 Oct.	1 Mar.–31 Oct.
Fallow deer	Bucks	1 May–31 July	1 May–31 July	1 May–31 July	1 Mar.–31 Aug.
	Does	1 Mar.–31 Oct.	16 Feb.–20 Oct.	1 Mar.–31 Oct.	1 Mar.–31 Aug.
Roe deer	Bucks	1 Nov.–31 Mar.	21 Oct.–31 Mar.		
	Does	1 Mar.–31 Oct.	1 Apr.–20 Oct.		

Notes ° J. A. Roll Pickering in *Deer*, vol. 6 (July 1985).
British Deer Society recommended close seasons for:
Muntjack, bucks and does : 1 Mar.–31 Oct.;
Chinese water deer, Bucks and does : 1 Mar.–31 Oct.

TABLE 22   Deer laws

England and Wales
Deer Act 1963 (ch 36).
Roe Deer (Close Season) Act 1977 (ch 4).
Deer Act 1980 (ch 49).
Wildlife and Countryside Act 1981 (ch 69), Sched 7.

Scotland
Deer (Scotland) Act 1959 (ch 40).
Deer (Amendment) (Scotland) Act 1967 (ch 37).
Deer (Amendment) (Scotland) Act 1982 (ch 19).
S.I.1984 No 76 The Deer (Close Seasons) (Scotland) Order 1984.
S.I.1984 No 899 The Licensing of Venison Dealers (Prescribed Forms, etc) (Scotland) Order 1984.
S.I.1984 No 922 The Licensing of Venison Dealers (Application Procedures etc) (Scotland) Order 1984.
S.I.1985 No 1168 The Deer (Firearms, etc) (Scotland) Order 1985.

Northern Ireland
S.I.1985 No 171 The Wildlife (Northern Ireland) Order 1985.

Various
S.I.1980 No 593 The Welfare of Livestock (Deer) Order 1980 (E, W, S)
S.I.1980 No 685 The Removal of Antlers in Velvet (Anaesthetics) Order 1980. (E, W, S)
S.I.1982 No 1884 The Welfare of Livestock (Prohibited Operations) Regulations 1982. (E, W, S)
S.I.1982 No 1885 The Veterinary Surgeons Act 1966 (Schedule 3 Amendment) Order 1982. (E, W, S, NI)

TABLE 23   Outline guide to permitted firearms for killing deer in the British Isles°

Country	England and Wales	Scotland	Northern Ireland	Republic of Ireland
Shotguns and ammunition	(Authorised persons only)	(Occupiers when defending crops and foodstuffs only)	(Authorised persons only)	
	Not smaller than 12 bore Min. AAA or rifled slug	Not less than 12 bore a. Roe deer AAA b. All deer SSG or rifled slug	Not smaller than 12 bore Min. AAA or rifled slug	
Rifles and ammunition	*Either* Calibre not less than .240 in. *Or:* Muzzle energy not less than 1700 ft/lbs	a. Roe deer expanding bullets min. 50 grains *and* Min. 2450 fps *and* Min. 1000 ft/lbs b. All deer expanding bullets min. 100 grains *and* Min. 2450 fps muzzle velocity *and* Min. 1750 ft/lbs muzzle energy	Min. Calibre: .236 in. *and* Min. projectile weight 100 grains	Min. Cal.: .22 in. *and* Min. proj. wt: 55 grains *and* Min. muzzle energy: 1637 ft/lbs
PROHIBITIONS	Any air rifle, pistol or gun	High-technology night sights	Handguns, air rifles, etc. gas weapons	

Note °J. A. Roll Pickering in *Deer* vol.6 (Nov. 1985). This outline guide is not intended to be a comprehensive or definitive summary of the permitted weaponry in each country–merely it is a brief summary of the present legislation.

Chapter XVI

ADVICE TO STALKERS, KEEPERS, FORESTERS AND OWNERS

The first part of the book is finished.It may not be as comprehensive as some would like, but there are several books on the market today that complement this, and fill the gaps. Hopefully, however, it provides that basic information on which to wean the young and train and develop the adults in the skills connected with stalking and managing deer.

Deer have staged a come-back in the life of the country and the last 25 to 30 years, since *Wild Deer* had appeared the attitude towards deer has changed for the better quite unbelievably; no longer is the interest confined to a small group of enthusiasts, the enthusiasm, interest and knowledge have grown, and deer have benefited.

To a large extent much credit is due to the self discipline which many owners, sporting and professional stalkers, foresters, stalking tenants and the deer-interested groupings have accepted, practised, encouraged and advocated, not only in the safe conduct in the field but in sensible selective approach to all aspects of conservation and control of deer.

The sporting and professional stalker has recognised that trophy hunting can not have a high priority — that trophy heads on mature beasts have to be left for tomorrow and only the old trophy beast is for today; so the stalker who finds a good specimen in its prime of life makes sure that this specimen is well looked after and is allowed to flourish and propagate.

When out stalking or merely watching deer, he must be constantly on the look-out for the things which can be done to improve the deer; he must cause the least possible disturbance and therefore move carefully, slowly and quietly, seeing everything and hearing everything, without being seen and heard.

This can be only done if he is well trained not only in the art of stalking but in such apparently trivial and obvious matters as making sure that the rifle is zeroed correctly before he goes out.

Some budding stalkers, finding the rifle and binoculars too much to carry and use, carry the rifle, and leave the binoculars (or telescope) behind, or let someone else carry them. Budding stalker! your duty is first to recognise the deer and then shoot it. Carry the binoculars yourself, leave the rifle, or let it be carried by a companion. When you use the rifle you will at least be sure that you know exactly what you are firing at, and thus decrease the chance of shooting the beast that should not have been shot. Mistakes are a human failing, but do make sure that the mistake was not made only because of your greed for a good trophy or insufficient interest which made you carry out the stalk insufficiently equipped.

When you fire, do make sure that the position of the animal is such that you have a chance of penetrating a vital part of the body, where a bullet will cut the web of life cleanly and neatly without causing undue pain. Your error of aim is an accepted risk, but your error of judgement in firing too far, at a running animal, or at one standing head-on, or facing away from you, are not the risks which can be accepted and forgiven.

If you are a guest, and your host suggests that you are accompanied by a keeper, forester or stalker, do not automatically think 'he does not trust me'; all he is doing is safeguarding his stock, or, specially if you do not know the area, ensuring that there will be no shooting accidents.

It does happen to the best shots and most experienced ones, that they have not killed the animal outright. Do not lose interest as soon as you see that the animal has fled. This is your test, specially if you find that there are signs suggesting that it may be wounded. A wounded animal will need your help to be put out of its misery; do not let it down!

If you are faced with a difficult shot, such as one through the bush, when you can see the animal clearly enough, but the bullet is likely to hit a twig before it hits the animal, do not take an unnecessary risk, unless you know that the beast is a wounded one, when any risk, other than that endangering a human life, may be taken.

Whatever you do, do not get impatient because you cannot see something at which to pull the trigger. Deer are sometimes difficult to spot unless they move, but they will spot any movement themselves. If you are impatient you will not be quiet, and you will never find a quarry.

When you have shot an animal learn as much about it as possible, not only memorise the antlers but try to estimate its age (even if it means admitting that you have made an error). On your return you are bound to be asked questions by those interested in the forest; help them by giving then the fullest possible information.

Having shot the deer, do not leave it where it was, make sure it is in as cool a place as possible where, specially in summer or early autumn, the sun warming it up will accelerate decomposition. And to follow up on the same trend, gralloch it. Too many people who are keen on stalking are unable to gralloch a beast. It may be a dirty job but it is not difficult, and in many parts of the world if you cannot gralloch you are not allowed to stalk. In summer this is very important, and the gralloch should be done as soon as possible and the animal left to cool in a shady dry place.

If you are calling but have not had a lot of experience do not forget that a faulty call can upset a large area; and therefore if you are not certain that your calls are correctly produced, do not wander from one place to another calling and upsetting everything everywhere.

Having secured one animal do not be greedy and ask for another; if you are meant to have more than one you will be offered it, but if you are not, you may place your host or your guide in the unenviable position of having to refuse your request. At all costs do not take the law into your own hands and shoot a second beast without even asking.

Remember that having accepted an invitation to shoot a stag or a buck you are under a moral obligation to accept an invitation to shoot a hind or a doe when the season for shooting the female deer comes

If you are to lead someone, a guest or even the owner, do not forget that he may be unaccustomed to the forest, which to you is your everyday bread and butter; if he makes errors do not hesitate to correct him; if he intends to make an obvious error, prevent it, but do it with tact.

Probably alongside the sporting-stalker the owner's or tenant's responsibility is the greatest.

He has the added task of economical running of the forest or estate, and the deer, as they are, represent an asset which is difficult to grasp. Only too often the economy of deer breeding and maintenance is placed on a warped platform, from which it slides, because of greedy tenants.

It may be worth to note the changes which have taken place in direct values of deer between 1958 and today. These are summarised in Table 24.

TABLE 24   Red deer stalking fees and venison prices, 1958–1986

	as quoted in 'Wild Deer' 1957/8	as quoted in 'Deer Management' at 1970 prices	as for 1985/86 season
Average stalking fees–red deer Scotland	£20	£20–40	£130–160
Compared with the Continent°	£200	£830–1250	£1,000–£3,000
Venison	1s.8d.=10p	17.5p	75–80p

If one accepts that stalking has a value, than one would have expected that this value would move with such forces as inflation or the law of supply and demand. And yet the analysis of stalking fees suggests that the movements have been no more than marginal in the last few years.

For instance, an estate that charged £100 per stag in 1978, charged £140 in 1985; inflation pressure alone, between these dates would dictate that the 1985 fee should have been about £185. If one considered also the international value of sterling in the same time had dropped by between 30% and 50%, a further increase in stalking fees would have been warranted on that account, specially considering that fair proportion of stalking in Scotland is being let to overseas visitors.

As against the stalking fees, the venison had retained its market value much better. °

It is interesting, in this context to note, that the Forestry Commission and some stalking agencies, have started charging fees for better quality antlers, on a scale related to the C.I.C. point scores, whilst others, including some private owners have developed other, simpler methods, some based on antler length and spread (for red deer), others on numbers of tines and weights (other deer).

Appendix 1/XVI: Proposal for Stalking Fees

In its concept, the stalking fee proposal in the example which follows is self explanatory. It aims at improving the benefit which estates derive from letting out the stalking.

In itself the method is clear, but maybe the 'Notional Fee' needs elaboration.

The Notional Fee at £300 and £120 for red deer and roe deer respectively had been plucked out from the sky. In reality it needs to be set so that, on one hand the level of fees do not frighten the potential tenant, on the other hand that it is realistic in consideration of the various forces. It is also necessary, to respond to these forces from year to year, and adjust the Notional Fee up (or down).

It can be said with a high degree of certainty, that most of the overseas stalkers, who have experienced the 'Trophy value' approach to the charges levied (say on the Continent) would understand an approach which dictates that they pay more for better heads and less for poorer. One could even simplify the concept and retain a flat charge (at a reasonable level) for poor quality heads, say red deer antler of 8 points and less and very light weight, or roe deer short and thin, and only resort to a graded charge for the higher quality trophies.

° Note: As a result of the Chernobyl accident and the consequent fear of contamination, the market value of venison originating from Northern Europe, has dropped; there are reasons to believe, however, that a recovery will be staged in the future few years.

Proposal for stalking fees

		Red deer	Roe deer
1	Take the best head from the previous year, shot under conditions of selective shooting (therefore *not* a privileged guest's trophy), and		
	a measure weight	3.5 kg	250 g
	b measure length	90 cm	21 cm
	Assume that this is the best the tenant is likely to obtain this year.		
2	Relate to a normally formed head of about CIC bronze standard and assume that the 'Notional Fee' for such head would be	4.5 kg 90 cm £300	325 g 23 cm £120
3	Make a weight percentage comparison between the best head (as at 1) and the CIC standard (as at 2) and apply to it the Notional Fee. This is the 'Local Fee for the Year'	$\frac{3.5}{4.5}$ x 300= = £233	$\frac{250}{325}$ x 120= = £85
4	Measure the head shot by the tenant	2.75 kg 105 cm	275 g 20 cm
5	Make a percentage comparison with the best head from the previous year and apply the Local Fee for the Year. This is: *The Head Fee*	$\frac{2.75}{3.5}$ x 233= = £183	$\frac{275}{250}$ x 85= = £93
	Additions:		
6	For weight and length in excess of CIC standard additional fee is as follows:		
	Excess *Additional fee(%)* 10–14.9% 10 15–19.9% 20 20–24.9% 30 25% and over 50	$\frac{105}{90}$ = 16.6% £36.60	
7	For CIC medal placing: Bronze medal 15 Silver medal 20 Gold medal 30		
TOTAL FEE DUE		£219.60	£93

Chapter XVII

STALKING RIFLES

Requirements — Choice of Ammunition — Safety

T he fact that the market today can offer a very wide variety of rifles for stalking, most of them with various types of ammunition, is in itself proof that some of them must be less suitable for stalking than others. Needless to say, each type and make has, especially in the gunsmith's sales talk, its advantages; the disadvantages are omitted, and it is left to the stalker to find them out.

The selection of a stalking rifle depends to a very large extent on the stalker's personality, his habits, likes and dislikes, and, of course, on the type of game to be stalked.

In the selection of weapon various features must be considered: safety in use (in relation to the inhabitants), humaneness in killing, and the weight of the weapon are primary considerations.

It must be admitted that a crack shot with expert knowledge of the animal's physiology and of ballistics, can be extremely effective with any of these weapons when shooting deer. Indeed Bell, the famous big game hunter, has shot a lion with a rim-fire .22 using long rifle ammunition; but how many stalkers can honestly compare themselves with Bell for marksmanship and skill in game shooting?

We must remember that the physical data of the bullet derive from the formula:

$$\text{energy} = \frac{m \times v^2}{2}$$

where m is mass (weight) of bullet in grams and v is velocity at the point of strike in metres/second.

It will thus be seen that for production of energy, bullet weight and velocity at the time of strike are all-important factors. When we consider further that a light bullet loses velocity faster than a heavy one when combating the resistance of the air or any other matter, solid, liquid, or gas, we realise that with constant value for m (bullet weight) the energy will drop quicker with a light bullet than with a heavy one.

Let us next consider the effect of the bullet on a living animal which is hit, and fit the energy, velocity and any other characteristics of the bullet into their right 'pigeon-hole' so as to get the bullet strike and its result in the right perspective.

The effect of the bullet strike is multiple. It consists of the effect on the nervous system, cardiac system, and on the living tissue. It is as a result of the destruction of tissue in certain areas that a subsequent haemorrhage is caused.

Considering these effects individually we find that upon impact of the bullet, the nervous reaction causes a condition similar, but not equivalent, to paralysis. We shall call the state pseudo-paralysis, though this is not the correct medical terminology. The pseudo-paralysis increases as the striking velocity of the bullet increases. At low velocities of about 1000–1400 ft/sec (305–427 m/sec) its value is so negligible that outwardly the state of pseudo-paralysis cannot be noticed; with the increase of velocity, however, the pseudo-paralysis increases and at a velocity of approximately 3000 ft/sec (914 m/sec) is very considerable.

The effect on the cardiac system mounts the nearer a strike of high energy is to the heart or the main arteries. This produces shock in the blood stream and causes, or may cause, a temporary stoppage of the bloodflow and heart action.

Both these reactions depend very much on the nervous condition of the animal at the time of strike. For instance, an animal not expecting a hit, i.e. unaware of anyone's presence, unalerted, will suffer a heavier shock, and a deeper state of pseudo-paralysis, than an animal on the alert.

The destruction of living tissue depends on a number of factors; it can be generally said, however, that the weight of the bullet, the velocity at the time of strike, the calibre and the expanding ability play important roles, and that all are primary contributory factors to which haemorrhage is only a secondary after-effect (taking the events in chronological sequence). It may thus happen that with a well-placed bullet the effect of the haemorrhage may appear only when the animal is dead or dying, or at any rate unconscious.

From the above it will be seen that there is one component in the consideration of killing factors which is within the control of the 'shooter' using a sporting weapon; that factor is the selection of suitable ammunition by weight and expanding ability.

We have thus introduced into our considerations a new factor, the expanding ability of a bullet. This ability is dependent on the bullet construction of which there are the following basic types:

(a) *The solid non-expanding bullet* (for thick-skinned animals only).

(b) *The soft-nosed bullet.* The bullet envelope (jacket) is left open at the nose end and a lead core is inserted from the front. The envelope is then compressed so that the lead and the envelope form an integral unit. The expansion of the bullet will be affected by the amount of lead exposed. In general the soft-nosed bullet offers a slow rate of expansion after impact, but deep penetration. As it may be ideal for a broadside shot, where a bone has to be penetrated before the vital organ is reached, so if a 'soft passage' is encountered, the bullet may pass through the body only partially expanding or only mushrooming, thus wasting the bulk of its expanding power.

(c) *The soft-nosed split bullet.* This is the soft-nosed bullet, the jacket of which has four or more longitudinal cuts. The cuts allow for more rapid expansion.

(d) *The capped bullet.* This is a bullet in which the envelope extends only a short way beyond the parallel, while the rounded nose is covered by a soft metal cap. A small hollow is left between the front end of the lead and the inside point of the cap. The degree and rapidity of expansion depend on the size of the hollow on the metal selected for the cap.

Let us imagine that the bullet is fired and strikes an animal. Having upon impact created shock and pseudo-paralysis, it starts to destroy living tissue.

The tissue the bullet can meet in the animal's body can be soft (skin, muscle, fat, etc) or hard (bone and gristle).

We have already decided that on soft-skinned animals, at any rate of the type one is likely to encounter in the British Isles, expanding ammunition must be used because the solid steel or cupro-nickel bullet will drill a hole and pass through the body, continuing to travel at a lethal velocity for a considerable distance. Furthermore, the solid non-expanding bullet entering and leaving the body at a high speed produces only small lacerations in a soft-skinned animal, in which the blood congeals quickly and the haemorrhage which occurs is often self-sealed; depending upon the location of the wound an internal slow haemorrhage may take place, in which case death caused by loss of blood may be slow, the animal being able to move a considerable distance during the time and may be lost, as it will not have left a blood trail. Thus for reasons of safety and humaneness in killing solid ammunition is excluded by current legislation.

All of us are aware of the fact that the vital organs in an animal are mainly contained on the front of the body, where the thickest bones can be encountered by the bullet. The thickest of all is the front portion of the shoulder blade. The bullets to be selected therefore must be ones which will be capable of penetrating that thickness of bone and of expanding fully just after the bone has been penetrated.

Admittedly, most bullets of the expanding variety on entering even a fragile body will start the expansion sequence and will mushroom, and the wound will be torn as opposed to clean cut; but the effect of expansion will not greatly benefit the killing sequence; furthermore the mushroomed bullet may still be lethal by the time it leaves the body. By ensuring therefore that the ammunition selected will expand inside the body of the animal, we shall achieve not only maximum safety but also the highest degree of humaneness in killing, provided that expansion takes place after the bullet has reached the vital organs of the body.

Taking into consideration therefore the ballistics of rifles and ammunition and the expanding values of bullets, the details of which are in Table 25, we will soon come to the conclusion that in order to ensure clean kills which will be humane, and to give maximum safety to the population, the fast expanding ammunition of calibre suitable to the type of animal to be shot should be selected.

How does this affect the safety of human inhabitants?

A bullet, having struck the animal's body, and having expanded into fragments (at least two, of core and jacket), must be considered as a number of projectiles. At the moment of fragmentation (expansion) each fragment parting company travels at the same speed; but with varying weights the energies of fragments differ, and their velocity will vary in direct proportion to their weight. The energy being in direct proportion to weight and the lethal power in direct proportion to energy, the weight of fragments is the deciding factor in the retention of lethal power, and the velocity of fragments in square proportion to lethal power.

The first object in safety has thus been achieved; the expanded and fragmented bullet will be less lethal than the bullet would have been as a whole.

This does not, however, mean that the fragments will be safe. We must strive to ensure that a bullet disintegrates within the animal's body. It may be that the fragments will lose so much power penetrating the bones, etc. that they will be unable to penetrate the whole body, or having penetrated the body will be able to travel only a very short distance at lower than lethal velocity. It may, however, happen that the fragments having had a soft passage will be lethal, and a stop will be essential.

In the forest a stop butt is not a difficult problem. Provided there is a solid background of trees, behind the target in which the fragments can lose their energy, maximum safety has been achieved. Problems arise in the open country which is populated, specially in the case of a bullet missing its target. Just as in forest we should not fire when there is an inadequate background, so in open country a background of earth provides maximum safety of fire. In flat countryside this may not be available and in the mountains, firing at animals standing on the line of the horizon should be excluded, and firing up the slope should be avoided.

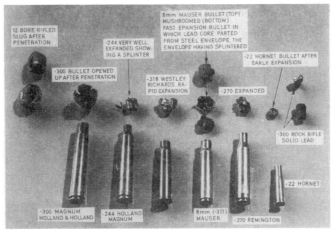

Plate XXIX Bullet expansion

TABLE 25   Typical ballistic tables*

Calibre bullet weight	Velocity-feet per sec.			Energy-ft/lbs			Sight at yards	Line of sight 1½ above centre of bore + indicates point of impact in in. above - in in. below sighting point.				
	Muzzle	100 yards	200 yards	Muzzle	100 yards	200 yards		25 yards	50 yards	100 yards	150 yards	200 yards
220 Swift 50gr/3.2 g	4110	3611	3133	1877	1448	1090	100	−0.9	−0.5	O	−0.2	−1.2
222 Rem. 50gr/3.2 g	3200	2650	2170	1137	780	520	100	−0.8	−0.3	O	−0.9	−3.2
22-250 53gr/3.4 g	3707	3192	2741	1616	1198	883	100	−0.9	−0.4	O	−0.5	−1.9
243 Win. 100gr/6.5 g	3070	2790	2540	2090	1730	1430	100	−0.7	−0.2	O	−0.9	−2.9
270 Win. 130gr/8.4 g	3140	2884	2639	2847	2401	2011	100	−0.8	−0.3	O	−0.8	−2.7
270 Win. 150gr/9.7 g	2800	2616	2436	2616	2280	1977	100	−0.7	−0.2	O	−1.1	−3.6
7 x 57 150gr/9.7 g	2755	2539	2331	2530	2148	1810	100	−0.7	−0.1	O	−1.2	−3.9
7 mm Rem. M. 150gr/9.7 g	3250	2960	2690	3519	2919	2410	100	−0.8	−0.3	O	−0.7	−2.4
7 x 64 150gr/9.7 g	2890	2625	2375	2779	2295	1879	100	−0.7	−0.2	O	−1.0	−3.3
30-06 130gr/8.4 g	3205	2876	2561	2966	2388	1894	100	−0.8	−0.3	O	−0.8	−2.7
30-06 150gr/9.7 g	2970	2680	2402	2943	2393	1922	100	−0.7	−0.2	O	−1.0	−3.4
30-06 180gr/11.6 g	2700	2493	2297	2914	2484	2109	100	−0.6	−0.1	O	−1.3	−4.1
308 Win. 130gr/8.4 g	2900	2590	2300	2428	1937	1527	100	−0.7	−0.2	O	−1.1	−3.7
308 Win. 150gr/9.7 g	2860	2570	2300	2725	2200	1760	100	−0.7	−0.2	O	−1.2	−3.8
308 Win. 180gr/11.6 g	2610	2400	2210	2725	2303	1952	100	−0.6	−0.1	O	−1.4	−4.5
303 British 150gr/9.7 g	2720	2440	2170	2465	1983	1569	100	−0.6	−0.1	O	−1.4	−4.4
303 British 180gr/11.6 g	2540	2340	2147	2579	2189	1843	100	-0.6	±0	O	−1.6	−4.9
8 x 57 J 196gr/12.7 g	2525	2195	1894	2778	2097	1562	100	−0.6	±0	O	−1.8	−5.8
8 x 57 JS 108gr/7.0 g	2976	2178	1562	2122	1137	585	100	−0.6	−0.1	O	−1.8	−6.1
8 x 57 JS 196gr/12.7 g	2525	2195	1894	2778	2097	1562	100	−0.6	±0	O	−1.8	−5.8

Notes
*Reproduced from Norma and Parker Hale Ltd catalogue; R. *Prior*, From *Modern Roe Stalking* (Tideline, 1985).

Part II

Deer Management Groups

Chapter XVIII

INTRODUCTION

There in increasing volume of evidence to prove that the management of red deer, and in some ways of other deer, based on the individual effort of an individual estate, is very difficult and in a long-term perspective success may be impossible unless the estate be a very large one and its deer well contained.

Deer wander, and under some circumstances migrate and spread and often therefore find themselves outside the jurisdiction or influence of a good manager. A given estate may be seriously implementing a sensible approach to its deer management, regarding the deer as an asset, only to find that having made a considerable effort, having invested time and money on improvements be it through selection of feeding, the deer have moved away, or someone else's deer have moved in.

To overcome this, the concept of Deer Management Groups had been developed and is increasingly practised to a lesser or greater degree of success, and an attempt is made here to present this concept, based on the experiences gained from working with one of the oldest and more successful Groups over a period of the last 20 years.

Many of the requirements may seem at first sight to be, to say the least of it, ambitious and at the onset may appear to be impractical, demanding and occasionally requiring a considerable change from the hitherto prevailing practices.

Such change, however, is needed. Many practices and customs which have originated in years gone-by have altered, more will do so in the future, and this applies not only to deer management. The changes which are advocated may take years before they are wholly accepted and implemented and this will depend on the flexibility of group members. The demands may seem frightening, but the benefits can be very considerable.

A large estate, self-contained as far as deer are concerned can apply everything that is being proposed, the only difference being that it may find many recommendations easier to implement as it does not require the cooperation of other estates.

If, some basic concepts of deer management are discussed in this part of the book, this is so because it is often more difficult to agree on a given course of action when there is a multiple participation in the decision-making process, than if the decisions are in the hands of one person.

197

Group Concept

A number of people with similar ideas can form a group; in the context of deer management, the Deer Management Group represents a number of estates. The Group must represent the estates within the natural deer range, the bio-mass within which deer move freely and naturally; hence the group is thrown together by the habits of deer within the range and not by the interests of a few isolated or dispersed estates. The estates must therefore be neighbouring.

Under normal conditions deer do not move very far. There is an increasing volume of evidence which suggests that deer, especially hinds, are localised, probably staying within a reasonable distance of their birthplace; they will move as a short-term measure to escape bad weather, to find better wintering with shelter, to find a mate during the rut, to escape seasonal human intrusion, but usually return to their home ground to drop the calves. Deer will of course also move as a long term measure when fenced off, when pressed by expansion of human habitation and industries or when shifted by development of new roads and railways or water reservoirs.

Deer ultimately become contained in their area (where there is no excessive intrusion) by geo-physical influence, mountain ranges, sizeable rivers, coastline or by artificial barriers such as major roads and rails or fences. Such containments are not absolute; deer will jump fences or find gaps in them, will cross even busy roads and railway lines and swim rivers, lakes and even seas.

The area within which deer are so contained and within which they freely move is referred to here as the deer range, and the Deer Management Group should comprise estates within such a range. It could be therefore that an estate divided by a motorway or a major railway line, or a major river or mountain range, which deer do not habitually cross, may find itself in two Management Groups; theoretically better this, than extending the Group activities to cover an area of two or more deer ranges, thus extending over land where conditions under which deer live, and problems which deer and owners face, are vastly different. The Red Deer Commission seem to have found at least a partial answer to this problem of different deer ranges by developing viable counting blocks.

Assuming that the Group representing a deer range decides to operate and co-operate, what are the problems which they are likely to meet?

Experience suggests that they are several.

An early problem is that of deer holding, how many deer are held by each estate, how many should there be and at what sex ratio; how many deer should be culled by the Group and how to distribute the cull in proportion to deer holding, acreage, practices and financial needs; how to distribute the cull in terms of stags and hinds. These are problems not only of the estates' manpower resources but also of revenue and capitalisation, issues upon which there may be conflicting views and interests affecting rates, possible rentals and use of resources where the agreement is central to the Group's success. The resolution to these problems may be crucial to each estate's well-being, leaving out for the time being opinions and practices which may be right or wrong and forgetting possible mistrust between the estates and their employees.

Then there is the problem of one-upmanship which may afflict the owners as much as the employees and which may affect the degree of co-operation between estates: I have better deer than you; you have shot my best stag in the area (or worse still you have shot my best stag when it strayed over the march); remarks like you attract my deer unfairly by feeding them.

Issues concerning economic standing of neighbouring estates can have a serious bearing on the level of co-operation within the Group; here the question may be that of being able to afford fencing or improvement of the hill, additional feeding or open winter grazing.

Another problem may be that emanating from the authority which representatives of the estates have, to commit to a certain course of action, this often concerns finances, utilisation of other resources, estate policy, etc.

There is the vexed question of selection of animals to be culled, the uniformity of the standards of selection.

A frequent problem may arise from the difference in the general approach to deer between the owner of the estate and the tenant, specially the tenant who takes the ground for a season or longer and therefore feels entitled to have more freedom to select what he wants, rather than a short-term tenant who is usually more controlled by the estate's stalker, keeper or other agent. A long term tenant may feel that he has the right to optimise the offtake of deer, if not in quantity then in quality; this may be a special problem with the trophy hunter who is ruthless and who not only wants to pack his house or his game book with royals and better, and see his name in yearly stalking reviews, but who will not shrink from bribing the stalker or keeper. In these circumstances, who is the rightful representative of the estate within the group, the owner or his factor, or the tenant.

Finally there are problems within the estate, each estate's working policies and practices: between the estates, the differences in policies and practices; between the Group and the environment in which they operate, and the different reaction to the pressures by each estate, be that pressure of political, economic, agricultural, silvicultural, industrial or even social nature. All pressures tend to create upsets.

Chapter XIX

A MATTER OF ATTITUDE

The success or failure of a Deer Management Group is a matter of team work, not only between each of the member estates, but also between the estates' employees.

Vertical co-operation within each estate, between the owner, agent/factor/manager, and employees at all levels is in general terms straightforward; co-operation between the estates and their tenants is more of a complex problem.

Co-operation within the estates may mean that during the stalking season and at odd times outside such seasons, the stalkers or keepers need help and support from others; this may be during the annual count, feeding on the hill, tending to ponies or other carcass retrieval methods. To be able to assist effectively, those estate employees should not only know the hill but need to know a fair deal about, and be interested in, deer and stalking, particularily if they help in deer counting, or if engaged in retrieval of shot beasts from the hill. The converse may also apply, the stalkers' and keepers' year may not consist of 12 months at full stretch on their primary job, so they, to secure willing and effective co-operation from others, need to be willing to offer help in other estate activities, be it shepherding, working in the forest, tending to live stock or anything else.

Equally important could be the co-operation with the tenant farmers, who often appreciate help from the estate or its employees, be it in loan of equipment or helping hands. They may suffer from marauding deer; how they react to them, or how willing they are to suffer from them, may well depend on the relationship between the estate and the tenant. The tenant should almost as of right, expect the stalker to help with marauders, and the stalker should react without hesitation, for this way he can ensure that his best beasts are turned off the ground instead of being shot.

A more difficult internal question is that co-operation from the stalking tenant, specially one who wants to optimise the return he gets from his stalking fees. To this end the tenancy agreement must be very carefully drawn up, not only stipulating what may be shot and who is in authority (usually the stalker), but include penalty and termination clauses even with forfeiture of fees, in instances of contravention of the rules (ideally without warning, i.e. for the first offence). A better method however, is an educational approach; such an approach seems to be practical with a long-term tenant who may be more amenable and educated in the moderm method of management of deer and be persuaded that he has an active role in it, by becoming involved and committed, gaining long-term interest and benefit himself.

But the greatest change of attitude is needed in achieving the total co-operation between the neighbouring estates' stalkers and in complete openness in exchange of information between the estates themselves.

To enable the Group to make decisions regarding their deer, all members of the Group must have a clear picture of each estate's approach to deer, their deer numbers, their culling figures, the quality of deer both culled and on the hill, the income from sale of venison and letting of stalking, intentions and plans regarding the beginning and closing of yearly cull, keepers perks, etc. In exercises such as the yearly count, the recovery of beasts from the hill, or access to the locations across the neighbouring estate where the very presence of the stalker with a tenant or guest could be questioned; culling near the march may be of critical importance to both estates and on such issues not only co-operation but complete trust in each other's integrity is needed, not only between the owners but even more so between the stalkers.

Such co-operation is not only sometimes difficult but is also often alien to the traditional privacy with which internal matters of the estate management have been treated, especially if they concern some important issues of policy and plans which in turn, if only peripherally, affect the deer.

Another change of attitude may be needed in the inter-estate rivalry; shooting better heads, heavier carcasses; higher calving rates; competition in better selection is always healthy, and even the rivalry such as mentioned may be healthy when the deer are all of top quality, but when it is a matter of one-upmanship at the Group development stage, it can be destructive.

Sometimes there may also be a difference in the prosperity of Group members; whether such prosperity is derived from the estate's profitability or from the owner's generosity is of secondary importance, what may be of consequence, however, is that the more prosperous estate can possibly afford better equipment, better access to the hill, improvement to the shelter and feeding of deer, etc. It is a nice gesture, often leading to better co-operation, if in such situations an estate offers help to its neighbour, not in finance, but in those little things which often make or break the life of the stalker.

The last change of attitude is that in respect of education.

An estate or group of estates forming a Management Group need to develop a progressive approach to deer. It becomes crucially important that deer both dead and alive can be aged, evaluated, carcasses checked for signs of disease; that records and statistics, such as have been agreed, are kept and shared. Many of these issues may be well understood within the member estates but all too often the understanding is not shared; there must be a willingness to exchange this information and if necessary to break away from some of the more harmful traditions of deer management looking for conservation and improvement of deer and through it improvement of prosperity of the Group and its members.

Chapter XX

THE COUNT

The annual deer count is probably the first activity that the Group must undertake. The count should be done by the combined resources of the Group involving at least the stalkers/keepers if not other employees, and covering the Group area as a whole. It is not good enough to rely on each estate reporting how many deer it holds. Deer have to be counted by a centrally directed team effort, and the count itself must be well planned, meticulously executed and fully reported. Only by such a combined effort will the count figure be accepted as being credible.

The organisation and conduct of the count can be a headache.

It is useful to carry out the main yearly count around about March, the time when deer are on the low ground and somewhat run down after winter; at such time they are less likely to move long distances when disturbed by the counting team. This time of the year also has other useful characteristics: firstly the stags have not shed their antlers and are therefore easily distinguished from hinds; secondly at that time the calves are not fully developed in body size, and can therefore be recognised and distinguished from the hinds. The count has of course to be carried out when the weather allows good observation and the staff engaged in it are not hampered by extremes of weather in which note making and map reading and marking can otherwise be difficult. As far as the weather is concerned therefore, fair weather should be forecast for a couple of days ahead as it is unlikely that the count over the entire area of the Group can be carried out in a single day.

How long the count will take and how many people are needed for it is a question which is impossible to answer in general terms. It very much depends on the size of the range and its geophysical characteristics; the more qualified people that can be assigned to the task the shorter it will last. Qualified counters need to be able to spot the deer effectively and therefore need to be adequately equipped, be able to read a map and make notes.

Ideally the arrangement for counting should be such that the employees of each estate cover at least partially the ground of other estates. The team should be positioned in a line abreast, members retaining intermittent visual contact with each other; they move forward along the ground retaining the line abreast, spaced in a manner whereby neighbouring counters can cover each other's dead ground. The general movement should be into wind, which moves deer either in herds or individually slowly ahead of the counters or sometimes allows them to break back between them.

It is quite usual to cover the area of a number of estates in several consecutive days; there are two approaches which are possible, one is to cover a comparably short distance by a large number of counters spread in a long line abreast, or covering a longer distance but on a narrower front; the counting on the following day starts where the first day's counting finished. The second approach is more useful in areas marked out by a number of natural barriers such as a range of mountains which divide the ground into a number of deer holding pockets like glens; several glens can thus be counted in one day. In either method the team moves on a predestined course marking the deer they spot on a map; as a minimum the marking should show the number of beasts spotted, their location, and a breakdown into stags, hinds and calves. More sophisticated counting would at the same time break down the deer into young and old (up to 4 years and over four years) and mark the stags as shootable and not shootable (see Fig. 37).

A very useful indication on the counting map is the direction in which the deer are moving for this helps in protection against double counting; it distinguishes between

deer moving into sight	→H15, C7
deer stationary	H15, C7
deer moving out of sight	H15, C7 →

Needless to say to be in radio contact is of enormous value as the information exchanged between neighbouring counters decreases the risk of double counting. By using walkie-talkies the counting teams can also be better controlled in their progress.

The Red Deer Commission suggest that an experienced stalker can cover an area of 3,000 to 5,000 acres in a day, although this may be somewhat ambitious unless the ground is fairly easy.

A deer count will provide working figures on which any subsequent plans can be built. It has to be remembered however that it will show the deer disposition figures in March/April, probably therefore on the deers' wintering ground, thus leading to a possible argument over each estate's holding of deer during the actual stalking season and there can be considerable differences between the two figures. This argument leads inevitably to the conclusion that from time to time a second count may be advisable, around the beginning of August, before the stalking (and game shooting) starts. Such a second count need not be done every year and of course by August, the calves that were counted in March/April will now be counted as adults, and new calves will be in evidence.

Why Count?

Counting is done to achieve the following:

1. To establish the number of deer within the group, and to provide a basis for working out the cull figure.

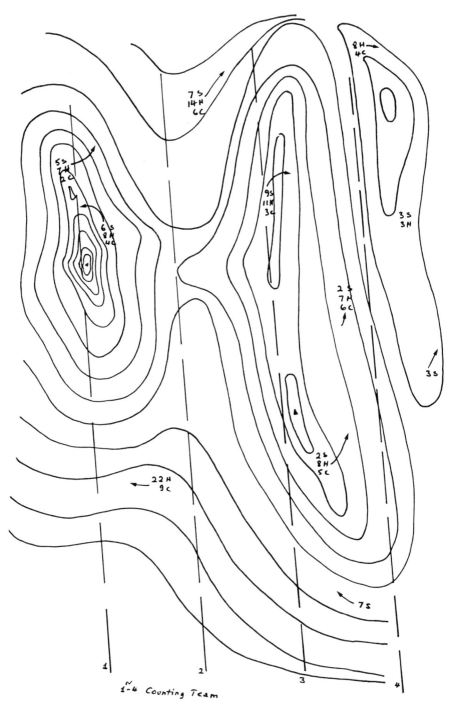

Fig 37   Deer count record map

2. To classify deer at least into stags, hinds and calves (but also to establish the quality of deer).

3. To increase the credibility of deer-holding figures within the Group, through counting as a joint inter-estate team effort.

How to Verify

Provided one has a fair assessment of natural mortality (including losses through poaching), it is possible to verify the count figure as follows:

TABLE 26   Count verification (or forecast)

	Stags	Hinds	Calves
Previous year's count	100	150	60
plus			
Calves (now adults) from previous year (50/50)	30	30	
plus			
Last summer calving (say 40%)			60
	130	180	60
less			
Shot last season	40	62	8
Mortality over winter	9	12	5
Expected for March	81	106	47

This method can also be usefully applied if the March/April count has gone disastrously wrong or had to be abandoned for whatever reason (usually the weather), and the culling quota for the year need to be established.

Forest Counting

In afforested areas, counting can be done as described above: other methods are described in Chapter III.

Chapter XXI

THE CULL PLAN

The cull plan for the Group and for each estate within the group must be discussed and agreed well in advance of the season. An early agreement (probably in April) will allow the estates who let their stalking to do so with the inclusion of the exact number of deer to be taken by the stalking tenants.

The agreement of cull figures may be difficult and several issues need to be resolved, some preferably in advance of cull discussion.

1. Total long-term holding of deer within the group must be clearly defined including an agreement on possible changes of deer-holding in the future. The total holding then must be broken down into stags and hinds.

2. An agreement must be reached on the accuracy of the last deer count.

3. If the total holding of deer is to remain unchanged, then the difference between the number of deer counted, and deer as the total holding indicates the size of the cull. This figure needs to be broken down into stags, hinds and calves.

4. From the total Group cull, each estates quota must be agreed recognising in relation to each estate the following:

(a) the size of each estate in terms of deer acreage and/or deer population;
(b) the importance of deer revenue to each estate or the commitment that the estates may have made in advance when letting their stalking;
(c) the resources which each estate has available and can allocate to deer stalking and culling (there is no point in allocating a quota which the estate is unable to fulfil).

5. The agreement must be wholehearted with complete commitment of each state as to its viability. (Therefore agreement by majority vote is not advisable.)

6. The agreed cull plan should be notified in writing as soon after the meeting as possible.

With a high level of overstocking of deer in parts of Scotland, it could be that the cull needs to be a savage one. In such instances it should be carefully considered how the heavy a cull should be undertaken, for increases in the cull in excess of 25–30% of the previous cull may disturb the animals too much; under such circumstances it may be necessary to extend the plan of reduction of numbers over a period of two or even more seasons.

Once the Group records have been kept for a few years, it is possible to adjust the various holding policies.

Firstly, it is likely that, no matter how diligently the annual counting has been done, the figure will show inexplicable peaks and troughs (over- and undercounting). These can be statistically smoothed out (usually on a four-year moving average basis, see Fig. 38).

Secondly, it is possible to review the effect of hind culls and their effect on the overall number of deer and make necessary adjustments, remembering that the effect of too low a cull will start showing itself after two and more years in the shape of increasing numbers of deer.

It is not usually appreciated that one hind left unculled may equal an addition of as many as 15 animals to the total population in a space of 7 years (see Table 27), hence it is always important to cull hinds rigorously, in this respect the stag cull is of lesser importance.

TABLE 27   One hind's 7-year 'production' achievement

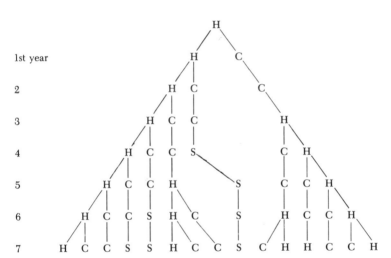

Note

This diagram indicates that the Hind (H), after a year has a Calf (C) so there are 1H and 1C; in the next year she has another Calf, resulting in 1H and 2Cs, in the third year the first Calf becomes a Hind (H) and starts producing her own; etc.

H–hind
C–calf
S–stag

Of course the size of the cull in relation to the total intended holding will be controlled to a large extent by the stocking policy of the Group, i.e. whether deer are to be managed for stalking or for venison and on the feeding potential which the range represents. Both issues are discussed in 'Group Policy'.

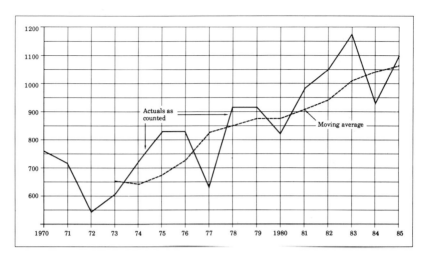

Fig 38   'Smoothing' of deer count by moving average

The Cull

The deer cull is the apex of deer management: not only is it the harvest, but also in the strife for improvement of deer, it is the most significant activity which has a direct bearing on the future, and when management of deer has been successful for a period of years, it provides the proof of success. The cull ensures that:

1. The number of deer taken off the hill reflects the stocking density policy.

2. The numbers taken of each sex are commensurate to and in accord with the sex ratio policy.

3. The poorest animals are culled, thereby maintaining the overall quality of the herds and any quality beasts taken are only those well past their prime and within sight of natural death.

4. There are no sanctuaries in which deer are protected by the difficulties of terrain, whilst others are overculled in more easily accessible areas, in order to fulfil the cull programme.

5. The cull numbers of each estate are:

(a) related to the estate's holding of deer;

(b) in accordance with the prearranged plan.

To be effective and economical, the cull should be carried out early in the season; stags should be taken before the rut, and hinds as early as possible during the season, before they start losing weight and before the bad weather hampers the already difficult selection process.

Such timing allows the estates to optimise their return from the sale of venison. A prudent stalker will however allow himself a small proportion of his cull quota to be kept in hand in case he finds a particular poor doer late in the season.

As explained before, it is essential for the well being of the deer that the poor quality specimens are ruthlessly taken out, even at the cost of marginally overshooting the cull quota.

Chapter XXII

GROUP POLICY

A t an early stage in the existence of the Group there is a need to establish clearly the general policy that the Group wants to follow and accept that unilateral changes to the policy as agreed, would have to be rediscussed.

Such policy will control the general approach to deer management and would cover such subjects as:

(a) the size of deer population;
(b) the business objectives of the group (deer for stalking or deer for venison);
(c) selection criteria (linked with business policy);
(d) deer population;
(e) feeding of deer;
(f) range sharing with domestic animals;
(g) forestry — access to deer;
(h) need for, and allocation of financial resources;
(i) approach to letting and venison sales;
(j) hikers, campers, etc.on the deer ground;
(k) method of dealing with possible internal and external pressures.

Whilst many of these topics are discussed in the appropriate chapters of Part I, some additional suggestions are outlined below, with a specific application to the Deer Management Group system.

Chapter XXIII

DEER POPULATION

The density of deer is a vexed question at the best of time, and is only marginally researched. An attempt to provide guidance is in Chapter III. The question of deer density needs to be explored by the Group and an understanding reached probably following and exploring topics such as:

General

What is the present density of deer?
What is the condition of deer at this density: calving rate; natural mortality age and rate; carcass weight; antler quality?
What is the condition of summer and winter grazing?
Are improvements of grazing possible/likely?
Is there an opportunity for additional feeding?
Is there a benefit to be had from improving the condition of the deer — is improvement practical?
Is there a marauding problem: attributable to overstocking; attributable to lack of winter feed/shelter; does it create social/political problem?
If deer improvements are desirable, could funds be made available?

Specific to Hill

Is adequate shelter available to deer in winter?
What are the owners intentions regarding range sharing with domestic animals?
Is there a likelihood of encroachment (agriculture, forestry, or other)?

Specific to Forestry

Is the age of the forest such that it needs: special protection; could be opened to deer (when)?
Is forest layout conducive to deer?
Is there an uneconomical level of damage?
Are the trees of a type especially vulnerable to damage?
Is forest cropping and replanting planned for the foreseeable future; what will be the effect on deer; can replanting be done with deer in mind? (See Chapter X.)

Chapter XXIV

BUSINESS OBJECTIVES

There are two basic business objectives of deer management which are incompatible.

1. deer for stalking — with venison as a useful by-product;
2. deer for venison — with stalking as a by-product.

The reason why the two objectives are not compatible is that they require completely different sex ratios and different age structures of the deer population.

The sex ratio at which deer are born, is about 1 : 1. Under natural conditions there is however a slight predominance of young hinds, the reason being that stags suffer a higher mortality rate at the young age (say up to three years), with a partial offset, in that hinds do not live generally to the same old age as the stags do.

For optimum natural development of species, one cannot beat what nature herself provides, and it is not surprising that deer thrive when the sex ratio is retained at the level of about 1 : 1 or very slightly higher hind population of say 1 : 1.2. Such a ratio gives a high number of stags available for culling, with a population retained to an advanced age, and it therefore suits the 'deer for stalking' policy. In a forest of say 2,000 heads equally divided between stags and hinds, and the calving rate (after first winter) of 40%, the yearly recruitment of animals would be that of 400 representing a cull of 400 (if the population density is intended to be maintained), and in such cull 200 stags and 200 hinds would be appropriate. In this policy, the age structure of stags would be 1 to 14 years (or older) and hinds 1 to 11 or 12.

A different picture is presented however in the deer for venison situation. Under this regime fewer stags are required, the stags are only needed in reality to fertilise the hinds and play their role in a high recruitment level. Here a sex ration of 1 : 3 in some instances even 1 : 4 or 1 : 5 may be acceptable in unfenced areas (bearing in mind the possible migration of stags in areas of high sex ratio situations), and even 1 : 8, a very high ratio indeed for normal conditions, might be acceptable in fenced areas.

Deer for Venison

In terms of selective culling, the deer for venison approach is much less demanding than deer for stalking, but there are two inherent problems; one is the size of the cull and the difficulties in culling a large number of males (calves and stags) in order to keep the stag population at a low figure. The other is the risk of population explosion if, for whatever reason, the hinds are underculled.

Let us assume that our deer forest is still the 2,000 head one — calves excluded. The lowest sex ratio that makes sense in deer for venison policy is 1 : 3, usually higher, bearing in mind that the higher the ratio the higher is the annual recruitment of calves, and the higher the recruitment the higher will be the cull of calves and yearlings. Furthermore, because the sex ratio of deer at birth is approximately 1 : 1, the higher the population sex ratio the more male calves and yearlings have to be culled (because fewer mature stags are required to maintain the overall population). The fewer mature stags there are, the fewer there are for stalking as a by-product of this policy (see Fig. 39).

At sex ratio 1 : 8 the number of stags is down to 222 and the complementing number of hinds is 1,778. Of the stags, 100 need to be at ages of 3 to the age of 6, thus say 25 at each age group, totalling 100, leaving space for 122 aged 2 year and yearlings, say 42 at the age of 2, and 80 yearlings. With the recruitment of 357 male calves, the cull should be 227. However to preserve the economic return from culling, this figure may have to be reduced, let us say by 50, with a corresponding increase in the more rewarding cull of yearlings by the same number. Such an arrangement, however, means that the overall number of adults (deer of age of one and above) becomes increased by 50 to above 2,000, and creates an extra pressure on the feeding capacity of the range.

The hind situation tends to be somewhat easier.

We have a total of 1,778 hinds aged 1 and above; their recruitment is also about 357 (the same as stags).

For breeding purposes we need hinds aged 3 to 7 and the simplest distribution of these is 220 at each age totalling 1,100, leaving a total of 598 for distribution between ages of 1 and 2; the equal distribution of 289 per age group, calls for a reasonable calf cull of 68 and no cull of yearlings. However, a high level of cull of calf-bearing hinds, may force us into higher calf cull because when a calf-leading hind is culled, her calf should be taken with her. In such a situation a cut may have to be made in the cull figures of young hinds aged 1 and 2 years to offset the calf-cull increase (Hoffman pyramid, see Fig. 40).

A similar logic can be applied to a ratio of 1 : 4 where we have 1,600 hinds and 400 stags.

In execution of this policy 400 stags are not needed for breeding purposes, so we can afford to optimise the return from stalking at a reasonable age by distributing 200 stags between the ages of 3 to 6, meaning that at each age group we have 50, thus allowing for a cull of 50 at the top of the age group. This leaves 200 to be distributed between the ages of 1 and 2 years, say 75 at the age of 2 and 125 at the age of 1. This distribution calls for a cull of 195 calves (to reduce the numbers from the 320 born to the required 125). Again an adjustment of numbers may be required for reasons of economics, and we could again reduce the calf cull by say 50, and increase the cull of yearlings by the same number. The same danger of increasing pressure on the feeding resources as mentioned in the 1 : 8 ratio above, has to be considered.

The situation on the hind cull is that we now have 1,600 hinds aged 1 year and over. The recruitment is 320. For breeding we need hinds aged 3 to 7, say 200 at each age group, totalling 1,000 and leaving 600 to be distributed between ages of 1 and 2, for the sake of simplicity this can be taken as being 300 yearlings and 300 two-year olds, thus leaving only 20 to be culled. Such a low cull may not be practical for reason's already mentioned (culling of calf-leading hinds) and an adjustment may be required in culling more calves and decreasing the yearling cull accordingly,

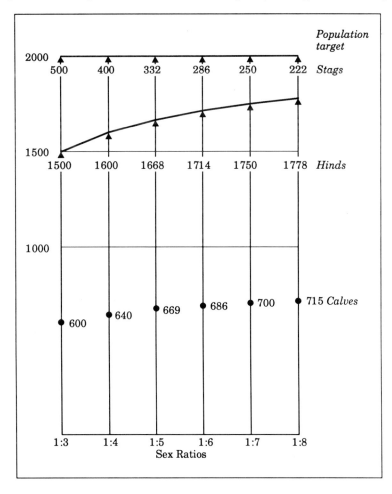

Fig 39   Deer for venison - headcount comparisons

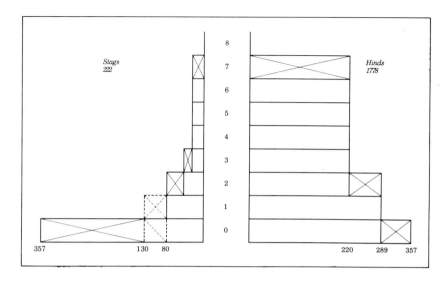

Fig 40 Deer for venison: ratio 1:8

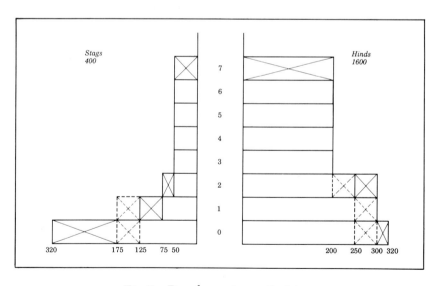

Fig 41   Deer for venison: ratio 1:4

and even spreading the adjustment to 2 year-olds (see also Hoffman pyramid, Fig. 41).

Deer for Stalking

For the sake of comparson using the same deer population of 2,000, we have 1,000 stags and 1,000 hinds all at ages of 1 year and over.

The recruitment from 1,000 hinds would be 400 calves, 200 male and 200 female.

The age pyramid and the culling structure are shown in Fig. 42.

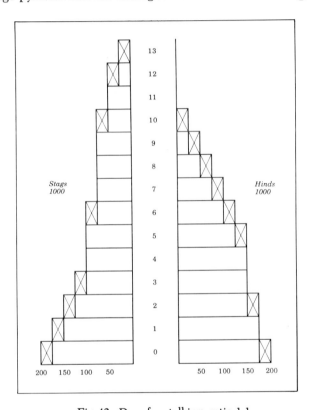

Fig 42   Deer for stalking: ratio 1:1

In Table 28 is a comparison of financial return one could expect from the different policies. Basic assumptions reflect the price levels at the time of writing. But in considering the relative advantages one has to pay particular attention to the following:

1. The price of venison has been slowly rising as a result of high demand for venison on the Continent. In response to this demand the venison production has increased through deer farms, and more venison is being supplied by New Zealand and Eastern European countries. At the same time the internal market within the United Kingdom has not been fully

exploited. It is difficult therefore to predict the future pricing of venison be it for export or for internal consumption.

2. Stalking on the other hand is perhaps more predictable. The popularity of stalking is increasing within the United Kingdom and abroad and the availability of stalking on the Continent seems to be slowly falling. At the same time, with careful management of deer and improvement of quality of trophies, the value of stalking could easily increase both in terms for basic fees (i.e. just for the privilege of participating in the sport) and in possible opportunities in the future of charging a premium for good heads, even if the achievement of quality standard at level of CIC medals, on the Scottish hill is unlikely. (Income comparison is in Table 28.)

TABLE 28   Deer management groups: revenue return:
stalking v. *venison policy*

Policy		Stalking		Venison			
Ratio		1:1		1:4		1:8	
Cull		No.	Value	No.	Value	No.	Value
A	Stalking fees £150/beast	150	22,500	50	7,000	25	3,500
B	Stalking premium on 25% of stags at £50	37	1,850	–		–	
C	Venison at 80p						
	stags 140 lb	150	16,800	75	8,400	80	8,960
	yearlings 140 lb	25	1,400	50	5,600	50	5,600
D	Venison at 80p						
	hinds 100 lb	175	14,000	250	20,000	289	23,120
	yearlings 100 lb	25	2,000	50	4,000	–	
E	Venison						
	calves male 70 lb	25	1,400	145	8,120	227	12,712
	calves female 70 lb	25	1,400	20	1,120	68	3,808
			61,350°		54,240		57,700°°

° An increase in stalking fee of £20/beast produces an additional £2,800, and increase in quality premium to 33% of stags equals an additional £2,500.

°° The penalty is in very high number of calves that need to be culled at uneconomical weights.

Chapter XXV

SELECTION

Selection of deer to be culled and retained will differ drastically between the two basic management principles of deer for stalking and deer for venison. In deer for venison, selection is of low importance.

Deer for Stalking

Stags

Our aim here is to improve the quality of stags and to develop a herd which is strong in antler, of a minimum of 10 points and better at the age of full maturity. To this end the aim is to cull stags with poor heads and those which do not show a promise of good development. We then preserve the stags with good potential both for propagation, and for stalking by the time they reach full maturity and possibly even at the age when they start to go back; rarely therefore would we aim at shooting a good stag younger than 9 or 10 years old. The main emphasis in the selection policy is to get rid of all poor quality antlers.

To this end deer recognition is a most important facet of deer management.

Hinds

As far as hinds are concerned we need a healthy stock of fertile hinds of good parentage. Those hinds which are good mothers and which produce strong calves are retained; also young and middle-aged hinds, and those healthy ones which are yield having a rest from production for one season, after which a strong calf is usually produced. The concentration is therefore on poorer quality hinds. As long as a hind produces good calves she should be kept and will produce between six and eight young in her lifespan. Those hinds which are leading hinds in a herd are also retained and shot only when we need to split the herd into smaller units.

All this having been said, the numerical control of hinds is still of a paramount importance, even if in it a proportion of good and valuable hinds have to be culled.

Chapter XXVI

FEEDING

Chapter IV discusses feeding of deer at some length. Here we are considering the Management Group's approach to it. It is important for the Group to make up its mind on the issue of additional feeding and the best method to introduce it. Artificial feeding once started, should continue throughout the winter and in quantities which provide for all the beasts; it should not be limited to small amounts, on the fringes of the estates or only in locations easily accessible, unless deer can be attracted to such locations.

As mentioned elsewhere, there is a danger in one estate feeding deer while others do not (assuming that deer dispersion is even throughout the estates). Such practice may attract deer from one estate to another, creating a concentration of deer artificially and leading to possible internal conflict. It could of course happen that one estate has poorer quality grazing on the hill and as a result has to provide additional feed to safeguard their deer. Such instances need to be discussed at the Group meetings so that everyone is aware of the position.

In many ways the most beneficial method is through provision of small areas with suitably selected feeding vegetation, even if the access to such areas is allowed only on a seasonal basis.

In a way a similar situation may develop with shelter.

Deer will seek shelter in bad weather: it may be provided by the terrain, to where they will soon find their way or it can also be provided by an unfenced woodland, which may be available on one estate and not on the others. Again, deer will find their way to it if they need it. In both instances however, shelter of long standing will not upset the natural disposition of deer; deer will return to their normal locations when the need for shelter has ceased.

A different situation arises if an area of forestry is unexpectedly opened to deer.

Being a new shelter, it will upset the normal routine of short-term migration in search of shelter. More deer than had been expected may possibly enter the newly opened forestry and this may have a two fold effect: some deer may take up permanent living there, others may use it as wintering shelter, but because they gather in numbers, the forestry may be exposed to an unexpected level of damage through excessive numbers of deer gathering in a small area.

It is also worth noting that once the forest has reached a height of some 3 to 5 metres, it also provides shelter, even when well fenced, because it creates a wind barrier; deer will tend to gather to the lee of it; this is of course the area where, during snow falls, drifts will form, and this is the time when deer may be able to jump the fence, the drifts forming a deer leap. For this reason it is important to plant trees a sufficiently large distance away from the fence to allow for drifting inside the fence.

Chapter XXVII

GROUP MEETINGS

To a large extent, the success of the Group will depend on the effectiveness of its meetings and how well and conclusively the members can discuss their problems and arrive at acceptable decisions in unanimity.

Group meetings are the formal opportunity for discussions concerning the Group and therefore are the occasions when the decision-making body which governs the activities makes its presence felt. Ideally the Group should have a chairman whether permanent and elected or appointed for the occasion is of no consequence. What is of consequence is the manner in which he conducts the meetings and steers them to the achievement of its objectives.

Practice suggests that there are many questions which arise at the meeting and which need a discussion and a conclusion and that in many discussions stalkers/keepers should participate. It is essential to the success of the Group that the views, opinions and advice of the stalkers/keepers be taken into account and they be included in the decision-making process; only this way will they be fully committed to the decisions.

It is also important that in all discussions all the necessary information is easily available.

One could envisage a standardised agenda for the meetings should include the following:

1. full record of last deer count;
2. previous seasons' cull programme and estates' quota;
3. report on fulfilment of cull quota;
4. presentation of previous season's heads;
5. proposals for next seasons cull and estates' quotas;
6. estates' report on condition of deer;
7. summary of Group's achievements;
8. disposal/sale of venison;
9. letting or stalking; tenants;
10. proposed policy changes.

It is quite likely that there may be issues which require further and more confidential discussion. To this end a second meeting should be convened to be attended purely by the owners or similar estate representatives.

Although mention has already been made of the level of estate represent-ation at the Group meetings, it is here that issue comes to its own. The Group needs to make decisions, discuss and commit to courses of action which may have far reaching consequences. An estate which is represented by someone who is not in a position to commit that estate to a course of action undermines the validity of the Group, and what is more destroys the purpose of the meeting. It must be accepted therefore by all partici-pating estates that the main representative of the estate has full authority to make decisions, and does do not have to refer elsewhere.

As far as discussion of the agenda is concerned the explosion of agenda points below may be of help.

Item 1.   *Record of deer count.* Has the count been successful, how could it have been better; was the timing correct; were arrangements adequate; does it stand up to scrutiny? What was the condition of the deer; were deer grouped in overlarge herds; were there any significant changes in location of deer? Does the count suggest over- or under-stocking; is the sex ratio as counted credible; is there a need for its adjustment to meet the group policy or as a result of a policy change?

Item 2 & 3. *Last season's cull.* Has the cull been met by the Group; has it been met by the individual estates? What was the condition of deer during the season; what were the weights in comparison with previous season(s)? What was the age structure of deer culled? Did the Groups and the estates meet any difficulty in completing the cull? Did any estate under- or overshoot the quota — why; how many had to be shot as marauders; what is the effect of marauder shooting on the overall cull?

Item 4.   *Presentation of last season's antlers/jaws.* All antlers of stags shot (including marauders) should be displayed, each set of antlers to be accompanied by the stags lower jaw. Lower jaws of hinds should also be presented. All deer shot should be aged; all antlers should be commented on (was the stag shot suitable for shooting) . Where antlers have been taken away by the guest or tenant large photographs of good quality should be displayed in the place of antlers. It is advisable that ageing and shootability evaluation should be done either by a team representing the estates but preferably by an unbiased assessor. Adverse comments about stags shot should be regarded not as criticisms but as learning points for the benefit of all concerned.

Item 5.   *Next seasons cull.* The total number of deer by sexes to be culled by the Group, and each estates quota, must be agreed by all. Any significant changes must be fully discussed and explored. Of special importance is the question of over- or under-population or any changes in sex structure of the stock and how should this affect the cull plan.

Item 6.   *Condition of deer.* This item is of special importance if an improvement programme has been in progress or a need for its introduction is perceived. If an improvement programme is to be introduced, it should be explored here and plans laid for the future.

Item 7. *Group achievements.* Has the Group been successful in achieving its aims and if not, can the rate of success be improved. In very large Group areas it may be worth discussing the differences in the Group's operation at the extremes of area and the difficulties which the size represents.

Item 8. *Disposal of venison.* Success and problems in the relationship with dealers; price structure for the forthcoming season.

Item 9. *Letting and tenants.* Have the estates experienced difficulties in letting their stalking; difficulties as regards control of tenants? Are prices acceptable and are there any possible changes. Do the estates optimise the return from letting stalking?

Item 10. *Policy changes.* (Sometimes needs discussion without stalkers/keepers present.)

Having gone through the agenda with the keepers present, the owners may need to continue their discussion on items which are confidential. In such case there should be no changes made to those decisions which directly affect the stalkers and which have been taken in their presence.

TABLE 29   Matrix of 4-dimensional pressures and influences upon deer management groups°

1	2	3	4
Deer	*Estate*	*External*	*Group*
Stock numbers	Available range	Local politics	Stock numbers
Sex ratio	Agricultural interests	Farmers & tenants	Sex ratio
Quality	Cattle & sheep on the hill	Forestry Commission	Quality of deer
Natural feed	Forestry	Roads and rails	Feeding of deer
Shelter	Business diversification	Tourism	Shelter for deer
Deer movements (weather/rut)	HIDB	Support/animosity	Movement of deer
Fencing	Manpower & other resources	Red Deer Commission	Fencing
Poaching	Letting	Development plans	Poaching of deer
	Impact of external developments		Disagreements
	Revenue/capital		Selective culling
	Personalities & emotions		Personalities & emotions

Note
°Nearly each of the items in each of the dimensions can interact with each or most items in the other three dimensions and there may be other pressures.

It is usually useful to make the Group meeting where stalkers are present into a social occasion where the stalkers and owners can meet and discuss any deer matters informally. A useful adjunct to such gathering is the presentation of last season's trophies.

Keepers' competition

It is a very useful addition to the meeting to have a keepers' competition (in which the owners could and should participate). Such competitions are useful educational exercises. The topics which can well be covered are:

1. age estimation by tooth formation, (probably about 20 to 25 sets of jaws to be aged by each keeper. This item can be repeated);
2. measuring of heads by British and Continental methods;
3. evaluation of shootability of stags from photographs; to include a short justification of keeper's decision (can be repeated);
4. comment on selected number of heads and jaws;

It is usually advisable to have an independent adjudicator for competitions who also provides a set of answers and explains his evaluation.

Annex to Part II:

SOME DISORDERS OF RED DEER (*CERVUS ELAPHUS*) IN SCOTLAND

Dr A. McDiarmid, D.Sc; Ph.D.; M.R.C.V.S; F.R.C Path; F.R.S.E.

Until comparatively recently the causes of death in deer have not been systematically investigated and very little has been published. Most of the records come from zoological collections where the animals are living under abnormal conditions and are often kept well beyond the age to which they survive in the wild. It appears that, on the whole, British deer are remarkably healthy.

Accidents and Mortality

Accidents are common in all deer and most injuries are associated with cars, snares (particularly those set for foxes), wire fences, nylon netting, shotgun and to a lesser extent rifle wounds. It is a remarkable fact that severe injury to the lower limbs does not necessarily lead to death. Sometimes the whole foot may be lost and yet the stump heals successfully. Broken legs heal well but with various degrees of distortion; infection rarely becomes established even in severe complicated fractures.

Ectoparasites

The warble fly in deer (*Hypoderma diana*) is quite distinct from that affecting cattle and the presence of deer does not therefore impede any warble eradication scheme in cattle. Warble damage to deer skins in the south of England has not be recorded but red deer in Scotland are frequently badly affected.

The nasal or bot fly (*Cephanomyia auribaris*) probably occurs in the southern counties of England and yet its presence in deer in those areas has never been proved; deer have been observed exhibiting the characteristic signs associated with the presence of these flies. The red deer in the northern counties of Scotland seem to be the ones mainly affected.

Occasionally, secondary strike occurs in wounds on deer but this is rare.

In Scotland the head fly (*Hydrotaea irritans*) can cause considerable distress in July and August, especially to stags in velvet, and could be a contributing factor to their diminished food intake at this time of year.

Lice, particularly the biting louse (*Damalinia meyeri Taschenberg*) may be more common than we think. Few records are available but infestation seems to occur mainly in the spring of the year, almost causing a premature moult in some animals. The deer keds (*Lipoptena cervi*) are unusual insects widely distributed in most deer. They seem to be at their maximum concentration in midsummer. Very large numbers can have a debilitating effect.

The tick (*Ixodes ricinus*) is probably the most important ectoparasite of deer. Hundreds may be present on one deer. Apart from the obvious damage they do, in heavy concentrations on red deer calves, the ticks are important vectors of disease such as tickborne fever, louping ill and redwater fever. Infection with tickborne fever is common in many deer herds. No clinical condition has, however, been attributed to this infection in deer, contrary to the situation in cattle and sheep.

Redwater fever has been found in red and roe deer, but attempted transmission to bovine calves has failed. Recently the infection has been passed to captive red deer. So far the parasites have not been shown to affect cattle and it is possible that those *Babesia* are species-specific.

Endoparasites

So far as helminths are concerned there is still very little known about these parasites in British deer. The vast majority of cervine helminths found in the intestinal tract are common to various species of deer and domestic animals. They are mostly *Trichostrongylus* spp in the abomasum, particularly *T. aexi*. The worm burden is low in the small intestine and deer do not appear to be important reservoir hosts for these worms. Under natural conditions in the wild, the nematodes in the intestinal tract seem to be of little pathological importance, although problems arise under intensive park conditions.

Hydatid cysts due to *Echinococcus granulosus* are, fortunately, extremely rare in all species, although small cysts *(Cysticercus tenuicollis)* are often found in the omentum and sometimes in the lungs and it is feasible that a fox/deer cycle operates in remote areas where dogs are not directly involved.

The two important helminths of deer are *Fasciola hepatica* and *Dictyocaulus* sp. although clinical disease is rarely encountered except in roe. Red deer appear to have a basic resistance to the parasite. For example, in an area of Wester Ross where an attempt was made to establish a health profile of the red deer, sheep died in hundreds during one particular winter from fascioliasis. Despite this, red deer on the same ground showed only slight scarring of the liver and no clinical disease. In many deer no eggs were detected and if they were, they never exceeded 50 per g of faeces. Recent work in Canada confirmed that the white-tailed deer (*Odocoileus virginianus*) is also extremely resistant to experimental infection with

Fasciola hepatica. One could argue that the behavioural pattern of the red deer on the hill takes them away from the infected snails at the time when they are most likely to be infective in midsummer. There can be little doubt that red deer are extremely resistant.

Parasitic pneumonia

This is probably the worst disease of roe. Fallow and sika appear relatively resistant under free-living conditions and red deer, although frequently infected, hardly ever exhibit clinical signs.

So far as roe are concerned, the lungworm performs the same role in some areas that the liver fluke plays in others. Many roe under a year old die from parasitic pneumonia and when roe are confined in a small paddock this is always the principal cause of mortality.

Protozoal Diseases

Recently, in the UK, it has been shown that roe and red deer carry Babesia without obvious ill-health. Transmission experiments in splenecto-mised bovine calves have so far failed, although the infection has been transmitted to susceptible red deer calves by experimental inoculation.

Rickettsial Infections

Tick-borne fever originally thought to be a rickettsial infection and now classified in the genus *Cytoecetes*, is common in all the main species of deer in the tick-infested areas in the UK, without apparent clinical disease. The infection can readily be transmitted to cattle and sheep by experimental inoculation and it can cause abortion in these animals: susceptible deer from a non-tick area might well exhibit similar symptoms on their first meeting with the TBF agent.

Bacterial Diseases

Many of the superficial pyogenic conditions probably arise from mech-anical contamination of wounds by bacteria such as *Corynebacterium pyogenes*; occasionally more deep seated abscesses in joints and tendon sheaths are found. Sometimes streptococcal infections occur at the site of tick-bite but do not compare with the staphylococcal infection of hill lambs.

Brucellosis

Some serological evidence of this infection has been obtained in free-living deer in the south of England, but a more recent survey has not shown any evidence of antibody, or clinical disease, e.g. abortion.

Leptospirosis

Although common in a great variety of wildlife, cases of leptospirosis in deer are rare. Isolated cases have been found in roe and red deer.

Salmonellosis

This is virtually absent from deer. Only one strain of *S. dublin* has been isolated from a New Forest fallow in the UK despite an intensive search for such organisms over a period of many years.

Clostridial infections are also virtually non-existent. This is surprising when one considers the opportunities that red deer have for contracting the sheep diseases, such as brazy, pulpy kidney and lamb dysentery. Anthrax and tetanus have never been encountered even in areas where the incidence of such infections is high in this country.

Tuberculosis

About twenty years ago, several golden eagles were found dead or dying in the Cairngorm and Grampian mountains in Scotland. Post mortem examinations confirmed these birds died from avian tuberculosis. Consequently, a detailed study was made of blue hares, grouse and ptarmigan to see if any of these could be a source of infection. All were free from tuberculosis. It was, of course, known that grallochs and carcasses of red deer dying naturally on the hill were also part of the eagle's diet. Shortly afterwards, a stag was shot near Braemar, the inside of the abdomen and thorax were studded with white nodules. Microscopic examination revealed masses of tuberculosis organisms; tests confirmed these to be the Avian type. Tuberculosis in mammals can be caused by any of the three main types of tuberculosis bacilli, i.e. human, bovine or avian, and post mortem findings can be virtually the same in some instances. The situation with regard to the golden eagles was now clear — it would be possible for them to ingest infection from deer carcasses on the hill.

The question still remained as to how the deer became infected. The predatory birds were too few to cause any trouble. Deer will, however, eat cast antlers and the bones of their deceased relatives to supplement their meagre source of minerals.

Another feature of this form of tuberculosis is the effect on the antlers. They were very thin in the beam, light in weight and light in colour — all indicative of a serious metabolic disorder. Local stalkers had seen similar heads associated with poor-bodied stags. Several hundred 'normal' deer were examined, from different areas. By removing the lymph node at the junction of the small and large intestines it was possible to isolate a number of strains of the organism by culture. About 5% of all red deer examined yielded cultures — stags and hinds seemed equally affected without clinical disease necessarily being apparent.

Nine cases of clinical disease have been recorded in red deer — all in Scotland. Maybe the rigours of the Scottish climate, overstocking through bad management, and consequent lack of food all helps to create a degree of stress so that the animals are more prone to disease.

Fortunately, human and bovine strains are rarely isolated from deer. Cases of both have occurred in the European Continent. In recent years 4 cases of bovine infection in roe and sika have been found in England near known infected badger sets. Unfortunately we still have a considerable amount of bovine infection by badgers, particularly in Cornwall, and it would not be prudent to set up deer farms anywhere near such infected areas.

Anyone finding suspicious looking nodules in a deer carcass should seek veterinary opinion before preparing it for the table or consigning it to the deep freeze. At the same time, 'piners' on deer forests should always be shot and, if at all possible, disposed of in such a way that the deer cannot gain access to them and thus perpetuate the infection.

Viruses

The distribution of viruses in British deer is not yet known. Fallow deer in Hampshire have shown evidence of mucosal disease antibodies but this is rare. Louping ill virus has never been isolated from free-living deer in this country although a very high proportion of Scottish red deer carry antibodies, as many as 40% in some areas, but no clinical cases have ever been recorded.

Foot-and-mouth disease

Free-living deer in Britain are susceptible to experimental foot-and-mouth disease to a varying degree ranging from a transient condition in the red to a severe form in roe. Fortunately deer have never been incriminated in natural outbreaks in this country although they have been found infected in the wild on the European continent. Deer are also liable to become infected with rabies if the opportunity occurs and in recent years many cases have been notified in roe in France, Germany, Luxembourg, Belgium and Switzerland.

Malignant catarrh

This infection is of considerable importance so far as red deer are concerned. Originally African buffaloes were considered the main reservoir hosts, but sheep are now of greater significance, little or no clinical disease appearing in them although they are a potent source of virus. One of the most interesting outbreaks ever recorded occurred in Pere David deer *E. davidianus* at Whipsnade Zoo. The infection was readily transmitted to red deer and one of the interesting features was the long incubation period of up to 48 days. The disease then had a sudden onset, the animals were dull and had muco-purulent discharge from the eyes and nose with considerable salivation. The source of the infection was never adequately explained. More recently, another small outbreak occurred in Scotland in a small group of red deer which had been moved into a paddock recently vacated by sheep. The first USA report concerned Axis deer *Axis axis* followed by other reports in white-tailed deer and mule deer *O. hemionus*. Cases in sika were also recorded; these deer had been in close contact with sheep.

Tumours

Tumours are rare in free-living wildlife and deer are no exception. Lymphosarcoma has occurred in roe and in fallow in southern England. A type of fibroma which occurs in red deer in Scotland, appears to be identical histologically to the tumours described in the Virginian white tailed deer (*Odocoileus virginianus*) in the USA.

Enzootic ataxia

Although not yet described in free-living deer, this disease is common in red deer confined to parks and because of the possible growth of deer farming enterprises, is worthy of comment here. The disease closely resembles swayback in sheep and is characterised by a bilateral demyelination of the tracts of the spinal cord. It has long been thought to be associated with a copper deficiency and appeared to be confined mainly to red deer. However, recently, cases have been seen in 'in contact' fallow. There can be no doubt that the affected animals suffer from a copper deficiency. Liver and blood analysis has shown this clearly but frequently 'in contact' normal animals in the same herd show normal levels. There is now some indication that the disease appears some years after the introduction of a new stag which may suggest a genetic factor. Under natural conditions it is extremely unlikely that a stag would serve his own progeny but this must frequently happen in an enclosed population. The disease is a fascinating one, not least for its close resemblance to multiple sclerosis in man; even the possibility of a 'slow virus' being involved is still under consideration. Mice and goats inoculated with suspensions of brain and spinal cords from affected deer have not, however, developed the disease.

Conclusion

The foregoing indicates that free-living deer in Britain, particularly the red deer on the Scottish hills, are remarkably healthy and pose little risk to 'in contact' farm livestock and man. It has yet to be seen what will happen when deer are confined to intensive systems for venison production, where they may be exposed to a variety of pathogens of which they have little or no experience. The impression at the present time is that they have a basic resistance to disease which is far greater that that of the conventional farm animals and if this is proved correct they could become a valuable asset to our economy, quite apart from their sporting value.

Much of this information has already appeared in the Proceedings of Working Meetings of the International Union for Conservation of Nature (IUCN) Survival Service Commission, Deer Specialist Group, at Longview, Washington State, USA in 1977, as published by IUCN Morges, Switzerland in 1978.
Further material has also been used from various articles on deer, by Dr. A. MacDiarmid, published in the Veterinary Record.

Part III

Deer of North America

Chapter XXVIII

INTRODUCTION

It is said that, at the time of colonisation and the wars of independence, 40 million white-tailed deer and 10 million black-tailed and mule deer inhabited North America as well as countless wapiti, moose and caribou. Their distribution, popularity and usefulness to the inhabitants is reflected in the great frequency of the word deer appearing in the names of geographical features like streams, rivers, creeks, etc.

By the early 20th century, the deer population had dwindled to about half a million white-tails; the black-tails and mule deer dropped proportionately in numbers, mainly because of skin and meat hunting, in which the white men have been more greedy and wasteful than the indians have been in the earlier days.

To anyone interested in deer it is the dynamics, resilience and scale of the deer population that are fascinating: for by 1950, the US Fish and Wildlife Service estimated the population at 5.1 million white-tailed deer and 1.7 million black-tailed and mule deer, with the more recent (late 1970s) estimates putting the population at 12.7 million and 3.7 million respectively. The total deer population of the USA is thus in the region of 20 million, spreading over an area of 3 million square miles, and producing a harvest of about 2 million beasts a year.

It is not only the total numbers that are staggering for those of us not used to thinking of such vast wildlife populations; it is also the variety of deer that North America presents in the number of species and sub-species: moose with 5 sub-species, wapiti with 4, caribou with 5, black-tailed and mule deer with 11 and white-tailed deer with 38; and the disparity of size alone between some sub-species, being as much as 100% and more.

When considering the climatic differences in which the deer live (between −40°C and +60°C; rainfall, between 10 ccm and 500 ccm per year, and living between high mountains and low prairie plains) it is not surprising that the development of the animals differs ecologically between any given areas.

And then there are deer of Canada, the same species, but some living in even more harsh climates.

The decimation of the deer population by the early 20th century gave rise to the introduction of the Buck Law in the USA in 1905. This banned the killing of female deer, thus giving rise to a fast increase of numbers, and a recolonisation of the deer into those areas from which they had been made extinct.

But the Buck Law has had another effect. The hunters, forbidden for some years to shoot the female deer (often referred to as antlerless) had been lulled into really believing the inpropriety of shooting them again. Came the time therefore when the shooting of females was re-opened due to the alarming increase of population, many hunters were reluctant if not downright opposed to the very idea, in spite of its ecological necessity. They have anyway discovered that, with the vast increases in overall numbers, there was a corresponding increase in male (antlered) deer, and that was what they wanted.

In the deer scene of the USA, politics both federal and state play an important role. Wildlife management, being organised on a state basis, is not only subject to the state political influences but, in some instances, the appointments to wild life services are political and not professional. This entails them being responsive to various political lobby pressures rather than to ecological needs. Thus the combination of ecological and political needs provides a staggering permutation of problematical situations.

In spite of these difficulties, the ecological problems are probably easier to reconcile, analyse and (ultimately) solve, than are the political ones; here one has to cope with election-minded officials who are faced with a great variety of often conflicting pressures: from anti-hunting lobbies to those who wish to maximise hunting, from long seasons to short seasons, from no shooting of females to shooting more females, to name just a few; none ecologically motivated, all politically dangerous.

The following statement from one of the works on the subject of American deer, made by an official, illustrates the thinking process: 'We are the servants of the public and therefore give heed to what the public wants'; one has to wonder how much is such sentiment a practical proposition; does it affect the payment of taxes, traffic control, judiciary, as well as the laws of sport, wild life and trade?

Maybe it is not surprising that, against this background, and in spite of the enormous attraction that deer in America could offer to the sportsmen of the Old World, the sporting exchange between the Old and the New Worlds tends to be one sided; few Europeans stalk deer in America.

Neither is it surprising that, although an enormous amount of research into problems related to deer has been and is being done, little of it is directly useful to those who manage deer or hunt, because only rarely it seems does it lead to clear and practical conclusions. For instance, there is a vast quantity of research into the fertility of female deer, the sex ratio of newly born calves and their survival, but very few conclusions are presented regarding the desirable sex ratio among the adult animals. Complex models for estimating deer numbers are developed alongside of the evaluation of food intake by deer and the analyses of the nutritional values of food in the deers' diet — but these are not coherently brought together, nor have attempts been apparently made to establish the capacity of the deer range, i.e. what the given areas should hold as far as populations of deer are concerned especially as related to overgrazing and damage of cultivated crops.

These are not criticisms of the researchers, but rather of the system; and the system does not seek this sort of information, perhaps because it may not be allowed to use it?

Chapter XXIX

SIMILARITIES IN DEER MANAGEMENT

Whether they be American, European or other, all deer belong to the family of Cervidae and therefore there are innumerable similarities between them; some of these are important in deer management, others not, and those that are can, in general terms, be related to much of the contents of this book.

Each of the species will survive in a wide spectrum of geophysical and ecological conditions, but they will not thrive in all. Caribou (European reindeer) for instance will live on a variety of food but require a period of cold frosty weather every year to rid themselves of certain parasites which they harbour. The few reindeer experimentally released in Scotand have found the Scottish weather too mild for them although, given time, they might even adjust to it rather as the Scottish red deer have adjusted to the poor quality and small quantity of food, by growing a smaller body and smaller antler.

Moose (European elk) on the other hand needs swampy, marshy land where they can feed on water-growing plants and so are unlikely to survive dry areas.

In a way, adaption like that of the red deer in Scotland, applies to most deer even to the extent that browsers will graze and grazers will browse, gregarious ones will live in small groups and those used to family life will adapt to living in small herds, like the roe deer in parts of Central Germany living on heathland or the hill moorland roe in some parts of Scotland. Deer are of necessity adaptable.

In terms of deer management however, if the objective is to optimise results in relation to management objectives and resources, then the techniques and practices to suit each particular species need to be developed and adopted, although some may have an all deer application and require no allowances other than those demanded the particular species size, shape, life span, etc.

Body Shape

Most people who practise deer management recognise the benefit of selective culling and within this the need for, and difficulties of estimating

232

the age of a live animal (that has not been tagged); and further, having made such estimation, then in having to decide whether after due consideration to condition, antler formation, etc. the animal is shootable or not. Most, through practice have tuned their eye to the basic body shapes, and from these are able at least to distinguish the young from the mature and the mature from the old, as well as also using the antler shape (in the male animals) as an additional source of information. Again most, over a period of time, develop a power of observation and retention of the tell-tale characteristics of the animal's appearance, a picture which is recorded in the mind as a point of reference which can then be compared with the other important clue which is only found when the beast has been shot: the tooth formation.

Hopefully the day arrives after many animals have been culled and several errors made, that our judgement is adequate for all practical purposes; but the day probably will never come when it can truthfully be said that we never have or will make a mistake!

Tooth Formation

In learning to age a beast by its tooth formation, one can reasonably quickly develop a level of fair proficiency, provided some basic logic is applied to reading the information presented.

There are two factors in tooth wear that are of crucial importance. One is the age at which the animals of the given species complete their permanent dentition (12 to 15 months in roe deer 24 to 26 months in red deer). The other crucial factor is the life span of the species (say 8 to 10 years in roe deer and 16 to 18 years in red deer).

Under natural conditions, most deer perish because they are no longer able to feed and chew; this happens when the chewing surfaces of the grinding molars in the lower jaw are so badly worn that the food cannot be properly chewed and therefore digested. So there is a scale of wear which can be calibrated, so to speak, by the span of life beyond the age at which the growing of permanent teeth has been completed and full dentition formed. Initially we may have to generalise — divide the tooth into three levels, the first third of the tooth for the first third of the deer's expected life span, the second third for its middle age and the last for its old age. Subsequently and through experience this process can be made more accurate, especially if by dissecting the tooth for an accurate estimation of age (see page 133) and relating this information to the molar wear and the recorded picture of the animal's shape in the mind's eye.

It is important to remember two points, however; firstly that the wear on molars depends very much on the abrasiveness of the deer's food; in sandy soil areas, where wind deposits sand on grass or leaves, teeth are worn more quickly than in good loamy soil with lush grasses and woodland leaves; and secondly that, like humans some deer have harder dentine than others; this can be estimated by colour, but the actual degree of hardness is difficult to define and only experience can help. (See also Table 17.)

Antlers

The least reliable factor in ageing deer on hoof is the formation of the antler. Once the antler is beyond the 'first head' or 'pricket spiker' stage, it can be misleading and needs to be related to the body shape. Antler growth is a function of many influences – heredity, local characteristics, the individual animal's health during antler growing time, the health of the animal and its mother during the time between the birth and feeding independance; all can have a reflection in antler form, shape and strength.

The best one can hope for is to develop a 'feel' for the local quality and 'judge' a given head of antlers against this local standard. The antler can later be related to the measuring formula of the CIC (Conseil International de la Chasse), for it is there that the premiums and penalties are clear to see.

All that can be said in terms of universal advice is: if the beast looks as if it has a good head and fine antlers, don't shoot but think again; and then think a third time before finally deciding to shoot. It is better to be safe than sorry for what is left now can always be taken later, but a mistake can never be rectified.

Chapter XXX

OVERVIEW OF NORTH AMERICAN DEER

Wapiti or North American Elk

Although considerably larger than even the largest of the European red deer, the wapiti is probably it's nearest relative and similar in body shape and antler.

Its normal habitat is the high mountain forest interspersed by areas of grassland where it will feed mainly on grasses, although will also browse on trees and bushes, mainly of the willow and aspen variety, stripping the bark in winter. Although not a migratory animal, it will move down hill to the valleys to escape from the snow and cold of winter.

The normal wapiti antler is 12 points (six aside) sometimes with a cup formed crown on top, although more points are possible. It is the length and thickness of the beam and the length of tines that indicate a good antler.

The colouring of the adults is brown red with light brown rump patch, changing to a lighter bay with dark brown legs and under-belly in summer.

The size is fairly uniform, about 5 ft at the shoulder and between 800 and 1,000 lb on weight, the females being about 15% smaller.

Reproduction

Calving takes place in June; the young usually single are light bay to light brown with white spots. The spots disappear with the first coat change after about 3 to 4 months. Sex ratio at birth is about 1 : 1.

The rut takes place during September/October.

Development

Full permanent dentition develops by the age of about 2½ years. Sex maturity is possible at 15 months but usually bulls (stags) are not fully mature until the fourth year and cows (hinds) 3 years reaching fully productive age at 5 years.

Antler

Antler development reaches the prime stage at 7 to 8 years and starts going back at about 11 to 16 years. Antler shedding takes between February and March, the older bulls shedding antlers first. Hard antler stage is reached in August.

Herd life

During the summer wapiti live in sex separation. Bulls collect their herds of hinds at the start of the rut, and separate after rut. Mixed herds are not uncommon in winter searching for food jointly, and separating again after winter.

Fig 43 Wapiti distribution

(Photo by Leonard Lee Rue III, Blairstown, N.J.)

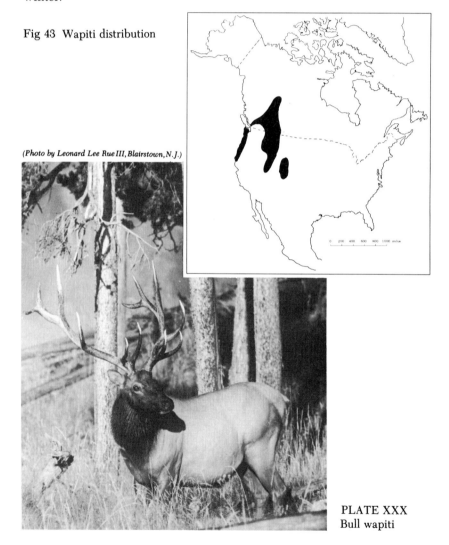

PLATE XXX
Bull wapiti

Fig 44   Wapiti measurement chart°

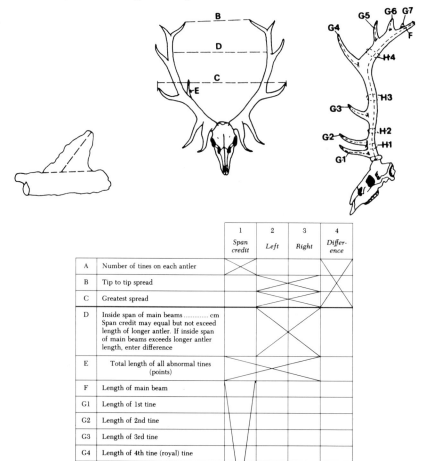

		1 Span credit	2 Left	3 Right	4 Differ-ence
A	Number of tines on each antler				
B	Tip to tip spread				
C	Greatest spread				
D	Inside span of main beams .... cm Span credit may equal but not exceed length of longer antler. If inside span of main beams exceeds longer antler length, enter difference				
E	Total length of all abnormal tines (points)				
F	Length of main beam				
G1	Length of 1st tine				
G2	Length of 2nd tine				
G3	Length of 3rd tine				
G4	Length of 4th tine (royal) tine				
G5	Length of 5th tine				
G6	Length of 6th tine (if present)				
G7	Length of 7th tine (if present)				
H1	Circumference at smallest place between first and second tines				
H2	Circumference at smallest place between second and third tines				
H3	Circumference at smallest place between third and fourth tines				
H4	Circumference at smallest place between fourth and fifth tines				
	TOTAL Lines D–H				
	Lines D–H	Total cols 1+2+3	Less col 4	FINAL SCORE	
	TOTAL				

°Based on *The Game Trophies of the World*, Conseil International de la Chasse (Hamburg, 1981, P. Parey).

Supplementary data

A. *Number of tines (points) on each antler;* in order to be counted as a tine a projection must be at least 1 in. (2.54 cm) long and its length must exceed the length of its base. All tines are measured from the tip to the base point on the beam as illustrated. Beam tip is counted as a tine but not measured as a tine.

B. *Tip to tip spread,* measured between the tips of the main beams.

C. *The greatest spread,* measured between perpendiculars at the right angles to the central line of the skull at the widest part, whether across the main beam or the tines.

D. *The inside span* of the main beams measured at right angles to the central line of the skull, at the widest point between the beams. Enter this measurement again in Span Credit column if it is less than, or equal to, the length of the longer antler.

E. *Total length of all abnormal tines (points):* abnormal tines are generally considered to be those non-typical in shape or location.

F. *Length of the beam* measured from the lowest outside edge of the burr (coronet) over the outer curve to the most distant point of what is or appears to be, the main beam.

G. 1, 2, 3, 4, 5, 6, 7.
   Length of normal tines (points): normal tines project from the main beam. They are measured from the nearest edge of the main beam over the outer curve to the tip.

H. 1, 2, 3, 4.
   Circumference – self explanatory.

Moose (European Elk)

The moose is basically a forest dweller, but the forest he will choose is one which is marshy and boggy since his feeding preference is for aquatic vegetation. This preference is so marked that the moose's nasal passages are adapted to enable the animal to dive, sometimes quite deep, in search of more tender morsels. Even in summer, when the bulls keep to higher altitudes wherever possible (probably to escape from flies whilst the antlers are growing), they will look for water where they can swim and dive for food. Apart from aquatic vegetation, they browse off trees and bushes being specially fond of willows, aspen, birtch and ash, which in winter they tend to strip, in addition to feeding off the young branches and buds.

There are two basic forms of antler. The first and typical antler is one with deep and wide palmation, with a number of short tines protruding from the outer edge of the palm and short brows between the palm and the burr. The other formation sometimes referred to as 'finger' formation, is one where palmation hardly develops and in its place the antler consists of long finger like tines. Whether palmated or not, the antler grows more or less horizontally sideways – unlike in other deer. A good antler spread can reach 5 even 6 ft.

Fig 45 Moose distribution

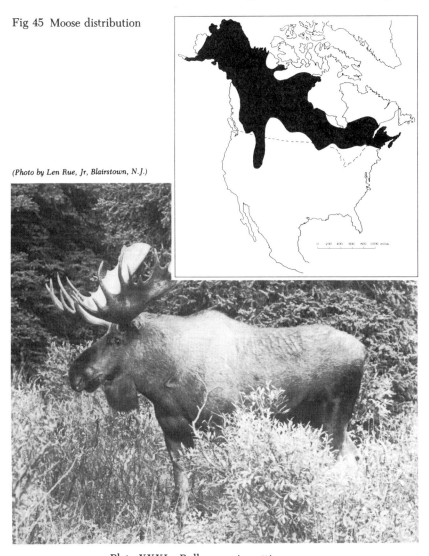

(Photo by Len Rue, Jr, Blairstown, N.J.)

Plate XXXI Bull moose in rutting season

It is the width and breadth of the palmation that distinguishes a good bull's antler from a poorer one.

Below the jaw and the upper neck the bull grows a long 'bell' dewlap which serves no known purpose.

The adult's coat does not differ much between summer and winter: brown with black tinges on the upper body with lighter brown legs and underbelly; colour variations from light brown to almost black are not uncommon.

There are five subspecies, between the Alaskan moose of some 90 in. at the shoulder and about 1,500 lb, and North American of 65 in. and about 900 lb. Females of each species are about 25% smaller than the male.

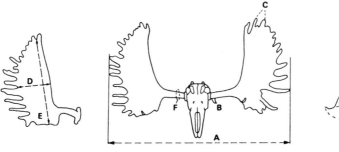

		1 Greatest spread	2 Left	3 Right	4 Differ-ence
A	Greatest spread				
B	Number of abnormal points on both antlers				
C	Number of normal tines (points)				
D	Width of palm				
E	Length of palm, including brow palm				
F	Circumference of beam at smallest place				
	TOTAL				
		Total cols 1+2+3	Less col 4	FINAL SCORE	
	TOTAL				

Fig 46 Moose measurement chart °

°Based on *The Game Trophies of the World*, Conseil International de la Chasse, (Hamburg, 1981, P. Parey).

Reproduction

Calving takes place in late May to June; twins are not uncommon. Calves are bay coloured and not spotted. Rut takes place late September to October.

Development

Full permanent dentition is developed by the age of 2½ years. Sex maturity is reached at the age of 2½ years but the reproduction potential is not at its peak until the age of 4 is reached. Longevity is up to 30 years.

Antler

Antler development to the prime stage takes 6 to 9 years. Antlers are shed at any time between November and March, older bulls shedding theirs earlier than the younger ones; antler re-growth does not start however until March, reaching the hard antler stage by late August–September.

Herd life

Except during the rut moose live in small groups separated by sexes. During the rut the bulls fight for possession of a cow and cows do become quite aggressive towards each other, thus large cow herds are uncommon during that time. During hard winter the sex groups may join up and seek food together.

Supplementary data

A. *Greatest spread* – measured in a straight line at right angles to the centre line of the skull.
B. *Number of abnormal tines (points) on both antlers:* abnormal tines are generally considered to be those non-typical in shape or location.
C. *Number of normal tines:* normal tines are those which project from the outer edge of the antler. To be counted as a tine a projection must be at least one inch (2.54 cm) long and the length must exceed the breadth of the tine's base.
D. *Width of the palm* – measured in contact with the surface across the underside of the palm, to a dip between the tines at the greatest width of the palm, and at right angle to the inside edge of the palm. Measure the width from midpoints between the tines.
E. *Length of the palm including the brow palm* – taken in contact with the surface, along the underside of the palm, parallel to the inner edge from the dips between the tines at the greatest length of the palm.
F. *Circumference of the beam at the smallest place* – needs no explanation.

Caribou (European Reindeer)

Caribou are one of the few deer that thrive in the cold of the sub-arctic. Even so the migration instinct sends them on a trek of several hundreds of miles, in their thousands, from the barren North to the more Southern tundra, just before the arctic winter storms cover the ground growth.

Their diet consists of grasses, herbs and lichens which they supplement seasonally with mushrooms, wild fruit and during winter wetland willows.

They are the only deer where antlers are grown by both species; during the winter months it is the females who seem to have a dominant influence on the herds, possibly because it is they that carry their antlers during that season.

Before the rut, the bulls grow striking buff to white mane which contrasts with the dark brown of the body and even darker chest.

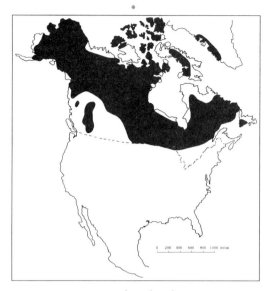

Fig 47 Caribou distribution

During the rut the bulls of adult age collect mature females driving away the younger bulls.

The quality of male antlers is gauged by the palmation of the brow (the shovel), the palmation of the top tines, beam thickness and the number and length of tines.

Reproduction

Young are born late May early June, and like moose are not spotted. At birth, the sex ratio is about 1 : 1. The calves are coloured light brown.

Development

Sex maturity is reached by both sexes at about 2½ years and females are productive till the age of about 11. Full permanent dentition is developed by the age of 2½.

Antler

Antler is grown by both sexes (not all females grow antlers). Old bulls shed their antlers in November soon after the rut, the young ones and females do not shed until March. Antler regrowth in all animals starts in March, reaching hard stage by about mid-August. Antler reaches the full development potential at the age of 7 to 8 years.

Herd Life

Bulls in herds feed away from the cows during the summer. Old mature bulls collect their cow herds for the rut keeping the young bulls away. During seasonal migrations bulls travel close to the cows.

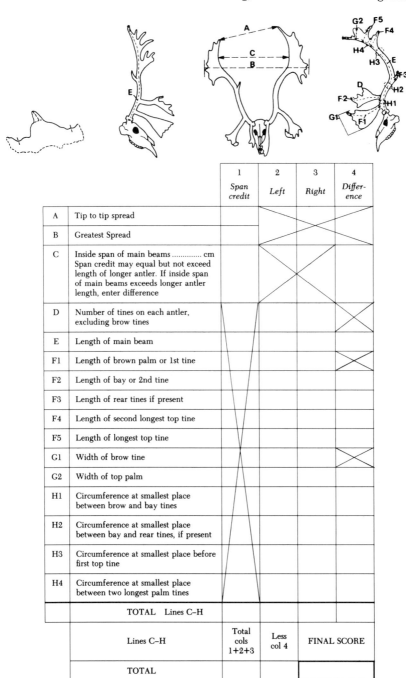

		1	2	3	4
		Span credit	*Left*	*Right*	*Differ-ence*
A	Tip to tip spread				
B	Greatest Spread				
C	Inside span of main beams .... cm Span credit may equal but not exceed length of longer antler. If inside span of main beams exceeds longer antler length, enter difference				
D	Number of tines on each antler, excluding brow tines				
E	Length of main beam				
F1	Length of brown palm or 1st tine				
F2	Length of bay or 2nd tine				
F3	Length of rear tines if present				
F4	Length of second longest top tine				
F5	Length of longest top tine				
G1	Width of brow tine				
G2	Width of top palm				
H1	Circumference at smallest place between brow and bay tines				
H2	Circumference at smallest place between bay and rear tines, if present				
H3	Circumference at smallest place before first top tine				
H4	Circumference at smallest place between two longest palm tines				
	TOTAL Lines C–H				
	Lines C–H	Total cols 1+2+3	Less col 4	FINAL SCORE	
	TOTAL				

Fig 48 Caribou measurement chart

°Based on *The Game Trophies of the World*, Conseil International de la Chasse (Hamburg, 1981, P. Parey).

Supplementary data

A. *Tip to tip spread* measured between the tips of the main beams.

B. *Greatest spread* measured between perpendiculars at right angles to the central line of the skull at the widest part, whether across the main beams or tines.

C. *Inside span of the main beams* measured at right angles to the central line of the skull at the widest point between the main beams. Enter this measurement again in 'Span Credit' column if it is less than equal to the length of the longer antler.

D. *Number of tines (points) on each antler:* to be counted as a tine, a projection must be at least one-half inch (1.27 cm) long and its length must exceed the breadth of the tine base on the main beam. Beam tip is counted as a tine but not measured as a tine.

E. *Length of the main beam* measured from the lowest outside edge of the burr (coronet) over the outer curve to the most distant point of what is, or appears to be, the main beam.

F. 1, 2, 3.
   Length of tines (points): these are measured to the upper line of the beam, on the shortest line over the outer curve, to the tip.

F. 4, 5.
   Length of upper tines; measurements to be taken from the tine tip to the appropriate outer edge of the beam at the right angle to the line of beam.

G. 1.
   Width of the brow measured in a straight line from top to the lower edge.

G. 2.
   Width of top palm measured from the rear edge of the main beam to the dip between the tines at the widest part of the palm.

H. 1, 2, 3, 4.
   Circumferences: if the rear tine is missing, take H. 2 and H. 3 measurements at the smallest place between the bay and the first top tine.

White-Tailed Deer

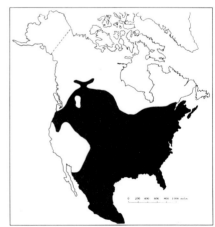

Fig 49 White-tailed deer distribution

(Photo by Leonard Lee Rue III, Blairstown, N.J.

Plate XXXII   White-tailed bucks

There are 38 sub-species of white-tailed deer, 31 living in North America. The differences are mainly those of size (between 25 and 40 in. at the shoulder and 50 lb and 300 lb weight) and pelage. Differences in body size are also reflected in antler size, the deer of the Northern areas being larger than those of the South. There are substantial antler formation differences within the sub-species as a result of different quantities and qualities of food available. Some antlers never develop beyond a single spike stage.

The white-tailed deer is basically a woodland and woodland fringe dweller, using woodland for browsing and shelter, and feeding mainly off grasses (and field crops). They are fond of water plants and where possible live in the proximity of cedar swamps specially in winter. Their diet includes mast, fruit, mushrooms and lichens.

During the winter both sexes may shelter in the woodland together, but apart from then and during the rut, they live in segregated groups, the females having the young of the previous two years and of both sexes with them, but abandoning the young during the rut.

In the rut, the buck seeks out his mate, but stays with her only for a short time and may cover several females.

The antler grows upwards and curves forward and inwards, with all tines other than brows growing from the rear edge of the main beam up-and-rearwards. A typical antler is of six or eight points aside.

The strong points of the antler in a perfect white-tail are: beam thickness and length and the symmetry of the tines.

The coat is coloured brownish-grey in winter and tawny in summer with regional variations: in the South the summer coat is cinnamon coloured. There is a lot of white on the body which remains all the year round: on the belly, inside the legs, under the tail and a throat patch, a stripe across the lip and patches around the nostrils and eyes; inside of the ears are also white.

When young, the white-tailed buck can be easily mistaken for the black-tailed, except for the colouring and tail.

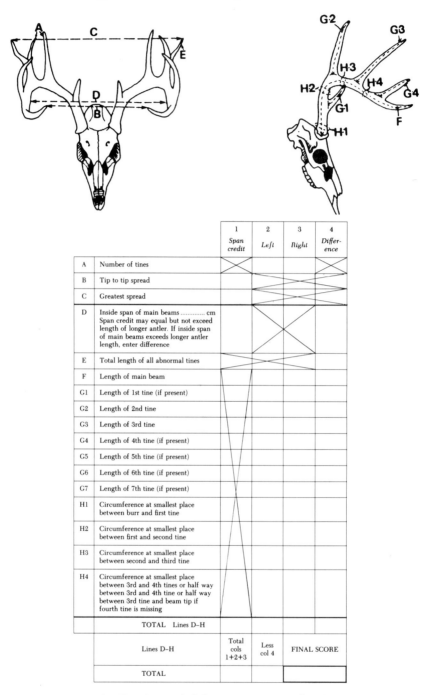

		1 Span credit	2 Left	3 Right	4 Difference
A	Number of tines				
B	Tip to tip spread				
C	Greatest spread				
D	Inside span of main beams .... cm Span credit may equal but not exceed length of longer antler. If inside span of main beams exceeds longer antler length, enter difference				
E	Total length of all abnormal tines				
F	Length of main beam				
G1	Length of 1st tine (if present)				
G2	Length of 2nd tine				
G3	Length of 3rd tine				
G4	Length of 4th tine (if present)				
G5	Length of 5th tine (if present)				
G6	Length of 6th tine (if present)				
G7	Length of 7th tine (if present)				
H1	Circumference at smallest place between burr and first tine				
H2	Circumference at smallest place between first and second tine				
H3	Circumference at smallest place between second and third tine				
H4	Circumference at smallest place between 3rd and 4th tines or half way between 3rd and 4th tine or half way between 3rd tine and beam tip if fourth tine is missing				
	TOTAL Lines D–H				
	Lines D–H	Total cols 1+2+3	Less col 4	FINAL SCORE	
	TOTAL				

Fig 50 White-tailed deer measurement chart°

°Based on *The Game Trophies of the World*, Conseil International de la Chasse (Hamburg, 1981, P. Parey).

Reproduction

Calving takes place in June°; twins are normal. The young are cinnamon coloured with white spots. Sex ratio at birth is about 1 : 1.

Development

Full permanent dentition is complete at 24 months. Sex maturity in both sexes is reached at 18 months°; calf production drops off at 8 to 10 years;° longevity about 15 years;° (19 to 23 years are on record).

Antler

Large regional differences in antler development. Full antler potential is reached at about 5 years;° antler starts going back at 8 to 10 years.° Antlers are shed in March,° hard by August.°

Supplementary data
A. *Number of tines (points) on each antler;* to be counted as a tine a projection must be one inch (2.54 cm) long and its length must exceed the length of its base. All tines are measured from the tip of the tine to the nearest edge of beam as illustrated. The beam tip is counted as a tine but not measured as a tine.
B. *Tip to tip spread,* measured between the tips of the main beams.
C. *Greatest spread* measured between perpendiculars at right angles to the central line of the skull at the widest part, whether across the main beams or the tines.
D. *Inside span of the main beams* measured at right angles to the central line of the skull at the widest point between the beams. Enter this measurement in 'Span Credit' column if it is less than or equal to the length of the longer antler.
E. *Total lengths of abnormal tines:* abnormal tines are generally considered to be those non-typical in shape or location.
F. *Length of the main beam* measured from the lowest outside of the burr (coronet) over the outer curve to the most distant point of what is, or appears to be, the main beam.
G. 1, 2, 3, 4, 5, 6, 7.
   Length of normal tines; normal tines project from the main beam. They are measured from the nearest edge of the main beam over the outer curve to the tip.
H. 1, 2, 3, 4.
   Circumference: if the first tine is missing, take H. 1 and H. 2 at the smallest place between the burr and the second tine.

Black-Tailed Deer and Mule Deer

There are 11 sub-species of the black-tailed deer and mule deer, spread from Canada to the South of the USA, but they are concentrated in the Central and Western states. The differences between the species are mainly

---

° Difference between North and sub-tropical South; timings shown above are for the Northern regions; South is 3 to 4 months later.

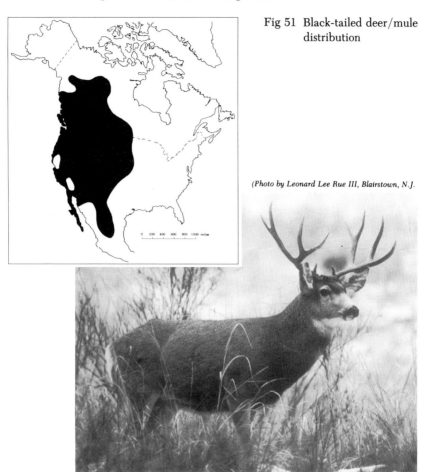

Fig 51 Black-tailed deer/mule distribution

(Photo by Leonard Lee Rue III, Blairstown, N.J.

Plate XXXIII   Black-tailed or mule deer

those of size (25–40 in.) weight (100–200 lb) and pelage.

The differences in body size are also reflected in the size of antler, both growing larger in the North than in the South. These differences are not as marked, however, as in white-tailed deer.

Colouring is basically browny-grey in winter (often sun bleached) to cinnamon brown and reddish brown with yellow tinges in summer, but there are variations. There are significant areas of white on the colouring of the body: forehead and throat patches, inside ears, belly and large rump patch; in some sub-species the white tends towards pale buff. There is a darker sometimes near-black spinal line leading to an always black tail tip.

The habitat varies from the plains to the high mountains and includes the sage bush desert, and through tree-less but bushy areas to the open pine hill.

The food covers a very wide variety of plant, from grasses, trees and shrubs, to mushrooms, mast and fruit; bark is stripped during the lean times.

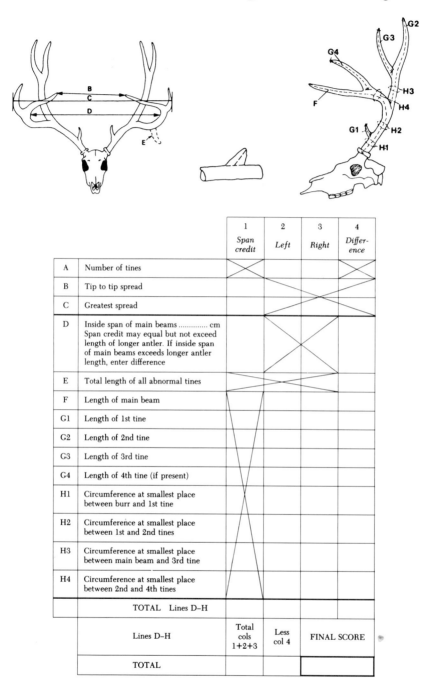

		1	2	3	4
		Span credit	*Left*	*Right*	*Differ-ence*
A	Number of tines				
B	Tip to tip spread				
C	Greatest spread				
D	Inside span of main beams .... cm Span credit may equal but not exceed length of longer antler. If inside span of main beams exceeds longer antler length, enter difference				
E	Total length of all abnormal tines				
F	Length of main beam				
G1	Length of 1st tine				
G2	Length of 2nd tine				
G3	Length of 3rd tine				
G4	Length of 4th tine (if present)				
H1	Circumference at smallest place between burr and 1st tine				
H2	Circumference at smallest place between 1st and 2nd tines				
H3	Circumference at smallest place between main beam and 3rd tine				
H4	Circumference at smallest place between 2nd and 4th tines				
	TOTAL Lines D–H				
	Lines D–H	Total cols 1+2+3	Less col 4	FINAL SCORE	
	TOTAL				

Fig 52 Black-tailed deer/mule measurement chart °

°Based on *The Game Trophies of the World*, Conseil International de la Chasse (Hamburg, 1981, P. Parey).

The adults are segregated by sex, the bucks often in pairs or groups of up to four, keeping to the higher ground specially during the period of antler growing. The doe groups, usually dominated by an older doe, include the young of the previous year or two. Bucks may join the females in winter when jointly they seek the shelter of the valleys and canyons, separating again when the weather improves.

The antler has short, forward-facing brow tines, with the main beam growing up and forwards; there is a bifurcated (forked) major tine and a forked beam-end, making the antler a five-aside formation. At a young age the antler can easily be mistaken for that of a white-tailed deer.

The characteristics of a good antler are beam thickness and length and the symmetry of the tine ends.

Reproduction

Calving takes place May and June, twins are normal, triplets do happen. Fawns are light coloured and spotted white. Sex ratio at birth is about 1 : 1 Rut takes place about October.°

Development

Full permanent dentition is complete at 18 months. Both sexes reach their sex maturity at 16 to 18 months. Longevity is about 15 to 16 years.°

Antler

Antler reaches its full development potential at about 4 to 6 years. Antlers are shed during December and January,° and reach the hard state in about August/September.° Antlers starts going back from the age of about 11 years.

Supplementary data
A. *Number of tines (points) on each antler:* to be counted as a tine, a projection must be at least one inch (2.54 cm) long and its length must exceed the length of its base. All tines are measured from the tip of the tine to the nearest edge of the beam as illustrated. The beam tip is counted as a tine but not measured as a tine.
B. *Tip to tip spread* measured between the tips of the main beams.
C. *Greatest spread* measured between perpendiculars at right angles to the central line of the skull at the widest part whether across main beams or tines.
D. *Inside span of main beams* measured at right angles to the central line of the skull at the widest place between the main beams. Enter this measurement again in the 'Span Credit' column if it is less than, or equal to the length of the longer antler.
E. *Total lengths of all abnormal tines;* abnormal tines are generally considered to be those non-typical in shape or location.

° Difference between North and South; timings shown above are for the Northern regions; South is 3 to 4 months later.

F. *Length of main beam* measured from the lowest outside edge of the burr (coronet) over the outer curve to the tip of the main beam. The starting point of this measurement is that point on the burr where the centre line along the curve of the beam intersects the burr.

G. 1, 2, 3, 4.
Length of normal tines: normal tines are the brow (or first) and the upper and lower forks as shown in the illustration. They are measured from the nearest edge of the beam over the outer curve to the tip.

H. 1, 2, 3, 4.
Circumferences:° If the first tine is missing, take H. 1 and H. 2 at the smallest place between the burr (coronet) and the second tine. If the third is missing, take H. 3 half way between the base and the tip of the second tine. If the fourth is missing, take H. 4 half way between the second tine and the tip of the main beam.

Fig 53 Unusual development of white-tailed and black-tailed deer

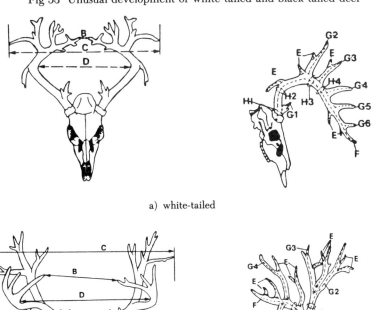

a) white-tailed

b) black-tailed

251

Chapter XXXI

LOOKING AHEAD

In the dynamic world of North America the management of deer has its problems, even apart from the obvious competition between human and deer interests, the conflict between deer and domestic animals, or even deer versus exotics like the imported wild pig, various wild sheep and goats, Asian deer species and ibex, in some areas.

Surprisingly, one of the main problems of the deer management seems to be hunting community itself. It is the hunter who often brings political pressure to bear in order to maximise the deer harvest, at the cost of ecological considerations; it is he who can bring hunting into disrepute through greed, carelessness and lack of consideration and also through lack of knowledge of deer.

All too often there are stories of wounded animals not being followed, illegal° animals being killed 'by mistake' and left, all providing the emotion laden 'conservation-at-all-costs' and anti-hunting lobby with powerful ammunition. That hunters in some areas need to wear distinctive, bright coloured, clothing lest they be shot themselves, in error, is in itself an indictment, as is the 'shoot first and look second lest someone else will beat you to it' practice which in no way encourages the care and discretion with which hunting should be conducted.

A hunter should consider himself as a 'second-line' deer manager.

What manager, of domestic animals, for instance, who cares for the quality and well-being of his stock, will randomly sell or butcher his animals at a flat price? What manager will not ensure that his animals have adequate food? And yet, translated into deer terms, the hunter, who should also manage deer if he cares for them, is prepared to cut down an animal at, or even before, its prime, merely for the flat price of a licence; or to demand that more animals should be available on the ground with no regard to their quality; he does not particularily care whether there is enough food available for the herds, and so sentences many animals to

---

° 'Illegal' are animals shot out of season, females in the buck only areas, spikers in the forked or better areas, etc.

inevitable death, for overpopulated and underfed, the herds are decimated by inclement climatic conditions in far greater numbers than they would have been had they been better cared for. And all this is music for the ears of the 'anti-brigades'.

Then too are the stories of the official deer managers who, under the influence of politicians and economists have to abandon the ecological considerations and long-term benefits of both deer and hunters, to meet the short-term pressures; or the scientists who conduct research with few practical benefits being obtained or deductions made, because such benefits, recommendations and efforts would only fall on deaf ears, not being politically acceptable. It is not surprising that so much effort lacks the sharp edge of practical and constructive conclusion.

Of course this all may be unfair to some, maybe many, who are careful, conscientious, considerate; there are many practical scientists and effective wildlife managers; there are even resilient politicians who place their responsibility towards the natural environment as a high priority for the future. But as in many walks of life, it takes only a few to damage and spoil what many are trying to create and repair, and those few usually invite bad propaganda. After all there are only comparatively few villains in the world and yet to combat them a vast security and judicial machinery is needed.

There are certain aspects of deer management, both in theory and in practice, which might benefit from examination. Basically they concern:

1. losses to predator; climate and influences beyond human control;

2. range capacity;

3. deer cull (harvest) in the context of this book

Much is written and said about the influences of predators, illness and climate upon the deer population. In a way these are provided by nature itself and indeed, in some parts of the world where predators have become extinct their controlling influence had to be undertaken by humans through increased hunting. There are also regions in which the climatic conditions are such that the climate does not act itself as a population control.

There are certain grounds of agreement; proportion of losses due to these influences in America (and elsewhere) is, so to speak constructive, in that in the main, it is the weaker, the diseased and the younger animals that fall victim; it is especially the numerical curtailing of the over-provision of the calves, that is beneficial, for the numbers of the young in their first year of life, in ecological terms, is excessive.

One could argue that, where predation is regular a correlation can be developed between the predator kill, population density and the harvest needed, almost as a statistical or computer model. One also has to bear in mind, that in many areas predators themselves are a hunting quarry.

It should also be possible to develop a correlation between the climatic influence and deer losses and to adjust the hunters' harvest accordingly, bearing in mind that some of these influences may have an effect more lasting than others; for example a heavy winter may not only cause the death of a number of animals but may, through undernourishment, influence the calf birth rate and even the subsequent years' fertility.

In their way, influences such as predation and climate do at least ensure that some control of numbers is enforced specially in those areas where numerical control by hunting is inadequate or where population is excessive in relation to capacity of the range.

That the numerical control of the deer population, and therefore numerical control of the herd and the cull (harvest) is essential is undisputed. An argument does exist, however, related to the level of the cull, which needs in turn to be related to deer capacity of the range; within this cull figure there must be a firm recognition that the animals retained after the cull (harvest) must not only numerically but also socially represent a healthy population.

A great deal of work in this direction has already been done; studies of food consumption by deer, as well as studies of nutritional value of foods that deer consume in various parts of the Continent, exist. These have not, however, been apparently correlated to show at what level of deer population the pressure on food supply (cultivated or wild vegetation) becomes economically or ecologically unacceptable or more so detrimental to deers' health.

The magnitude of the problem of deer density may be illustrated by the following figures: there are 4.7 million black-tailed deer and 13.7 million white-tailed in North America, some 2 million being killed every year.°

The plight of these animals is reflected by the density in which they sometimes have to survive; 1961 figures show density in some areas as high as 18. 9 deer per 100 acres, (L. L. Rue III, op. cit.) (in many areas the figures are of course lower) with the inevitable consequence of a very significant drop in body size, condition, winter survival rate, plus the devastation of the natural vegetation in the environment.

If the consideration is to be that of the economics of deer management, and the deer regarded as a harvested crop from a given area in relation to the capacity of that area, then the following points arise:

1. What is the annual calf recruitment and calf survival?

2. What is and should be the sex ratio within the population?

3. What is the proper age structure of the population?

Again, there is in existence a considerable volume of information on calving rates and calf survival. But calving needs to be viewed annually not in absolute terms but in proportionate relationship of calves to the total population of deer, so that the age structure within the deer population can be controlled.

Some writers talk in terms of maximising the deer harvest; but the numerical maximisation is not the best approach to the economics of deer management. Indeed the analyses of cull figures suggest that the cull of both sexes takes out the animals mainly in the age bracket between 1½ to

---

° Leonard Lee Rue III, *The Deer of North America* (Outdoor Life, C. Crown, 1984).

4½ years, whereas the natural longevity is about 12 years. Maybe in terms of a meat harvest such a cull would be beneficial, because it is done at the age when the animals reach their full body development, and their further feeding would provide only a marginal body weight gain. However, in the terms of ecology, and of deer management for the health and quality of herds (and therefore sporting trophy) this approach is counter-productive, because the males have not nearly reached the peak of antler development and the females are only just entering their age of full reproductive capacity.

From the social, psychological, physiological, ecological and economic standpoints, there is a need to ensure that, within the deer herds, there is a fair distribution of ages throughout the useful span of animals' lives. Such a useful life span starts at the bottom of the scale with the calves, and extends, at the top of the scale, to an age just below that at which the animals tend to die through natural causes, having gone through the peak of antler development in males, and calf bearing in the females. These structures are illustrated in Figs 2, 3, 41, 42, and 43 in relation to the roe deer and red deer populations, and presented in the shapes of the Hoffman Pyramid. (This pyramid could easily be adapted to the life spans of the various species of the American deer.)

One has to accept that the Hoffman pyramid is overpedantic for practical purposes, but it, however, represents the general concept and for practical use, a grouping of ages is usually resorted to.

This approach is clearly explained by Bubenik° in his discussion regarding the wapiti.

Bubenik widely draws on experience of red deer management, making parallels with the needs of wapiti management. Thus he is able to provide guidelines of social structures and age/sex relationships within the population which should provide for the well-being of the deer. His models recognise the basic criteria of reducing the numbers of calves by 50%, culling out 30% of young animals between the ages of 1 and 3 years (maybe 4 years), culling 7% of adults between the ages of 5 and 10 years, not only in order to keep the age structure correct, but also by proportionately culling males and females, maintaining the sex structure at the level of about 1: 1.2 (males to females) . These age and sex structures contribute to what he calls the Social well-being of the herds.

One can follow Bubenik's concepts and apply them, after certain adaptations to the other deer species. In the meantime one can only deduce that most deer live, to his way of thinking in an unbalanced age and sex structure and are therefore in a state of what he call Social Misery.

Surprisingly, there is comparatively little written about the value of antlers to the hunter. Even if one accepts that not all hunters are trophy hunters, most would, given a choice, seek to a good head or an interesting

---

° J. W. Thomas and D. E. Tweill (eds), *Elk of North America* (Stackpole Books, 1982) ch. 3 'Physiology' by A.B.Bubenik.

set of antlers from their sport, and for true sport seek out a wily old beast
rather than take the first youngster that comes along.

This fact is exploited in most of the European deer forests where the
level of fees paid for deer shooting is based on the quality of antler (in
better forests this can run to several hundred or even thousands of dollars
per beast). To this end the quality is often related to the CIC formula, even
if only in some simplified form. (CIC formulae for various species of deer
are shown in the text.)

In the deer world one thing alone is sure: a young male cannot have
developed a full-sized antler of quality: and therefore to benefit from the
concepts of quality antlers, a proportion of deer in the herd must be of full
maturity, that proportion needs to be of the magnitude which suggest to
the hunter that he will at least have a chance of securing a good trophy
(Bubenik talks in the terms of 17% of the harvest). Such a chance is a
function of nothing else but continuously good deer management.

But to have this possibility, the hunter must also accept that he is bound
to have a discipline imposed on him to shoot selectively. Selective shooting
does not mean selecting the best, but accepting that a large proportion of
deer shot must be those of poor quality, or those which are young with
poor development potential, so leaving for next year a good but immature
beast which is not ready, as yet, for culling. This approach certainly calls
for a great self-restraint and integrity, both personal and belief in the same
in others.

Selective culling is not, in some respects and in some areas, supported
by some of the state laws, for the state law which prohibits the shooting of
spikers is suspect on two grounds; firstly, the age structure approach calls
for harvesting of some yearlings and two year olds, although one needs to
be selective and shoot only short antlered weaker head spikers. Secondly,
if all spikers are protected then spikers which are not merely young, but
in fact those that are poorly developed older ones will also always be
protected and their poor quality will be propagated.

The other aspect of numerical control and age structuring concerns the
culling of females and calves. If a sex ratio is to be achieved and maintained
at about the level of 1 : 1 or 1 : 1.5 (see Bubenik, op.cit.) , then much
higher number of females need to be harvested than is the current practice;
furthermore a large number of calves and yearlings is also necessary
(Bubenik talks of 50% of the calves).

Here we have also a question of ethics. Published analyses suggest that
in the USA for instance ratio between the females and calves shot is in the
region of 4: 1 even as high as 8 : 1.

For reasons of ethics if nothing else, it is usually accepted that when a
female deer is shot, her calf is also shot. Theoretically therefore with the
calving rate of 30% to 40%, one could expect in the harvest females to
calves ratio to be in the region of between 3 : 1 and 2.5 : 1. This is not
always practical but an improvement on the current ratio would certainly
seem possible.

In both the female deer and calf harvest, the selection based on quality
is very difficult if not impossible, for it takes no mean expert to differentiate
between a shootable and non-shootable animal. Such is the importance of

this part of the harvest, to the deer management principles and deers' own well-being, that one has to forgo the principle of selection for that of numbers, otherwise the numerical control of deer population becomes impossible; it follows, that if one had to chose between the harvest of males and females, in terms of good management the harvest of females and calves is of greater importance.

The suggestions in this chapter have serious implications: they call for wider and stricter controls, and such increased control means more man-power and inevitable opposition; they call for a considerable self-discipline among the hunters; they may mean a reappraisal of the economics of deer management, specially in the transitional stage.

But above all they call for a modicum of education on the sides of both the management and the hunters (as well as the antis), all of whom need to accept that overpopulation and overgrazing are bound to result, in the long run, in the deterioration or decimation, if not disappearance of deer, either on account of poor nutrition or on account of excessive damage which, being economically and politically unacceptable, may lead to a pressure for extermination of the species from the devastated environment.

We can and should learn from the examples of devastation which are available to us from throughout the world. Both domestic and wild animals in excessive numbers had led to the erosion of the environment. This alone should be enough to persuade the intelligent and educated, that there is a case for a fairly drastic action often calling for personal sacrifices in order to protect the future of deer for posterity.

Annex

BIBLIOGRAPHY AND REFERENCES

Banner and Baxter, *Husbandry of Red Deer* (Rowett Institute & Highlands and Islands Development Board).

Brodner, M., *Deer Stalking in Britain* (The Sportsmans Press, London 1986).

British Deer Society, *A Field Guide to British Deer* (1971).

British Deer Society, *Deer Control* (1970).

British Deer Society, *Deer of the World* (1968).

Bubenik, A., *Das Geweih* (The Antler), (Hamburg, P.Parey, 1966).

Burrard, Sir G., *Notes on Sporting Rifles* London, Edward Arnold, 1953).

Chapman, N and D., *Fallow Deer* (British Deer Society, 1970).

Chaplin, R., *Reproduction in British Deer* (Sunday Times, 1960).

Chaplin, R., *Deer* (Dorset, Blandford Press, 1977).

Clutton-Brock/Guinness/Alban, *Red Deer Behaviour and Ecology*, (Edinburgh Univ. Press, 1982).

Coles C. (ed.) *Shooting and Stalking* (Stanley Paul, 1983).

Conseil International de la Chasse (W. Trense, Ed)., *The Game Trophies of the World* (Hamburg. P. Parey, 1981)

Delap, P., *Red Deer* (British Deer Society, 1970). Delap. P., *Roe Deer* (British Deer Society, 1970).

de Nahlik, A. J., *Wild Deer* London, (Faber & Faber, 1959).

de Nahlik, A. J., *Deer Management* (Newton Abbot, David & Charles, 1974).

Department of Agriculture & Fisheries for Scotland, *Farming Red Deer* (London, HMSO, 1974).

Deutscher Jagdschutz Verband — Jagd u.Hege in *Aller Welt DJV* (1957) (Game Shooting and Customs of the World.

Dziegielewski, H., *Jelen (The Red Deer)*, (Warsaw, 1970).

Eidmann, H., *Untersuchungen am Gebiss des Rothirsches* (Research into dentition of red deer), Forstwirtschaft und Forstwissenschaft, (Hanover, 1939).

Eisenhardt, B., *Fahrten und Sperrenkunds* (Footmarks and Tracking), (Hamburg, P.Parey, 1953).

Frevert, W., *Das Jagdliche Brauchtum* (Shooting customs), (Hamburg, P.Parey, 1951).

258

Game Conservancy, *Forestry and Fame,* Report on symposium (1971).

Haber, A. (ed.) *Gospodarstwo Lowieckie* (Management of Shooting), Warsaw, *Panstwowe Wydawnictwo Naukowe.*

Halls, L.K. (ed.) *White-tailed Deer — Ecology and Management* (Harrisburg, Stackpole, 1984).

Heck, L., *Der Rothirsch* (Red Deer) (Hamburg, P. Parey, 1956).

Hetschild, W and Vorreyer, *Das Ansprenchen des Rotwildes* (Red Deer Recognition), (Hamburg, P. Parey, 1963).

Kerschagl, Dr W., *Rehabschuss, Abschussplannung und Altersbestimmung beim Reh* (The Cull, Cull Planning and Age Estimating in Roe Deer), (Richter 1942).

Krebs, *Young or Old* (Munich, F.C.Meyer, 1966).

Lotze, K., *Das Ansprechen des Hirsches* (Recognition of Red Deer), (M. & H.Schaper, 1950).

Marshall-Ball R., *The Sporting Rifle,* (Pelham, London 1986).

Meyer, W., *Zur Herstellung von Verbissmitteln* (Towards the Manufacture of Anti-Browse deterrents), (Seifensiedelzeitung, 1959).

Mottl, S., *A Case against Damage by Deer* (Czechoslovak Government Publication, 1954).

Mottl, S., *Feeding of Deer* (Prague Biologia, 1957).

Nature Conservancy *Red Deer Research in Scotland,* (1967).

Paslawski, T., *Lowiectwo* (Game Shooting), (Warsaw, 1971).

Parker. *et. al. Shooting by Moor, Field & Shore,* (Seeley Service).

Pielowski, Z., *Sarna* (The Roe), (Warsaw, P. W. R-L, 1970).

Portland, the Duke of, *The Red Deer of Langwell and Braemore,* (London, Blackie, 1935).

Prior, R., *Roe Stalking* (Percival Marshal, 1963).

Prior, R., *Deer of Cranbourne Chase.*

Prior, R., *Trees and Deer* (London, Batsford, 1983).

Prior, R., *Modern Roe Stalking* (Tideline, 1985).

Raesefeld F. von., *Das Rotwild* (Red Deer), (Hamburg, P. Parey 1967).

Raesefeld F. von., *Das Rehwild* (Roe Deer), (Hamburg, P. Parey, 1956).

Raesefeld F. von/A.H. Neuhaus, *Das Rehwild,* (9th ed.) (P. Parey, Hamburg, 1985).

Red Deer Commission (Dr B. Mitchell) *Red Deer Management* (London, HMSO).

Red Deer Commission *Annual Reports* (London, HMSO). and their uses), (F. C. Meyer, 1953).

Rowe, J. J., *High Seats in Deer Management,* Forestry Commission, (London HMSO, 1979).

Rue, L. L. III, *The Deer of North America,* (Outdoor Life — Crown, 1984).

Ruffle, The, *The Sporting Rifle* (Batchworth, 1951).

Sartorius, B., *Das Ansprechen des Rehwildes* (Recognition of Roe Deer), (M. & H.Schaper, 1950).

Schmidt, J. L. and Gilbert, *Big Game of North America* (Stackpole, 1978).

Stelinski, J., *Odstrzal Zwierzyny Plowej* (Culling of Hoofed Game), (Warsaw, Polski Zwiazek Lowiecki, 1957).

Schultze, H., *Der Waidegerechte Jaeger* (Experienced Game Shot), (Hamburg, P. Parey, 1955).

Taylor Page, F. J., *Red Deer*, (Sunday Times, 1962).

Taylor, W. P., *The Deer of North America*, (Stackpole, 1965).

Tegner, H. S., *The Roe Deer*, (Batchworth, 1951).

Thomas J. W. and Tweill, D. (eds) *Elk of North America* (Stackpole, 1982).

Türcke, Dr F., Mittel gegen Wildschvden und ihre Anwendung, (Game Deterrents and their Use), (F. C. Meyer, 1953).

Türcke, Dr F., *Mittel gegen Wildschvden Richtig Anwenden*, (Correct use of Game Deterrents), (F. C. Meyer, 1953).

Ueckerman, E., *Wildstandbewirtschaftung und Wildschadenverhuttung* (Management and Damage Protection with Roe Deer), (Neuwid, 1970).

Ueckerman, E. *Das Damwild* (Fallow Deer), (Hamburg, P. Parey, 1956).

Vesey Fitzgerald, B., *British Game*, (London, Collins, 1946).

Vogt, F., *Das Rotwild* (Red Deer), (*Oesterrichischer Jadg - u Fischerei Verlag*, 1947).

Wagenknecht, Dr E., *Rotwild* (J. Neumann, Meslungen and Berlin, 1981).

Waldo, C. M. and Wislocki, G., *Observations on Shedding of Antlers in Virginia Deer* (American Journal of Anatomy, 1951).

Walace, F., *British Deer Heads, Country Life*. Wallmo, O. C., *Mule and Black-tailed Deer of North America*, Lincoln, University of Nabraska, 1981).

Whitehead, G. K., *Deer and their Management, Country Life*, (1950).

Whitehead, G. K., *Deer of the World* (London Constable, 1972).

Whitehead, G. K., *Hunting and Stalking Deer* (London, Batsford, 1980).

Whitehead, G. K., *The Deer Stalking Grounds of G. B.* (Hollis & Carter, 1960).

Whitehead, G. K., *Practical deer-stalking*, (Constable, London, 1986).

Wooding, F. H., *Wild Mammals of Canada*, (Ryerston, Toronto, (McGraw & Hill, 1982).

INDEX

261